RHODESIA:
The Road to Rebellion

RHODESIA:
The Road to Rebellion

JAMES BARBER

Published for the
Institute of Race Relations, London
OXFORD UNIVERSITY PRESS
LONDON   NEW YORK
1967

Oxford University Press, Ely House, London W.1

GLASGOW NEW YORK TORONTO MELBOURNE WELLINGTON
CAPE TOWN SALISBURY IBADAN NAIROBI LUSAKA ADDIS ABABA
BOMBAY CALCUTTA MADRAS KARACHI LAHORE DACCA
KUALA LUMPUR HONG KONG TOKYO

PRINTED IN GREAT BRITAIN
BY EBENEZER BAYLIS AND SON, LTD.
THE TRINITY PRESS, WORCESTER, AND LONDON

To June

Author's Preface and Acknowledgements

This book has been written in Rhodesia in the year following the Unilateral Declaration of Independence. It has been a time of strong emotions, great tensions, and hardening of the already polarized political opinions. It has also been a time when a peaceful compromise solution between the conflicting ambitions of the Africans and Europeans has seemed well-nigh impossible. Doubtless this atmosphere has influenced the judgments I have made.

Although I have written the book while living in Rhodesia it is the work of an outsider, who is temporarily resident in the country. As an outsider I hope that I have been able to understand the predominant feelings and ambitions of the racial groups, but I do not pretend that I can share all their emotions and certainly I have felt isolated from the extreme thinking currently so strong among Europeans and Africans.

I should like to record my thanks to the following: to my colleague Christopher Hill, who read the manuscript and made many useful suggestions for revisions; to Larry Bowman who gave me information and advice; to the many people—including Sir Roy Welensky, Mr. Winston Field, Dr. Ahrn Palley, Mr. Matthew Wakatama, Mr. Enoch Dumbutshena, Mr. Brian Oliver—who patiently and courteously answered my questions; to the stimulating and enthusiastic members of the adult education class on whom I tried many of my ideas; to the staff of both the Rhodesian National Archives and the library of the University College of Rhodesia who have been unfailingly helpful; and finally to the staff of the Institute of Race Relations, and especially Simon Abbott and Claire Pace, who have been so patient and helpful in publishing this book.

Contents

List of Tables and Illustrations

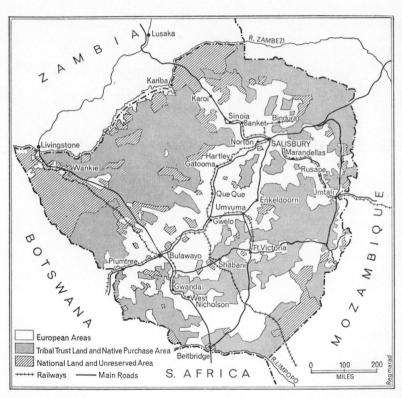

Rhodesia, showing Land Apportionment Act.

CHAPTER I

The Origins of a Divided Society

This book is an attempt to examine the political and constitutional developments in Rhodesia[1] during the 1960s which led to the Unilateral Declaration of Independence (U.D.I.). The U.D.I. has made Rhodesia the centre of an international crisis, but the act cannot be isolated. It is one part of a political and constitutional pattern; a pattern created by relations between Africans and Europeans.[2]

After more than seventy years of European rule the outstanding feature of Rhodesian society today is the division between the races, not so clear or formalized a division as in South Africa but a division which largely dictates the range of jobs open to a man, the education his children will receive, what wages he is paid, where he can live, and how he behaves to his fellows and to men of another race. The Africans are clearly predominant in numbers: about 4,000,000 against about 220,000; but in all else Europeans predominate. There are almost no social contacts between Africans and Europeans. The main contact is in working relationships in which Europeans hold all the top posts while Africans provide all the manual and menial labour. In between, some jobs are shared between the races; there are African doctors and schoolteachers, lorry-drivers and nurses, clerks and foremen, but normally Africans are given authority only over Africans. Where there is direct contact between the races the European is master and the African servant. There are strong arguments to explain why the Europeans, with their long background of education and acquired skills and resources,

---

[1] 'Southern Rhodesia' is the official name, but when 'Northern Rhodesia' obtained independence as 'Zambia' in 1964 the 'Southern' was dropped from general use.

[2] There are also approximately 12,500 Coloureds and about 8,000 Asians in Southern Rhodesia, but in political terms they are not of great importance.

are the predominant race. There are strong arguments to explain why the races live apart and have little social contact. These arguments help to explain but they do not remove the fact that there are still in Rhodesia 'The Two Nations'.[1]

There are certain unique features in the Rhodesian situation which add to its complexity. First, Rhodesia is on the frontier between 'black' and 'white' Africa. To the north in Zambia, Malawi, the Congo, and East Africa there are black African governments. To the south is the great bastion of white supremacy, the Republic of South Africa. On either side of Rhodesia, to the east and the north-west, are the Portuguese territories of Mozambique and Angola, anachronistic reminders of the great European empires of the recent past. The geographical division is not absolute, for, to the south of Rhodesia, Botswana and Lesotho have moved to independence as 'black' states, and will soon be joined by Swaziland, but all three are small, relatively poor countries, and do not substantially affect the generalization that north of the Zambezi is 'black', south of the Limpopo is 'white'. Between the two great rivers lies the land-locked Rhodesia, uncertain of which side of the racial fence she will fall, and open to direct pressure from both camps.

Rhodesia is an ideological as well as a geographical frontier. Although the white minority has dominated the country's government and economy, this dominance has never been translated into the ideological claims of South Africa. In Rhodesia there has been much talk of creating racial partnership, of a society based upon merit not upon race, although in practice the races have as yet kept apart. Mr. E. S. White, the Town Clerk of Bulawayo, addressing a South African Local Government Conference in 1953, said:

In other words this legislation [the Land Apportionment Act] aims at residential segregation and, therefore, has some features in common with policy in the Union. But it differs in that it was not conceived as a permanent solution of what is miscalled the 'native problem'—i.e. the problem of two races of very different cultural and technical levels living together. It obviously owes a lot to Union thought on the subject, but it was designed more as an

---

[1] See Richard Gray, *The Two Nations*, London, Oxford University Press for the Institute of Race Relations, 1960.

interim measure to protect the natives from losing their lands to shrewder members of any other race. Whether the passage of time will have the same hardening effect as senility has on the heart, it is too early to say.

The Town Clerk was re-emphasizing what Lord Hailey had called the 'conflict of attitudes towards the relation between Africans and Europeans, typified by the contrast between Cecil Rhodes' phrase—"Equal rights for all civilized men south of the Zambesi"—and the clause from the original Constitution of the Transvaal—"There shall be no equality between black and white either in church or state." '[1]

For Britain the Rhodesian crisis has been especially difficult and galling. Britain, once the possessor of the greatest empire in history, has in her decline transferred power to her ex-colonial territories with relatively little bitterness on either side. But in Rhodesia the two strands of British imperial history have met and clashed. One strand has been in territories where large numbers of people of British stock have settled and been given control of their own affairs, in Canada, New Zealand, Australia, and South Africa. The other strand has been in territories where small numbers of Britons, acting as trustees, have administered large native populations until the indigenous people themselves have assumed control. In Rhodesia the white population has been large enough to claim a substantial degree of self-government, but not large enough to convince Britain that she should abandon completely her trusteeship of the black majority. Britain has therefore found herself in the worst of positions: she has claimed responsibility but retained few powers.

Britain's restricted role in Rhodesia is an inheritance of the past. From the first European occupation, when Cecil Rhodes and his British South Africa Company extended the British Empire north from South Africa, the European settler community has held the initiative and most of the power. In 1923 Company rule came to an end. The small, predominantly white electorate rejected the opportunity to join South Africa and chose to become a British colony with a large degree of

---

[1] Lord Hailey, *An African Survey*, London, Oxford University Press, 1938, p. 130.

responsible government, although the British Government retained some reserve powers over legislation and administration affecting Africans.[1]

In Southern Rhodesia the Europeans formed a small *élite*. Until the end of the Second World War their numbers increased steadily but not spectacularly. In 1913 there were 25,500; in 1930 48,000; in 1945 80,500. Then after the War came a rapid increase; by 1950 there were 125,000 and by 1960 219,000. From the earliest days the predominant European stock has been British and South African (British South African rather than Afrikaner). This predominance has never changed. In 1951 the origins of the European population were: 32·7 per cent born in Rhodesia, 30·5 per cent in South Africa, and 28·8 per cent in the British Isles. In 1951 13·5 per cent of the European population claimed membership of the Dutch Reformed Church, and this probably gives a reasonably accurate figure for the Afrikaner element.[2]

The European population retained a strong loyalty to Britain, which revealed itself very clearly during the two World Wars, but the basis of the loyalty was a general, vague emotion. It was associated with pride in being 'British', in loyalty to the Crown and the flag, in upholding the standards of an idealized homeland. The loyalty satisfied the need for an identity in an alien continent, but in peacetime its limitations

[1] The reserve powers were 'provided in the Letters Patent in the following ways, viz.:

   (*a*) Section 28 provides that "any law, save in respect of the supply of arms, ammunition or liquor to natives, whereby natives may be subjected or made liable to any conditions, disabilities or restrictions to which persons of European descent are not also subjected or made liable", must be reserved for the signification of the pleasure of the Crown, unless the Governor, prior to its passing, shall have obtained instructions upon such proposed legislation through the Secretary of State, or unless it contains a clause suspending its operation until such pleasure has been signified.

   (*b*) Section 40 provides that no such discriminative conditions shall be imposed, without the previous consent of the Secretary of State, by any proclamation, regulation or other instrument issued under the provisions of any law, unless they have been explicitly prescribed, defined and limited in such law.

   (*c*) Certain supervisory and other powers in regard to native administration were vested in the High Commissioner for South Africa . . . One important provision in the Letters Patent vested the Native Reserves in him' *Bledisloe Report* (Cmd. 5949, 1939).

[2] See Leys, *European Politics in Southern Rhodesia*, London, Oxford University Press, 1959, p. 59.

were always near at hand. Any British Government and all British politicians, especially Labour politicians, were suspect for they threatened Southern Rhodesia's freedom of action. Better, thought the Rhodesians, to retain a strong emotional tie but to keep the political power for the men who knew, the Southern Rhodesian Europeans themselves.

The increase in European numbers was more than matched by an increase in the African population. In 1901 it was estimated that there were 500,000 Africans, in 1920 850,000, in 1940 1,430,000, in 1954 2,820,000, and in 1960 3,400,000.[1] The increase in African numbers was helped by the peace, order, and organization of the modern state and the extension of European medical facilities.

The relationship between the races has been greatly influenced by economic conditions. In the early days mining and farming became the two major industries; Europeans providing the skill and capital and Africans, reluctantly at first, providing the labour. After the 1939–45 War there was rapid economic expansion. The traditional primary products became more valuable and new secondary industries were developed. In 1939 the gross national product was £28·2 million, by 1954 this had risen to £168·6 million and in 1958 to £240·6 million.[2] As the balance of the economy shifted away from the old dominance of mining and farming to the new industrial developments so the population concentrated itself in the urban areas.[3] The majority of the new European immigrants settled in the cities and towns, especially Salisbury and Bulawayo, and they were joined there by an influx of Africans from the rural areas. The expansion is clearly shown in the population figures of the main cities:

[1] The earlier figures probably underestimate the African population. The last two (1954 and 1960) are taken from the Final Report of April–May 1962 Census of Africans (Central Statistical Office, Salisbury, June 1964), p. 7.
[2] Central African Statistics, Vol. VI, No. 3.
[3] The increasing concentration of Europeans in urban areas is reflected in figures given in the European Census, 1961 (Central Statistics Office, Salisbury, p. 6). The figures are:

Percentage of total European population	1936 %	1946 %	1961 %
(a) main urban areas	55	60	76
(b) remainder	45	40	24

TABLE I

POPULATION OF SALISBURY AND BULAWAYO, BY MAIN RACES

	SALISBURY		BULAWAYO	
	African	European	African	European
1936	c. 46,000	11,392	c. 30,000	12,321
1946	c. 65,000	21,294	c. 50,000	17,544
1951	c. 104,000	40,433	c. 90,000	32,163
1961	c. 215,000	88,710	c. 154,000	50,000

Naturally the rapid increase in the urban populations caused major social problems. This was especially true for Africans, many of whom had known no other life than rural, tribal society, and who found that the services and accommodation provided for them in the towns were very poor. Within the urban areas the economic division between the races was re-emphasized. There were a few rich Africans, businessmen, bus-operators, and the like, and in the new industries some Africans were drawn into skilled and semi-skilled trades. But, in general, the Europeans continued to be an economic *élite* and the Africans the working class. In 1958 the average European wage was £995 per annum and the average African income £80 per annum. (These figures include rural as well as urban incomes.)

Another problem closely associated with economic development was that of landholding. The problem had arisen in the early days as European farmers spread themselves over wide areas. To protect the Africans the Company created Native Reserves from which Europeans, other than missionaries and government officials, were excluded. These Reserves were recognized in the 1923 Constitution. However, the rapidly expanding African population and Africans' lack of capital to purchase holdings in the theoretically 'free' land market outside the Reserves made a redistribution essential. A Land Commission was appointed under the chairmanship of Sir Morris Carter, and on the basis of the Commission's report the Land Apportionment Act was passed in 1930.

The Commission found that:

However desirable it may be that members of the two races should live together side by side with equal rights as regards the holding of land, we are convinced that in practice, probably for generations to come, such a policy is not practicable or in the best interests of the two races and that until the Native has advanced very much further on the paths of civilization it is better that points of contact in this respect between the two races should be reduced.[1]

Based on the Commission's recommendation, Southern Rhodesia was divided into racial areas. The African reserves were increased in size and much of the land outside the reserves was specifically designated as European. All the major towns were included in the European areas. The division of land, which came into operation in April 1931 was:

TABLE II

THE LAND DIVISION OF 1931

European Area	49,060,000 acres approx.
Native Reserves	21,600,000 acres approx.
Native (Purchase) Area	7,460,000 acres approx.
Forest Area	590,000 acres approx.
Undetermined Area	90,000 acres approx.
Unassigned Area (i.e. Unassigned to any race or other category)	17,800,000 acres approx.
	96,600,000 acres approx.

The land division was based upon the anticipated needs of the two races, including room for future expansion but, while it was estimated that each African farmer would require only a few acres, it was assumed that the European would require hundreds or even thousands of acres. However, the estimates again undervalued the pace of African population expansion and soon some of the Reserves were under great pressure, while considerable sections of the European area lay idle, from under-farming or because of absentee owners or because no purchases had been made. In 1941 there was a further expansion of the African Reserves, which took their total area to approximately 30,000,000 acres, but the population expansion more than kept pace with this and so the pattern remained that in many of the

[1] Carter Commission Report Salisbury, 1926, para. 63.

Reserves there was considerable land pressure, while in European areas there was still room for expansion.

The Land Apportionment Act was also important in its implication that the races would live apart and therefore could be administered and governed apart. This thinking was closely associated with 'the Two Pyramid Policy'.[1] This policy envisaged a predominantly white and a predominantly black pyramid standing side by side. At the base of the white pyramid was a layer of unskilled black labour, while the apex of the black pyramid contained Europeans; native commissioners, missionaries, and the like. Within the black pyramid detailed control lay with the native commissioners, who would, helped by the chiefs, exercise a paternal administration.

Within Southern Rhodesia direct participation in politics was confined to a small section of the population. From 1923 the Legislative Assembly had consisted of thirty members who were directly elected on a 'colour-blind' franchise, which had been inherited from the Cape Colony, but the right to vote was restricted to those who could satisfy set standards of income, property and education. These standards which were designed to distinguish 'the responsible', 'the civilized' citizen were naturally related to European standards and so the vast majority of those on the voters' roll were Europeans, while few Africans qualified. This is revealed by the following figures:[2]

TABLE III

THE VOTERS' ROLL, 1928–58

	Total Electorate	Africans on Roll
1928	26,629	62
1933	28,515	58
1939	28,894	39
1948	48,000	258
1953	49,068	380
1958	55,082	560

[1] See Gray, op. cit., p. 151.

[2] The figures are derived from G. C. Passmore and M. T. Mitchell, *Source Book of Parliamentary Elections and Referenda in Southern Rhodesia, 1898–1962*, Salisbury, U.R.C.N., 1963; plus Palley, *The Constitutional History and Law of Southern Rhodesia, 1888–1965*, London, Oxford University Press, 1966; plus Leys, op. cit., p. 196.

Because political activity was confined mainly to a minority distinguished by its race and economic strength, the ebb and flow of politics was based upon attempts to balance the interests and groups within that minority. But while the administration of Africans was regarded as a technical subject to be handled by experts (the native commissioners) rather than by politicians, native policy often intruded into politics to provide one of the distinctions between the political parties. The Europeans' attitude to African advancement was largely empirical but there was a wide divergence of views, extending from those who accepted that in time Africans would emulate European achievements to those who believed that Africans would always be a servant race.

The ruling group in government and politics was a tight circle of men who knew each other intimately. Politicians, senior civil servants, leaders of agriculture, commerce, and industry moved in the same social circle and settled many of their problems informally. The line between government and private enterprise was often difficult to distinguish, particularly with the creation of statutory bodies, such as the Tobacco Industry Board, the Electricity Supply Commission, and the Rhodesian Railways. On these boards and commissions, government and private interests shared control of large sectors of the Rhodesian economy.

The confined political circle emphasized the importance of personality. There was no mass electorate to please, no great party machine to be organized. For the potential leaders it was important to mix well, to be known, liked, and trusted within the circle. Likewise the small electorate preferred a man whom they could trust, in whose hands the government could safely be left. Thus Sir Godfrey Huggins, who was trusted and liked, could dominate Southern Rhodesian politics for twenty years.[1] Thus in 1958 Garfield Todd fell when he encountered friction within the circle, and when the electorate felt that he could no longer be trusted.

Although between the 1920s and 1950s political parties arose, merged, and disappeared in considerable profusion, there was a clear pattern in Southern Rhodesian politics. There was a

[1] See L. H. Gann and M. Gelfand, *Huggins of Rhodesia*, London, Allen and Unwin, 1964.

'Government Party', which went under a variety of names—the Rhodesian Party, the United Party, the United Rhodesian Party, and the United Federal Party; and an 'Opposition Party' which, at various times, was called the Progressive Party, the Reform Party, the Liberal Party, and the Dominion Party.[1] The 'Government Party', which was closely allied to big-business interests, became known as 'the Establishment'. In the political groupings the same names appeared, the same reliance was put upon general policies—'the general development and advancement of all races in the Colony'. The 'Opposition Party' offered only one consistent point of difference: a greater emphasis on the need to defend European interests against potential African economic and political competition. Until the 1960s this voice of caution, or of fear, was never persuasive enough to gain a majority vote.

The only break in the Government/Opposition relationship was the Labour Party. The party was active in the 1930s and 1940s, drawing its main support from European artisans, but the great mass and weight of numbers that a Labour Party might hope to attract was African and voteless. In the late 1940s the Labour Party quickly lost support, partly because of internal disputes but more because its *raison d'être* disappeared as, with increasingly high standards of living, the identity of interests between European capital and labour became stronger than their differences. This identity of interests was explained in 1938 by Sir Godfrey Huggins:

The Europeans in this country can be likened to an island of white in a sea of black, with the artisan and the tradesman forming the shores and the professional classes the highlands in the centre. Is the native to be allowed to erode away the shores and gradually attack the highlands? To permit this would mean that the leaven of civilization would be removed from the country, and the black man would inevitably revert to a barbarian worse than ever before. I say this because the ancient controls and inhibitions of tribal custom and superstition on which Bantu society rested are going, or have gone, never to return. But the white man's law, religion and example can take their place. Rightly or wrongly, the white man is in Africa, and now, if only for the sake of the black man, he must

---

[1] Leys, op. cit., Chapter V.

remain there. The higher standard of civilization cannot be allowed to succumb.[1]

Outside formal politics were important European pressure groups, such as the farming community, the mining companies, the trade unions. Within the tight circle of Southern Rhodesian politics these pressure groups were important in helping to shape and to criticize the Government's actions.

The changing economic pattern after the Second World War affected the old 'two-pyramid' approach to race relations. It became evident that, with the growth of industries and the increase of the African urban population, the races would have to co-operate closely at least in their working relations. Huggins recognized this change. In 1941 he said: 'You cannot plan for the unknown, to state that the lines will never meet is stating what is not and cannot be known.'[2] He spoke of black and white as brothers who had grown apart because of environmental differences. Huggins's change of opinion was within the established Southern Rhodesian empirical approach. He told Guy Clutton-Brock: 'You know, I used to believe in separation once but I found it wouldn't work so I gave it up.'[3] The clearest practical expression of Huggins's change of policy was in the townships, where he legislated to improve living and accommodation standards.

Huggins and his party were prepared to accept the changing social and economic order but were determined to retain political power in 'responsible' hands, and at that time they regarded 'responsible' and 'European' as synonymous. While Huggins was arranging improvements for Africans in townships, his party was planning to exclude Africans from the common voters' roll for the foreseeable future. Huggins decided that the British Government would not accept this but, in 1951, he introduced amendments to the franchise qualifications which he said did 'almost as much as closing the Roll for fifteen

---

[1] Gray, op. cit., p. 152.
[2] Gray, op. cit., p. 276.
[3] G. Clutton-Brock, *Facing 1960 in Central Africa*, London, Africa Bureau Anniversary Address, 1959, p. 3.

years' and preserved 'what we call civilized government, which is the only important thing'.[1]

The growth of a large urban African population encouraged African organizations. These organizations were stimulated and shaped by the major political and ideological changes which swept through Africa after the Second World War, and found their expression in the nationalist movements. In Southern Rhodesia the trade unions were particularly active in the formative years and threw up leaders like Joshua Nkomo, General Secretary of the Joint Industrial Committee for Railway African Workers, Jasper Savanhu of the African Workers' Union, and Charles Mzingeli of the Reformed Industrial and Commercial Workers' Union. In September 1957, the first major political party, the Southern Rhodesia African National Congress, was formed under the leadership of Joshua Nkomo, when the existing but inactive Congress merged with the more militant City Youth League.[2]

The first clear demonstration of the potential strength of Africans was not directly related to any of the formal organizations. It was an unorganized but major strike in Bulawayo in 1948. The strike failed in its immediate objectives but it shocked many Europeans into realization of the very real if ill-organized strength of Africans and dispelled any doubts that Africans would increasingly demand a stronger voice in the affairs of the colony.

In 1953 Southern Rhodesia joined the British Protectorates of Northern Rhodesia and Nyasaland to form the Central African Federation. Some form of association between the

---

[1] Gray, op. cit., p. 309. The main changes in the qualifications concerned property and income. They were:

Old Qualifications + 1951 changes (in parentheses)

(a) Occupation of immovable property within the Colony value £150 (£500); or
(b) Ownership of registered mining location in Colony (same); or
(c) Receipt of income of £100 p.a. (£420 p.a.)
   plus the ability to complete and sign claim form unassisted (ability to speak and write in English language and to complete and sign claim form unassisted).

(Passmore and Mitchell, op. cit., p. 10.)

[2] For an account of the early African parties and movements see N. Shamuyarira, *Crisis in Rhodesia*, London, Deutsch, 1965, chapters 2 and 3.

territories had been canvassed for many years but, for the Europeans of Southern Rhodesia, there was always a delicate balance between the advantages and disadvantages it offered. When an association with Northern Rhodesia had first been proposed in 1915, Northern Rhodesia had been a poor, undeveloped territory with a small European population. At that time the proposal offered little to the Europeans of Rhodesia but an economic burden and the threat of being overwhelmed by African numbers. The discovery of copper in Northern Rhodesia changed the whole economic picture. As the Copperbelt revealed its great wealth, so the attractions of an economic association became obvious. But there were other considerations which counselled caution. There was always the fear that what were regarded as the excessively liberal policies of the Colonial Office might filter into Southern Rhodesia via the northern territories. Many Europeans thought it was better to shape Southern Rhodesia's future independently and avoid the excesses of the Colonial Office or of South Africa.

However, in the years following the Second World War conditions became very favourable for a federation in Central Africa. The growth of extreme political attitudes in South Africa, where Dr. Malan's Nationalist Party took a firm grip, and the spread of African nationalism in the north gave Southern Rhodesian Europeans a feeling of uncomfortable isolation. Building a large state in Central Africa, with a strong diverse economy and based upon traditional Rhodesian lines, offered obvious advantages. The economic advantages seemed to grow clearer every year as the Northern Rhodesian copper industry flourished and the expanding manufacturing industries of Southern Rhodesia searched for wider markets. Also it was reasoned that the combined internal economic strength would attract additional external capital for further expansion.

In the post-war years British opinion also moved towards support for a federation in Central Africa. British Ministers and officials saw the opportunity of creating a powerful economic unit upon which could be built a moderate racial policy, a *via media* between black and white nationalism. When the Federation emerged, with its complex constitutional and franchise arrangements, the hand of the British official was heavy upon it. It was British influence and insistence which persuaded the European politicians to accept federation rather than amalgamation, which many of them favoured, and to accept the small and economically poor Nyasaland Protectorate as a member.

When the British and Central African politicians and officials had agreed to a federation it was put to the Rhodesian electorate for confirmation. 25,570 voted in favour and 14,729 against.

The Central African Federation was a most complicated constitutional arrangement. It consisted of three territories which were separately under British control. Two were Protectorates controlled by the Colonial Office, while the third, Southern Rhodesia, was a colony with responsible rule and channelled its relations with Britain through the Commonwealth Relations Office. Within the Federation each territory retained its own government, but superimposed on the whole was the Federal Government with its own legislature, ministerial organization and civil service but in its turn ultimately responsible to Britain. Central Africa had a superabundance of government.

The division of powers in the Federation was made on the basis that 'these services which have a specially close relation to the day-to-day life and work of the African peoples' should remain with the territorial governments but, while the territorial governments continued to administer a wide range of services, the Federal Government was responsible *inter alia* for external affairs, defence, economic planning and development, income tax, major communications, electricity, health, and prisons. Some services were placed on a concurrent list but with the federal law prevailing in case of inconsistency. Colin Leys concluded that: 'The territorial governments had relatively few powers, apart from "provincial and native administration", which are not possessed by local governments in most unitary states.'[1]

In the years of federation the attention of Southern Rhodesians moved from the confines of their own country to the wider borders of Central Africa. The attraction of governing the larger

[1] For an extensive list of powers see C. Leys and C. Pratt, *A New Deal in Central Africa*, London, Heinemann, 1960, pp. 25–27. The quotation is from pp. 26–27.

area drew many leading Southern Rhodesian politicians and civil servants into the Federal Government. Sir Godfrey Huggins (soon to become Lord Malvern) became the first Federal Prime Minister. The enthusiasm with which Southern Rhodesians accepted the Federation and the decision to make Salisbury the federal capital heightened the already strong suspicions of many Africans that federation was a form of Southern Rhodesian sub-imperialism. The explanation is probably much less sinister. The Federal Government, which appeared to offer wide scope for ambitious men, naturally attracted the Southern Rhodesians away from the parochial territorial government, and Southern Rhodesia, with years of responsible government behind it, had a much larger reservoir of experienced men on whom the Federal Government could draw than had the two northern territories combined. But, while the preponderance of Southern Rhodesians is easily explained, these politicians and officials brought with them the ideas and ambitions of their own society. They saw the Federation as a larger Southern Rhodesia, not as a larger Nyasaland.

The composition of the Federal Government reinforced the impression that the Southern Rhodesian pattern was to spread across Central Africa. There was the significant difference that Africans sat in the Federal Legislative Assembly, but control lay firmly in European hands. The right to vote, as in Southern Rhodesia, was based upon property, income, and educational qualifications. The franchise and arrangements for return of members were complex, but Colin Leys has estimated that twenty-nine of the thirty-five seats in the original Federal Assembly were controlled by the European population of the Federation.[1] In 1958 the franchise and Constitution of the Assembly were amended so that two voters' rolls were established—an 'ordinary' roll, which had a predominant voice, and a 'special' roll with much more restricted powers. The number of seats in the Assembly was increased to fifty-nine. Again Europeans predominated.

In 1959 the registration figures were 64,465 Europeans, 1,638 Asians and Coloureds, and 1,024 Africans on the Federal 'ordinary' roll, and 161 Europeans, 49 Asians and Coloureds,

[1] Leys and Pratt, op. cit., p. 27.

and 750 Africans on the 'special' roll.[1] These voters followed the established Southern Rhodesian pattern by returning 'the establishment' to power in the Federation. In 1958, under the leadership of Sir Roy Welensky, who had succeeded Huggins as Federal Prime Minister, the United Federal Party (U.F.P.) won forty-four seats against the eight seats of the right-wing Dominion Party (D.P.) led by Mr. Winston Field.

While these constitutional and political patterns were emerging, the economy of the Federation had been expanding at a satisfactory rate. The copper industry of Northern Rhodesia was booming, the Southern Rhodesian industrial complex was expanding, and Nyasaland was receiving considerable financial aid from the Federal Government. This side of the picture looked bright, but underlying the whole federal structure was a major weakness. The Federation was bitterly opposed by the vast majority of Africans. This opposition had existed from the very beginning. It was particularly strong in Northern Rhodesia and Nyasaland where there was deep fear of white settler domination. This African opposition had, in 1951, created doubts among the British Labour Party Ministers who had originally supported the idea of a federation. In September 1951 a conference at Victoria Falls broke up in deadlock and uncertainty, but in the following month the Labour Party was defeated at a General Election and the new Conservative Government decided to go ahead with federation. The Conservatives reasoned that the advantages of the scheme were so great that in time they would become obvious to the Africans and therefore gain their support.

This change of heart did not materialize; indeed African opposition steadily increased. The opposition was reinforced by decisions taken in 1957. First the British Government supported the Federal Government in rejecting the objections of the African Affairs Board (a 'safeguard' device for African interests) to the new proposals for the franchise and composition of the Legislative Assembly. Then in April Sir Roy Welensky succeeded in negotiating further concessions from the British Government. In return for an agreement that Protected Persons (all Africans born in the Protectorates had this status)

---

[1] P. Mason, *Year of Decision*, London, Oxford University Press for the Institute of Race Relations, 1960, p. 261.

could obtain a federal vote without abandoning this status, Sir Roy obtained assurances that the British Government, in areas of concurrent authority, would only legislate at the Federal Government's request, that the civil service, federal and territorial, would be locally based, and that a conference to review the Constitution would meet in 1960 at which constitutional advances and a programme leading to independence would be considered. A deep fear spread among Africans that the Federation would achieve independence as a white-dominated state.

With the establishment of the Federation the centre of interest moved away from Southern Rhodesia but in the colony there were some important developments. After an investigation made by Sir Robert Tredgold an Electoral Amendment Act was passed in 1957, which, while not as liberal as Sir Robert had recommended, did extend the franchise. The electorate was divided into those with 'ordinary' qualifications and those with 'special' qualifications. Registration of 'special' voters was restricted to one-sixth of the Roll as a whole, and once this proportion was reached no further 'special' registrations were to be made. The basis of the qualifications to vote (income, property, and education) was retained but, while the standards of qualifications for the 'ordinary' voter were made substantially higher, qualifications for the 'special' voter were lowered.[1] The arrangement meant that more Africans obtained the right to vote, but that European predominance continued. In November 1960, from a total electorate of 75,061, there were 3,129 registered African voters of whom 1,861 had special qualifications and 1,268 had ordinary qualifications.[2] (It was thought that many Africans who were qualified to register did not do so.)

In Southern Rhodesia 'the establishment' (the U.F.P.) continued to govern but, in 1958, the Government faced a crisis when Garfield Todd, the Prime Minister, was forced to resign partly because of personal differences with his colleagues, and partly because of his supposedly over-liberal policy towards

[1] For details of the franchise, see Appendix III.
[2] Palley, op. cit., p. 312. For a detailed account of the changes, see Leys, op. cit., pp. 215 ff.

Africans. Sir Edgar Whitehead was recalled from America to replace Todd but, after failing to gain a seat at a by-election, was forced into a general election. At this election the opposition Dominion Party (D.P.) ran the U.F.P. very close and, in fact, gained more first preference votes but, by the operation of an alternate vote, Whitehead's U.F.P. gained seventeen seats against the D.P.'s thirteen.[1] The 'liberal' United Rhodesia Party, led by Garfield Todd, gained 11·72 per cent of first-preference votes but failed to gain any seats.

1959 was a troubled year for the Federation. In the early months violence broke out in Nyasaland, as Dr. Hastings Banda and his Nyasaland African National Congress Party, proclaiming their support for African majority rule and their opposition to the Federation, clashed with the Nyasaland Government. A state of emergency was declared, additional troops and police were summoned to break up the disturbances and, in incidents throughout the Protectorate, fifty-two persons were killed. The nationalist leaders, and many of their followers, were imprisoned.

In Southern Rhodesia the Government, fearing similar troubles, declared a state of emergency, and in a dawn swoop on 26 February arrested nearly 500 leaders and supporters of the African National Congress. The Party was banned. The Government followed this up by introducing new restrictive legislation, including the Unlawful Organizations and the Preventive Detention Acts. Under the Unlawful Organizations Act, the African Congresses of Central and South Africa were declared illegal in the colony. Among the Government's powers under the Preventive Detention Act any person could be imprisoned without trial who 'appears to the Governor' to have been concerned in any of the activities, or has been associated with or has supported directly or indirectly, any of the activities which led to the state of emergency. Philip Mason commented that the new legislation went 'far to remove from the inhabitants of Southern Rhodesia—and particularly from the "native"—that protection of the law against executive

---

[1] The D.P. gained 45·7 percent first-preference votes against the U.F.P. 42·4 per cent. Passmore and Mitchell, op. cit., p. 180.

authority which has been built up by generations of struggle in Britain'.[1]

Sir Edgar Whitehead explained that his Government had declared a state of emergency because the nationalists had systematically undermined the Government's authority, because they had ruined government schemes for the development of the country, and because violence and disturbances had been planned to coincide with those in Nyasaland. It is difficult to know whether there was a real danger of major violence and disorder, but what was clear was that African nationalist aspirations and the plans of the European Government were running directly counter to each other. It was a situation heavy with danger and potential tragedy.

[1] The implications of the legislation are examined by Mason, op. cit., pp. 218–23 and in Leys and Pratt, op. cit., pp. 128–31.

CHAPTER II

1960: The Year of Doubt – The Federation

1960 held out great hopes, fears, and expectations for Central Africa. At the beginning of the year it was known that the British Government was to appoint a Royal Commission (the Monckton Commission) to investigate the workings of the Federation and that this would be followed at the end of the year by a Federal Constitutional Conference. It was confidently predicted, therefore, that the future political and constitutional course of the Federation and its three constituent territories would be settled in 1960. Philip Mason, writing at the beginning of the year, called it a 'Year of Decision'.[1] The formalities for making decisions were completed; the commission made its investigations, the conference met at the end of the year; but in fact, except for Nyasaland where an important constitutional advance was made, no decisions were taken. By the end of the year the prevailing mood in Central Africa was one not of decision but of doubt and uncertainty. This was particularly true in Southern Rhodesia where the white minority Government was becoming increasingly conspicuous as African political rights were accepted elsewhere in the continent. By 1960 the road ahead for predominantly black countries like Nigeria, Tanganyika, or even Nyasaland seemed clear, but there was no clear or obvious road for Southern Rhodesia.

The doubts in Southern Rhodesia centred around two major themes: the future of the Federation and the role of Africans in the political and social life of the territory. Southern Rhodesians were reminded of both issues at the beginning of the year. On New Year's Eve Sir Roy Welensky, the forceful and forthright Prime Minister of the Federation, called for greater independence for the Federation. He demanded that the African

---

[1] Mason, *Year of Decision*, 1960.

Affairs Board, a checking device within the constitution to protect African interests, be abolished, and that Southern Rhodesia should obtain independence in the territorial field 'forthwith'. He also urged constitutional changes in Northern Rhodesia and Nyasaland to reduce British power, and to increase the powers of the local Legislative Assemblies. While Sir Roy was making these claims a group of men with very different ambitions were organizing themselves in Southern Rhodesia. On New Year's Day in the Salisbury African township of Harare a new political party was formed, the National Democratic Party (N.D.P.), with Michael Mawema as its first President. It was a multiracial party, but from the beginning drew the great bulk of its support from Africans, replacing for them the banned African National Congress. The new party aimed at quick majority rule.

The two themes of the Federation and African aspirations were closely related, but in Southern Rhodesia, unlike Northern Rhodesia and Nyasaland, it is possible to treat them separately. In the northern territories African political leaders realized that, if they could secede from the Federation, future political power would be theirs, but this was not so clear in Southern Rhodesia. There the immediate problem for Africans was to obtain a role in the exclusively white territorial Government.

A striking feature of federal politics was the number and variety of interests involved in it. The principal participants were the British Government, the Federal Government, the Southern Rhodesian Government and opposition parties, the colonial administrations in the two northern territories, and the African nationalist parties in each of the territories. Although 1960 failed to produce concrete decisions about the Federation's future, the constitutional debates and discussions gave these interests the opportunity to air and clarify their attitudes, and in doing this a balance of interests and powers began to emerge which was to shape the future of the Federation and Southern Rhodesia.

In 1960 the British Government was uncertain and confused about the future of the Federation. This uncertainty bred distrust on all sides. Sir Roy Welensky, who fervently wanted to retain and strengthen the Federation, was deeply suspicious of the British, but so also were the nationalists, who equally

3

fervently wanted to destroy the Federation. The British
Government was caught in the dilemma of trying to reconcile
its initial enthusiasm for the Federation with the growing
realization that opposition within and without Central Africa
was damaging Britain's international image and that if the
internal opposition continued to grow the only way to save the
Federation might be by the use of force. Initially the Conservative Government had given every impression that the
Federation was a permanent arrangement but, by 1960, with
changes in ministerial appointments, with the sustained and
increasing criticism of the Federation, and with a shift in
British policy towards the African colonies, the seeds of doubt
had been sown.

The change of attitude was apparent, but the degree of
change was unknown, and upon this imponderable hinged the
decision whether the British Conservative Government would
support the existing Federation despite all criticism, whether it
would demand a greatly revised Federal structure, or whether
it would allow the Federation to collapse entirely. The British
attitude was obviously open and flexible. It awaited pressures.
It did not take the initiative in finding a solution, and because
of this it had a tortuous—almost a deceitful—character for
those who were firmly committed to a particular stand. The
British were prepared to await events, to bide time, and to try
to gain as large a degree of agreement as possible. In Central
Africa this was no easy task. But at the same time British policy
was dictated by beliefs which were relevant not only to Central
Africa but to the whole empire. These beliefs were that rapid
and irresistible changes were taking place, that these changes
had to be accepted, and that while one might mourn the past
it was unrealistic to imagine that it could be resurrected.

For Central Africa the first clear indications of British thinking came in January when Mr. Harold Macmillan, then the
British Prime Minister, visited Commonwealth and British
territories in Africa including Central Africa. He claimed that
he was going to Africa to listen and learn, but the visit will
always be remembered for his assertion of British policy in his
Cape Town 'winds of change' speech. Before arriving in the
Federation Mr. Macmillan visited West Africa, where, in a
speech at Lagos, he declared that in no circumstances would

British protection be removed from Northern Rhodesia and Nyasaland until political machinery was available to express the will of the majority of the population. He made it clear that in Nyasaland at least the majority of voters would soon be Africans. When the speech was reported in Central Africa the European response was one of suspicion and mistrust.

However, at that time the British Prime Minister was a popular figure in Central Africa and when on 18 January he arrived at Salisbury Airport he was greeted with cries of 'Welcome, Supermac!', and 'Good old Mac!', by a crowd of about 1,500 Europeans. Also among the crowd were some African demonstrators who tried to display placards near Mr. Macmillan's car, but the good nature of the Europeans did not extend to them. The Africans were attacked, their placards torn down, and the police forced to break up the mêlée. It was an early, significant lesson for the British Prime Minister.

On the day of Mr. Macmillan's arrival *The Rhodesian Herald* carried the headlines: 'Anxious Federation looks to Macmillan for Guidance'. Mr. Macmillan did not provide that guidance. He answered questions in vague and general terms and showed a masterly ability to avoid commitment on specific issues such as the terms of the Monckton Commission or the franchise in the two northern territories. Both white Rhodesians and African nationalists felt frustrated and dissatisfied, but at least part of the fault lay in the nature of their hopes. British policy was unsettled. Macmillan was not prepared to give opinions on specific problems, but what he did do was to outline the broad and general British policy. In retrospect it appears obvious where this policy was pointing, but at that time it was not so clear for his Central African audiences. Because the speeches were made in general terms many people were able to listen for what they wanted to hear but ignore the rest.

Macmillan's major speech in Southern Rhodesia was given in a large cinema in Salisbury. Even here the petty, persistent discrimination of race could not be forgotten. The cinema was normally restricted to Europeans because, as was required by municipal by-laws, separate toilets for non-Europeans were not provided. For Macmillan's visit the law was suspended, but some African and coloured leaders refused to attend because they thought that they were being asked to participate in a mere façade of multiracialism to impress the British Prime Minister. The façade, they contended, would disappear when he disappeared.

In his speech Mr. Macmillan asserted his faith in the future of the Federation and the high ideals on which it was based. He said that the function of the Monckton Commission was 'not to destroy the Federation—far from it. It is to advise us how the Federation can best go forward.' However, he reaffirmed that the consent of the northern peoples to the Federation must be obtained. The United Kingdom Government 'has made it clear—abundantly clear—that we will not remove the protection of the British Government to either of the northern territories—Northern Rhodesia or Nyasaland—until it is clear that the expressed wish of these people is to enter into a full and independent Federation.' Then, in what was probably the most important part of his speech, he dealt with African nationalism. He stated that, immediately after the war, when similar nationalist movements had swept across Asia, Britain had accepted the reality of their strength and had not stood in their way. 'Now,' he continued, 'we are faced with a similar growth of national consciousness in Africa. This is one of the facts of the African situation today. We must take it into account in framing our policies. . . . My journey has already taken me to two countries in West Africa [Ghana and Nigeria] where we have followed the same policy as we did in Asia. It has been equally successful.' He said that the economic future of the Federation looked good, 'but our economic life must be set in a political framework. Indeed it cannot thrive unless the political basis of society is sound. The great challenge to you here in the Federation is to establish a sound basis, a social and political structure which reflects the political realities of your country in these days of change.' He stressed that men must be judged as individuals, not by their race. But he also stated that the British Parliamentary system could not work without a high degree of tolerance and self-discipline, qualities which he said could not be developed overnight.[1]

Mr. Macmillan re-emphasized and reiterated the main theme of his Salisbury speech in subsequent speeches on the

[1] *The Rhodesia Herald*, 19 January 1960.

tour. At Lusaka in Northern Rhodesia he said: 'Africa today all over this great continent is on the move and the attitudes and ideas of people all over the continent are changing rapidly. That tide of change is flowing strongly and it cannot be stemmed —but it must be guided so that it does not undermine the steady natural growth of a new country into nationhood.' Then in Cape Town he crowned his tour with the famous 'winds of change' speech.

Harold Macmillan left the Europeans of the Rhodesias confused and uncertain but suspicious. For some of those who believed in the long-term retention of European rule the suspicion turned to downright opposition. A housewife wrote to *The Rhodesia Herald* to 'thank Mr. Macmillan for his speech at the Rhodes Theatre. I now know for sure that the Federation is no place for my children or myself'.[1] But many more white Rhodesians were prepared to wait and see how the general policy was to take particular shape in Central Africa.

If Mr. Macmillan laid down the broad lines of British policy in Africa, it was left to Mr. Ian Macleod, the Colonial Secretary, to complete the details and to give substance to the policy. While Macmillan filled white Rhodesians with confusion, Macleod filled them with fury. When the Colonial Secretary arrived in Salisbury in March he was not greeted with cries of 'Good old Mac'; instead, a welcoming poster declared 'Mau Mau Macleod'. Although the Colonial Secretary did not deal directly with Southern Rhodesia, for that was a Commonwealth Relations Office responsibility, he became for whites throughout the Federation the symbol of British policy. It was a policy which most of the whites despised. Macleod was blamed for the 'sell-out' in Kenya; he was disliked and distrusted because he was prepared to meet and even to negotiate with African nationalist leaders, such as Kenneth Kaunda and Hastings Banda. He was accused of recklessness and bowing to intimidation when he used his influence to end the emergency in Nyasaland and release Dr. Banda. Among African nationalist leaders Macleod's actions made him a trusted and respected politician, but in the eyes of the Europeans these same actions damned him.

When the Nyasaland Constitutional Conference opened in

[1] *The Rhodesia Herald*, 21 January 1960.

London in July, not only were Dr. Banda and his followers present, but it was clear that it was they and not the Federal Government with whom Ian Macleod intended to make his settlement. Before the conference there had been gloomy predictions about its chances of success, but in an atmosphere which bred mutual admiration between Hastings Banda and Ian Macleod, a quick and unanimous agreement was reached. It did not satisfy all Dr. Banda's pre-conference claims but it made clear that Nyasaland's political future lay in African hands.[1] This acceptance of African political rights in Nyasaland was the one clear constitutional step taken in Central Africa during 1960 but, while it offered Nyasaland some certainty for the future, it only increased uncertainty for the Federation. Could the existing Federation continue as Nyasaland fell increasingly under the control of Africans who were bitterly opposed to its existence? Did African political advancement in Nyasaland mean that the British Government planned rapid developments to African majority rule in the two Rhodesias? After the constitutional conference Dr. Banda confirmed that he was opposed to the Federation whether he was in or out of office while Orton Chirwa, one of Dr. Banda's close supporters, said: 'Federation is dead. It was already dead before the conference put the last nail in the coffin.'[2]

By the end of 1960 the British Government had revealed in word and deed that the policy it had followed in West Africa was to be extended to East and Central Africa. African nationalism was not only a force to be recognized; it was a force with which agreement must be reached. African nationalist leaders who were recognized as the leaders of African opinion were to be included in any negotiations about future constitutional arrangements. In Kenya Britain had demonstrated that the claims of a small but important white minority were not to stand in the way of the majority African claims. Within the Federation the Nyasaland constitutional conference had

---

[1] The franchise was greatly extended to embrace an estimated 100,000 people on two Rolls; eight members of the Legislative Assembly would be returned by voters on the upper qualifications Roll and twenty by the lower Roll. The twenty-eight elected members would be joined in the Legislative Council by only three *ex officio* and two nominated members. Also half the Executive Council would consist of elected members of the Legislative Council.

[2] *The Times*, 6 August 1960.

revealed that the future of that territory lay with Africans, and thereby the future of the Federation would eventually depend upon the goodwill of these Africans.

The trend of British policy was against the interests of the Federal Government. Although the British Government continued to protest that it wished to preserve the Federation, in paying heed to African nationalists the British were listening to the very men who were determined to overthrow the Federation. The growing divergence between the British and Federal Governments was caused by this change in the British attitude. Federation had been imposed in the teeth of strong African opposition. By 1960 the Federal Government was still prepared to accept this opposition but the British were hesitant and doubtful. To defend their shift of policy the British Government argued that the anticipated change in African opinion as the benefits of Federation became apparent had not taken place, and, as we have seen, great stress was laid upon the need to accept change in Africa, to retain a flexible approach in a continent in transition.

Sir Roy Welensky was the dominant figure of the Federal Government. He is a large, affable man of great charm and friendliness, but volatile and emotional, which has sometimes clouded his political judgements. In 1960 Sir Roy stood as firmly for the Federation as he had from the very beginning. His policy had not changed. Sir Roy was so committed to the federal idea that he was prepared to try to weather any opposition, African or British. His immediate aim was to gain for the Federation increased independence from Britain, leading to a completely independent Federation in which the dominant power would lie with the Federal not the territorial governments. For Sir Roy the Federation was indestructible. He frequently quoted at the British Government the early promises of the permanence of the arrangement, and also Mr. Macmillan's protestations that the British Government's aim was to devise a means of preserving the Federation.

Sir Roy's chief emphasis was on the sound economic base which the Federation provided for the development of Central Africa. It would, he said, be a bastion against the spread of Communist influence, for while economic expansion was taking place power would remain in responsible hands.

Political advance would not be allowed to run ahead of economic development. Sir Roy always laid great emphasis on this. In a speech to the Northern Rhodesian Legislative Council when he was urging the creation of the Federation, he had said that progress depended on 'the economic development of these territories . . . Political rights, after all, mean very little to a man with an empty stomach. If we are genuinely concerned about the Africans let us give them economic development and political rights can come later. This is a secondary consideration.'[1]

Sir Roy was publicly committed to a policy of racial partnership, a policy in which it was said that merit not colour was the criterion. But 'partnership' was a very imprecise term open to a wide variety of interpretations. Sir Roy's interpretation, which accepted at least for the present the dominant role of the white minority, was anathema to the African nationalists. In 1949, when discussions were taking place about the Federation, Sir Roy had said: 'The European community will not under any circumstances recognize a paramountcy of African interests. I am prepared to work in partnership with the African people—and for as long as I can see, in that partnership we will be the senior partner—but I will never accept that Northern Rhodesia is to be an African state.'[2] Eleven years later, at the Federal review conference, Sir Roy as Federal Prime Minister revealed a difference of tone but not of substance. He said: 'I am opposed to domination by either black or white which is what most politicians want . . . Nevertheless we cannot afford to overlook the vital contribution which has been made and is still being made by the Europeans. "Africa for the Africans" is a tragically impossible slogan.'[3]

In Sir Roy the Federation had a champion of great forcefulness and courage, but he was becoming an increasingly isolated figure. By the middle of 1960 he was the only major political leader who was still uncompromisingly in favour of the existing Federation. Not only did the African nationalist leaders persist in their opposition, but the European leaders of Southern

[1] Sir Roy Welensky; *4,000 Days*, London, Collins, 1964 p. 35.
[2] Op. cit., p. 34.
[3] Op. cit., p. 288.

Rhodesia had increasing doubts. The Africans feared that the Federation meant the extension of white minority rule over all Central Africa. The Europeans of Southern Rhodesia feared that with Britain's increasing acceptance of African nationalism the Federation would become the means of extending African extremist rule into their country. There were still strong hopes among Europeans that some form of Federation could be preserved, but doubts were growing and these doubts showed themselves even in the Southern Rhodesian Government. The African leaders of the north had long realized that their objective of black majority rule could more easily be obtained outside the Federation. As doubts grew, the Europeans of Southern Rhodesia began to realize that their interests might also be better served by concentrating their strength in their own territory and abandoning the wider aims of Federation.

Uncertainty and doubt revealed itself even in the Federal Assembly. The predominantly European opposition party, the Dominion Party (D.P.), had never been particularly enamoured of the existing Federal structure, and increasingly it stressed that changes would have to be made. Mr. Winston Field, the leader of the Federal D.P., sponsored a plan, the Central African Alliance, for reorganizing the Federation, whereby Southern Rhodesia and the section of Northern Rhodesia which followed the railway line, that is, the areas in which most Europeans lived, including the Copper Belt, would be amalgamated, while the remaining, predominantly African, areas of Northern Rhodesia and Nyasaland would be shaped into loosely affiliated African protectorates or states.

Criticism from the opposition in the Federal Assembly was to be expected but, even among Sir Roy Welensky's United Federal Party (U.F.P.) supporters, there were critics of the trend of events in the Federation. The principal critic was Mr. Ian Smith, the Chief Government Whip in the Federal Assembly. At that time Mr. Smith was not even the smallest of clouds on the British Government's horizon, but his future importance warrants an examination of his opinions in 1960. In speeches in the Federal Assembly he expressed his opinion not only on the Federation but on political developments elsewhere in Africa. In a speech on 11 April 1960, he said that it was essential to settle the Federal Constitution for 'the whole future seems so uncertain, when we see the possibility of losing everything we have fought for and built up over the years.' The D.P. opposition had suggested a united political front for the negotiations with Britain and this appealed to Mr. Smith, although he wanted the terms of the united front to be defined. He attacked 'the long-haired critics' of the Federation both inside and outside its borders. 'We should,' he said, 'have some sort of united front for this conference so that we will know within our own borders just precisely where we stand, just precisely who is on our side and who is going to be on the other side, aiding and abetting the effect of the big sell-out of Western civilization in Central Africa.' Obviously Mr. Smith was already thinking in terms of a crusade in which the forces of right and wrong were clearly defined. 'Our fight,' he continued, 'is for full independence—there can be no compromise on that particular issue . . . We have no such word as defeat in our vocabulary.' Then he spoke of 'the ghastly mess' which had been caused elsewhere in Africa by giving independence with majority rule to people 'who have no more than a veneer of civilization'. This he blamed on the United Kingdom Government which, he said, was 'riddled with arrogance, believing that it has a divine right to guide the affairs of this country' but it 'must be precluded from doing so for all time henceforth'. He believed that the United Kingdom Government had persistently given way to extremists and violence, represented by the African nationalist leaders, some of whom he described as 'political criminals'.

Finally Mr. Smith emphasized that Southern Rhodesia was the kingpin of the Federation and that minimum requirements must be met if it were to remain within the Federation. According to Mr. Smith one of the main objects of the Federation had been to spread 'the Southern Rhodesian way of life' into the northern territories, but this had been frustrated by British Colonial Office policy. He spoke of 'the model system of race relations we have evolved' in Southern Rhodesia where 'we have done so much for the people of this country and in particular for the African people', much more than the Colonial Office had done for the northern territories. The views of Southern Rhodesia must be predominant. 'We have succeeded, without any doubt, where the Colonial Office has failed so lamentably.[1] During his speech D.P. opposition members called upon Mr. Smith to cross the floor of the House to join them. Mr. Smith did not do that but it was clear that he was far to the right of his own U.F.P. party, so far in fact that he was prepared even publicly to lay down his terms for continuing to support the Federation.

Mr. Smith's independent attitude was re-emphasized in April when he gave evidence to the Monckton Commission. Again he stressed that he was only prepared to support the Federation under the conditions that it be granted independence and that it be modelled on Southern Rhodesia for, he said, 'since Federation it had become more and more apparent that the Southern Rhodesian way of life was best.'[2]

Even in 1960, therefore, Mr. Smith's speeches revealed a strong determination to fight for what he considered a righteous cause against the combined forces of African nationalism and the untrustworthy British Government, and a strong conviction that whatever was in Southern Rhodesia was right.

Like the Federation, Southern Rhodesia was ruled by a U.F.P. Government. However, the leaders of the two Governments provided a striking contrast. Against the robust, extrovert figure of Sir Roy Welensky stood the academic, remote, bachelor figure of Sir Edgar Whitehead, the Southern Rhodesian Prime Minister. Physically Sir Edgar was the antithesis of a Rhodesian European caricature. He was obviously a man of sedentary life with a withdrawn, introspective air. He was well liked and respected by those who worked close to him but socially his reticence made him a poor mixer. He suffered from physical disabilities in sight and hearing which further emphasized his isolation. However, as a politician he had great determination, a logical mind and the ability to speak with clarity and force, but, in his isolation, he later failed to see that what he thought desirable was not immediately possible.

Sir Edgar led a party that was closely associated with the Federal image, and indeed his territorial U.F.P. party continued to support some form of federation right to the end, but the territorial party was in a very different position from Sir

---

[1] Central African Federation Hansard, 11 April 1960.
[2] Monckton Commission, Vol. V, p. 116.

Roy's Federal Party. Its main concern was obviously with Southern Rhodesian affairs. Its support for the Federation was based upon the advantages which the territory gained from the federal association. Also, the territorial party was in a much weaker parliamentary position than its Federal brother. Initially, with only seventeen seats against the D.P. opposition's thirteen, Whitehead realized that his hold on power was precarious. Naturally, therefore, the Government had to listen carefully to any shifts of opinion among the predominantly white electorate. As doubts about the Federation grew among the electorate, so they grew among the Government. Sir Edgar and his colleagues proclaimed their support for the Federation, but laid down terms for the continuation of this support. Late in January 1960, Sir Edgar stated that Southern Rhodesia was prepared to remain in the Federation provided that the remaining reserve powers which the British Government enjoyed in the Southern Rhodesian Constitution were removed, that the Federal Government remained in 'civilized hands', and finally, that the two northern territories did not fall under African nationalist rule. In the Legislative Assembly he explained that: 'I thought it very advisable to give the minimum conditions beyond which we would never retreat in any circumstances . . . As far as I am concerned, I would not retreat from these minimum terms, and I have informed the country publicly that if we are unable to obtain these terms I will feel it my duty to come back and take the view of the electorate on the next step.'[1]

Sir Edgar was soon under attack for his statement not so much for his doubts about the Federation, but because of the impracticability of his suggestions. Who, he was asked, was to define 'civilized hands'? How could anybody guarantee that nationalist governments would not rule in the north? These were valid criticisms, but much more serious for the U.F.P. was the dilemma which Sir Edgar's statement revealed. The Southern Rhodesian U.F.P. never really resolved its ambivalent position.

The Government's dilemma was not shared by the opposition party—the territorial Dominion Party, led by William Harper. The D.P. was opposed to the Federation in its existing form and

[1] S.R.L.A. Hansard, 10 February 1960.

warned of the future implications for Southern Rhodesian Europeans. In the Southern Rhodesian Legislative Assembly Mr. Harper said that the present Federation 'will inevitably lead to a lowering of European standards in this country, and it is my view that this year [1960] is not so much a year of independence, but is the year of the battle for the maintenance of standards.' He believed that majority rule in Southern Rhodesia 'would be a resuscitation of the dark ages'.[1]

Clearly support for the Federation was uncertain in Southern Rhodesia, but it was not dead. Again and again the U.F.P. stressed the economic importance to the Federation. They stressed the dire economic consequences which would follow a complete break of the federal ties. Most Europeans therefore thought it in their personal economic interests to retain some form of federation even if the existing one was unsatisfactory, but against this was the fear that membership of the Federation might imply acceptance of rapid African political advance. These two factors created a delicate balance for European opinion in Southern Rhodesia. Sir Edgar had truly reflected this in his stand as a supporter of the Federation, provided that certain conditions were met. But who was to confirm these conditions and ensure that they were maintained? Certainly the British Government, and even more the African nationalist leaders, would never leave such decisions to the white electorate of Rhodesia.

The strongest opposition to the Federation came from Africans. Not all Africans opposed it and African Members sat in the Federal Parliament, but the nationalist leaders opposed Federation and in all three territories they had the support of the majority of Africans. Their stand was clear and unequivocal. The Federation was an attempt to extend and perpetuate white rule in Central Africa. It was directly opposed to African desires and interests, and had, from the very beginning, been strongly opposed by Africans. The anti-Federal appeal was clearest in the two northern territories of Northern Rhodesia and Nyasaland. There militant, unswerving opposition to the Federation was an integral part of the nationalist appeal of leaders such as Kenneth Kaunda and Hastings Kamuzu Banda. Africans who supported the Federation were branded as traitors and

[1] S.R.L.A. Hansard, 25 February 1960, cols. 3042 and 3047.

sometimes physical violence was used against them. There can
be no doubt of the strength and determination of nationalist
opposition. The Monckton Commission found that 'the dislike
of Federation among Africans in the two Northern Territories
is widespread, sincere and long standing. It is almost patho-
logical.'[1]

During 1960 the nationalist leaders in Northern Rhodesia
and Nyasaland noticeably gained ground. Both Kenneth
Kaunda and Hastings Banda were released from detention,
and both returned to lead strong militant movements which
were firmly married to the ideas of majority rule and secession
from the Federation. Ian Macleod's recognition of these leaders
was an acceptance of the strength of the movements they led,
and from the recognition came enhanced prestige and power
for the leaders.

In Southern Rhodesia the African attitude to Federation was
less clear. The African nationalist leaders were firmly against
it, but there were some Africans in the country who thought
that it was directly in African interests to remain within a
Federation which held out hopes that the more liberal policies
of the northern territories might spread to Southern Rhodesia,
and that in time the sheer weight of African numbers in the
Federation would mean African predominance in the Government. Nationalist supporters in Southern Rhodesia did not
give evidence to the Monckton Commission, but other Africans
did. What stands out in their evidence is that they wanted more
functions, such as African education and labour, transferred to
the Federal Government, presumably because they had more
faith that an African voice would be heard by the Federal than
by the Southern Rhodesian Government. Mr. J. Nyamakanga
said that he wanted to retain the Federation, but under British
control. He wanted education and labour to be Federal responsibilities, he wanted more African representation in the
Governments, especially in Southern Rhodesia, and he wanted
an end to discrimination.[2] Mr. W. Mugadza wanted the
Federal Government to legislate against racial discrimination
in Southern Rhodesia. He thought that the Federal franchise

---

[1] Monckton Commission Report (Cmnd 1148), p. 16.
[2] Monckton Commission Evidence, Vol. V, p. 39.

should be amended to give greater African representation and he also asked that all education should be a Federal subject.[1]

The atmosphere in the Federation at the beginning of 1960 did not lend itself to compromise solutions of complicated constitutional issues. Nyasaland was still gripped in emergency regulations, with its major African nationalist leaders, including Dr. Hastings Banda, in prison or restriction. In Southern Rhodesia also many African leaders languished in prison after the banning of the African National Congress in 1959. Obviously the atmosphere was not good, but Sir Roy Welensky suspected that for his purposes it might grow even worse, as opinion in Britain seemed to be turning against the Federation. The Devlin Report on the emergency in Nyasaland had reinforced the wave of sympathy for African nationalist aspirations and had caused grave embarrassment to the British Conservative Government. Therefore Sir Roy urged that the Federal constitutional conference should go ahead as planned.

To aid the conference and to give it a basis of discussion, a Royal Commission, under Lord Monckton, was appointed. The Commission was to make recommendations on the future working of the Federation. For much of 1960 the shadow of the Commission lay across Central Africa. From the beginning controversy surrounded it. There was confusion and dispute about its terms of reference, and in particular whether it had the right to recommend the secession of a territory from the Federation. The British Government was studiously and irritatingly vague about this issue, while Sir Roy Welensky denied that the Commission could consider secession and reacted angrily when Sir Hartley Shawcross, a member of the Commission, said on British television that it could. The British Labour Party wanted secession considered, as of course did African Nationalist leaders, and because of the doubts about the terms of reference the Labour Party refused to participate, while the African political leaders and their followers refused to give evidence. Added to these difficulties was the cumbersome composition of the Commission, with eleven British Government nominees, including the Chairman and Vice-Chairman, one member each for Australia and Canada, four nominees of

[1] Op. cit., p. 214.

the Federal Government, and three from each territorial Government. It was hardly surprising that the Commission's report was peppered with minority findings.

Obviously any attempt to find a consensus of opinion about the Federation was well-nigh impossible. Yet the Commission was set the task of recommending ways in which the Federation could continue and carry support with it. In collecting its evidence the Commission, which Mr. Macmillan acknowledged was 'free in practice to hear all points of view from whatever quarter', became a sounding-board for the great spectrum of interests and opinions within the Federation. It became a means of collecting and assessing these opinions. In this, and not in producing an agreed formula for the future, lay its importance.

What became clear, as the Commission collected its evidence, was that even excluding the outright opponents there was little unanimity of opinion about the aims of Federation or its future organization. Among its supporters the Federation had meant all things to all men. Many laid stress on the economic advantages and gave political development a minor role. Others saw it as a great experiment in racial 'partnership'; others again as a means of spreading white settler rule across Central Africa. In the early years of Federation these diverse views had flourished side by side without stifling each other, because the precise implications of Federation had not been challenged, but by 1960 the divergences were marked and obvious. The evidence to the Commission revealed that the supporters of each interpretation appreciated that their aims could only be realized if the hopes of others were dashed. The Commission had therefore to attempt the impossible; to balance irreconcilables.

On some important issues the Commission reached agreement. It was unanimously accepted that some form of Federation should be retained. It was also accepted that African representation should be increased and the franchise extended, but there were differences over the detailed implications of this. A small majority of the Commission recommended that the Federal Legislative Assembly should be divided equally between Africans and Europeans, thirty members from each race, with a Speaker drawn from outside. In relation to the franchise the Commission thought that it was important to give the vote to many more Africans so that they realized that the Federation was not just for Europeans.

The dominant problem which the Commission faced was to decide how, if a Federation were to be retained, the African peoples of the northern territories could be reconciled to it without completely alienating the Europeans in Southern Rhodesia. The majority report, after noting the deep dislike for Federation in Northern Rhodesia and Nyasaland, said: 'The expectation that the opposition would decline as the economic advantages of Federation became apparent have not been realized . . . In brief, the opposition to Federation which, as we have seen, was strong at the time that Federation was introduced has gathered further strength by African disappointment in the manner of its operation. Partnership, in their view, has been a sham.' The Commission thought that this made the existing Federation untenable. 'Ultimately', said the report, 'Federation must rest on a general willingness to accept it, or it must be preserved by force. To hold the Federation together by force we regard as out of the question.' The alternative which the Commission offered was to give greater recognition to African rights, and within the federal framework to alter the relationship between the Federal and territorial Governments.

In addition to increased African participation in government, the Commission wanted to see the removal of all racial discrimination, for although, said the Commission, there had been some improvement, the pace had been too slow. It proposed that there should be a Bill of Rights, which would help allay the fears of racial discrimination on either side and also provide a criterion for political and judicial rights.

The Commission dealt harshly with two treasured beliefs of the Federal Government. The first was that economic development was an adequate substitute for political progress. The Commission praised the economic achievements of the Federation, and stressed the dire economic consequences that might follow its break-up. But economic success did not remove the political obligation. The Federation could succeed, claimed the Commission, only if the majority of the population, including the African population, participated in its political as

4

well as its economic activities. Economics could not be divorced
from politics, and to succeed in one it was necessary to succeed
in the other. The second cherished opinion was that race
should not be the basis of a political division. The majority
recommendation that parity should be granted to black and
white in the Federal Legislative Assembly was a clear acceptance that race created a political distinction in its own right
which should be recognized in the constitutional arrangements.

Obviously these recommendations would be difficult for the
Federal Government and the European electorate to accept,
but even more controversial were the recommendations about
the relations between the Federal and territorial Governments.
The Commission in fact recommended that the balance of
power within the Federation should shift towards the individual
territories. It proposed that the constitutional advance of each
territory should not be hindered by membership of the Federation and that the functions of the territorial Governments be
extended to cover all subjects 'affecting the day to day life of
the inhabitants'. In the view of the majority of the Commissioners, these subjects should include education, health
services, agriculture, roads, and prisons. The Federal Government would be left with matters connected with external relations, including trade relations and defence, but not internal
security.

Finally the Commission took the step which aroused the
greatest controversy. The majority report read: '. . . we are
convinced that no form of federal association, however reformed, can succeed so long as many of its peoples feel that they
are being kept in it against their will and can break out only
by force. We therefore recommend that under certain conditions there should be an opportunity to withdraw from the
association.'

The great increase proposed in territorial rights, including
the right to secede, was another attempt by the Commission to
contain the racial fears which threatened the Federation. By
increasing territorial powers it was hoped that the fears of the
whites of Southern Rhodesia and the blacks of the northern
territories would be overcome; that the territories as ultimate
masters of their own fates would realize that their interests lay
in retaining the federal link.

Despite the substantial changes which the Commission recommended, it emphasized that its aim was to preserve and indeed strengthen the Federation. The idealism of the early days found a voice, but a voice tinged with doubt. To break up the Federation would, the report read, 'amount to an admission that there is no hope of survival for any multiracial society on the African continent and that differences of colour and race are irreconcilable. We cannot agree to such a conclusion.' But how realistic were the Commissioners' hopes? They, themselves, had heard the interminable conflict of opinion and interest. When they made proposals to retain the Federation they asked for concessions which could be achieved only by cutting across firmly held beliefs and by seeking compromise from those who were unwilling to compromise. Indeed the Commissioners' report seemed to pose the very question they had set out to answer. How realistic was it to hope for the preservation of the Federation on any terms without using force?

Inevitably the Commission's report had a mixed reception. The British Government expressed its 'warm gratitude to Lord Monckton and his colleagues on the Commission for this important report which provides a valuable analysis of a very complex problem'.[1] For the opposition Labour Party in Britain, Hugh Gaitskell described it as 'a most impressive document'.[2] The enthusiasm in Britain was not matched in Central Africa. The African nationalist leaders dismissed the report because it did not recommend the immediate dissolution of the Federation. In Southern Rhodesia, Mr. T. G. Silundika of the National Democratic Party said that his party resented 'most strongly the fabricated conclusion by the Commission that the Africans in Southern Rhodesia favour Federation'.[3] The Europeans of Southern Rhodesia were equally dissatisfied. The report was published at a bad time: in the hot days of October, shortly after there had been serious African riots and strikes in Salisbury and Gwelo, and when the prevailing mood was to deny to Africans what they had tried to achieve by force. There was much sympathy among Europeans for Sir Roy

[1] *The Times*, 12 October 1960.
[2] British Parliament Hansard, Vol. 629, col. 25, 1 November 1960.
[3] *The Times*, 13 October 1960.

Welensky, but at the same time a growing feeling that to check African extremism Southern Rhodesia would have to stand alone.

The strongest adverse reaction came from Sir Roy and his close associates. Sir Roy was bitterly disappointed at the Commission's report, especially its acceptance of the right of secession. This, he claimed, was a subject outside its competence and indeed he continued to affirm that secession was even outside the terms of a constitutional conference. The conference which was planned for the end of the year was, he said, to 'consider a programme for the attainment of such a state as would enable the Federation to become eligible for full membership of the Commonwealth.'[1] This implied independence for the Federation, not its break-up.

When he spoke of the report in the Federal Legislative Assembly, he stressed that the Commission was only advisory, and that the decisions had to be made by the Governments. He attacked the emphasis on political rather than economic development. 'The result,' he claimed, 'was a classical Report on how to underdevelop an economy, how to fiddle while wealth burns.' Also, he attacked the franchise proposals and the recommendations for the transfer of functions from the Federal to the territorial Governments. 'The Federal Government will not,' he declared, 'allow itself to be influenced by any consideration of political expediency in judging what functions might be exchanged or transferred between governments.' On one major point, the need for the Federation to continue, he was able to agree with the Commission, but, said Sir Roy, 'it has given the benediction with one hand and the death-stab with the other'.[2]

In the same Assembly Ian Smith described the report as 'the most mischievous in dealing with the future of this country that I have ever had the misfortune to read'. It was, he thought, a 'scandalous betrayal' of all the British promises. He rejected all the proposed concessions to African nationalists. He thought that racial discrimination in the Federation had been much exaggerated, for similar discrimination existed everywhere in the world including Britain. Mr. Smith said that the members

[1] *The Times*, 12 October 1960.
[2] C.A.L.A. Hansard, Vol. XIV, 25 October 1960.

of the Monckton Commission should first clean up their 'own backyard'. In Southern Rhodesia, 'we are not prepared to accept anything which smacks of political revolution'. Change, which must be slow, must also be controlled by the people of the territories. He re-emphasized the necessity of independence from Britain, of freedom from the meddling British politicians who had done so much harm in Southern Africa. In passing he mentioned the freedom the Americans had gained by their revolution. He again praised the European contribution in Central Africa without which 'the country would so very quickly revert to barbarism and chaos'.

After describing British policy in Africa as 'too little too late' based upon 'incompetence and ignorance', he laid down five points. These were: the complete removal of Britain's reserve rights in the Southern Rhodesian Constitution; full control of its own affairs for the Federal Government; the assurance that in Northern Rhodesia and Nyasaland government would be placed 'in the hands of responsible, civilized opinion'; a precise and unambiguous plan of constitutional advance for the two northern territories to 'ensure a continuous control in civilized hands for all time'; and the assurance that any deviation from these standards would receive the approval of all the Parliaments in the Federation. In a not untypical phrase Mr. Smith said that there was 'no compromise on these matters'.[1]

Obviously the Monckton Commission had failed to resolve the differences of opinion. There seemed therefore to be little chance of a successful constitutional conference at the end of the year, but what chance there was disappeared because of the nature of the conference. It was called for mid-December. Around it centred a series of disputes which seemed almost a convention of such conferences. There were disputes about who should attend, about what the agenda should be, and, once it had started, some African delegates staged a walk-out. The dramatics were more impressive than the conference. It met apparently without an agenda. The delegates made their statements and then it was over without any real discussion and certainly without any agreement. Winston Field later called it 'farcical', for it had 'no agenda and no apparent plan'.[2]

---

[1] C.A.L.A. Hansard, 25 October 1960.
[2] Cmnd 2073. Field-Butler, 13 June 1963.

Obviously the British Government had decided that agreement at that time was impossible, and so the formality of the conference was completed but nothing else.

For the Federation the expectations of 1960 were unfulfilled. No constitutional settlement had emerged. But it would be wrong to conclude that the developments of the year had been unimportant. The Monckton Commission did not lead directly to a settlement, but it had provided a channel for the expression of diverse opinion. This opinion, plus the Commission's recommendations made it clear for most people that the existing federal structure could not survive. Only Sir Roy Welensky and a small group around him continued to believe otherwise. Most Africans continued to oppose Federation on any terms. Most Europeans accepted that the existing structure was unworkable but hoped that some looser link could be preserved to retain the economic advantages.

After the break-up of the constitutional conference, consideration of Federal affairs was suspended. For two years the Federation existed in a constitutional twilight, vague and uncertain of its future. Concentration moved to the three individual territories, but this concentration was in itself a decision in relation to the Federation. The Federation as a unit was not to decide its own future: the decision hung upon the developments and settlements within the territories.

CHAPTER III

1960: The Year of Doubt – Southern Rhodesia

The need for reconciliation between the races was the chief problem which faced the Federation. It was also Southern Rhodesia's main problem. With increasing concern the question was asked: 'What role are Africans to play in the country's political, economic and social life?' The question taxed Europeans and Africans alike.

Divisions in politics are necessarily relative. By some standards almost all white Rhodesian politicians who were active in 1960 were right-wing and reactionary. There were, for example, no Southern Rhodesian Members of Parliament appealing for 'one man, one vote', or even calling for African majority rule within a decade. But to use such standards is to use a blunt instrument. What was striking in 1960, and all the more striking when subsequent developments are remembered, was the clear and deep division between the two exclusively white parliamentary parties. It was a division based upon their attitude to African advancement. The two parties were the governing United Federal Party (U.F.P.), led by Sir Edgar Whitehead,[1] and the opposition Dominion Party (D.P.) led by William Harper. The U.F.P., the 'Establishment' party, was associated with urban and business interests, especially the great mining companies, while 'the opposition' had traditionally drawn most of its support from rural areas. 'The Establishment's' hold on political power had often appeared unchallengeable, but the 1958 election had revealed that this was no longer so.

The U.F.P. Government pursued a policy of 'partnership'. Already, in relation to the Federal Government, we have seen

---

[1] For a list of the U.F.P. Cabinet, see Appendix I, p. 307.

that this was an imprecise term, but in 1960 Sir Edgar's interpretation was an acceptance that Africans would play an increasing role in national affairs including politics; that racial
discrimination, with its humiliation and indignity, should be
removed; that in the long term the races could not be divided;
that Africans, like Europeans, must share the rights, privileges,
and obligations of full citizenship. It was a policy which turned
its back on *apartheid* and racial separation. The most effective
demonstration of the policy had been in the Industrial Conciliation Act of 1959, which had removed racial distinction in
labour negotiations and conciliation. In introducing the legislation Mr. Abrahamson, the Minister of Labour, had said:
'We wish to deal here with fundamental matters in an emergent
multiracial society in a non-racial way.'[1] However, Sir Edgar
stressed that, to succeed, the policy of partnership must be implemented gradually. For example, he opened the higher
grades of the civil service to Africans but said that it would be
twenty years before an African would hold a top post. Sir
Edgar also stressed that in political terms 'partnership' would
be implemented by those with 'a stake in the country', the
Europeans and the more prosperous Africans, not by a mass
popular movement. This slow and gradual approach, with its
emphasis on property and established interests, was strongly
attacked by African nationalists and by the more liberal Europeans. These critics doubted whether in the end Sir Edgar
was prepared to accept the full implications of the policy by
sharing political power with Africans and then accepting
majority African rule.

   In the Legislative Assembly Sir Edgar faced a very different
opposition. The D.P. rejected 'partnership', claiming that it
was too liberal, that it endangered the existing stable and satisfactory structure of Southern Rhodesian life. The D.P. based
their policy on the belief that, for the good of all Rhodesians,
control must remain in 'civilized' hands, which for the foreseeable future, meant European hands. They thought that
Africans were too inexperienced and socially retarded to take
an immediate and active part in governing the state. Their
opponents in the Government accused them of preaching
racialism based upon a belief in African inferiority. 'It is crystal

[1] S.R.L.A. Hansard, 12 May 1959, col. 1540.

clear', said A. E. Abrahamson, the Minister of Labour, 'that what has been represented by the Opposition from the very beginning of this Parliament has been the voice of white supremacy and that completely impossible hope of preserving it for ever on the basis of the white skin.'[1]

The difference of approach to race relations was at the root of all parliamentary disputes. There was no longer any attempt to pretend that policy towards Africans was a technical, 'non-political' problem. It was the subject which divided the white political parties and was accepted as such by both sides. When, in August 1960, the Prime Minister introduced a Bill to increase the size of the existing Legislative Assembly from thirty to fifty members, he explained that the existing House was too small for the volume of work it was asked to perform, but then he continued: 'This is where hon. members opposite and myself are in entire disagreement. I want to be perfectly frank on this. I believe that with fifty members for the first time, it is almost certain that we shall have Africans elected to the Southern Rhodesian House.' He thought that three or four Africans would be returned, and he said: 'I believe, and I know hon. members opposite disagree with me at this stage, that it would be for the real benefit of Southern Rhodesia as a whole if that were to happen.'[2]

The Prime Minister's prediction of opposition reaction was accurate. In reply, Mr. Harper stated:

I may say that in general the public [i.e. the Europeans] do not favour the idea of African representation in Parliament at the present moment. . . . No doubt he [the Prime Minister] has not paid sufficient regard to the ineffectiveness of Africans in administration. Already with regard to rural Native Councils the Native Commissioners in the Native Reserves have great difficulty in getting effective co-operation from natives on such a simple level of administration, yet the Prime Minister feels it right and proper that they should be in a position whereby they have a substantial say in running of a modern state.

Then Mr. Harper analysed the root of the political dispute. He claimed that he had no objection to Africans in the House on a colour basis. 'There is,' he declared, 'no question of

[1] S.R.L.A. Hansard, 12 December 1961.   [2] Op. cit., 17 August 1960.

colour as far as I am concerned. It is what goes with it that I am concerned with, or the lack of what should go with it.' It was clear to the Prime Minister and himself:

that the difference between us really depends on the question of whether we want Africans in the House in the next Parliament or whether we do not. . . . We simply do not want them in the next House. We feel that it is premature. We feel that it would be damaging to social conditions in this country. I myself can visualize that if we have them in the House here no doubt they will share the restaurant with us and they will share the bars with us. We will be living cheek by jowl with them and what sort of legislation can the people of this country expect when we ourselves are being conditioned to living cheek by jowl with Africans.[1]

As can be seen, the division was fundamental. While Whitehead believed that the races could and should work and develop together, even if the process was gradual, Harper believed that, 'If you take the two main races alone, you cannot suit the Africans entirely without the Europeans complaining.'[2] There was no doubt whose interests Mr. Harper thought should predominate.

As the Government took steps to implement its policy of partnership, so it was steadfastly opposed by the D.P. Nowhere was this more clearly demonstrated than in the Government's acceptance that the Land Apportionment Act must be amended, and perhaps even repealed. The Government's thinking was strongly influenced by the second report of the Select Committee on the Resettlement of Natives, published on 16 August 1960. The committee had carried out its task with great diligence. For two years it had pursued its investigations, touring all parts of the country. The all-party committee had been asked to make recommendations for:

finding land for and resettling 111,261 African families who cannot obtain so-called 'economic' holdings in the areas in which they are at present farming, or who are occupying land illegally (unalienated Crown land, alienated farms in the European Area or the Forest Area), or under conditions which do not apply to that land (portions of the Native Purchase Area occupied under tribal or communal conditions), or occupying mission land, or Native

---

[1] S.R.L.A. Hansard, 23 August 1960.
[2] Op. cit., 30 June 1960, col. 74.

Reserves which should be evacuated in order to preserve natural resources.[1]

The committee advised that the country simply could not afford to move these people, for it would cost about £28,000,000. The solution which the committee offered was to leave the people where they were but to declare the land 'African land'. The emphasis which the committee wanted to see was an improvement and development of lands under existing occupation, not the expensive task of opening up more land. Southern Rhodesia did not have a land shortage but was using inefficiently and wastefully the occupied areas.

The committee did not confine itself to the problem of resettlement. It grasped the nettle of examining the whole implication of the Land Apportionment Act. It concluded that, while in the past the Land Apportionment Act had been justified, it had now outlived its usefulness. The division of the races was only holding back the efficient development of the country's natural resources. The report stated: 'Whatever justification there may originally have been for this attitude [reserving areas for races] it is difficult to justify this artificial barrier in 1960 when the crying need is for more development and for an increase in the national output' (para. 214), and: 'Because of the restrictions which have prevented Europeans and Africans from participating in the development of areas designated for the other race, much development which might otherwise have taken place has not occurred' (para. 184). The committee recommended: 'It should be the ultimate aim to be achieved as soon as possible, for agricultural land anywhere in Southern Rhodesia to be purchasable by any person, irrespective of race or colour, since your Committee does not believe that the Act can, or should, in the best interests of the country remain in force much longer' (para. 227). The committee then went further and recommended that 'land in general whether urban or agricultural should be purchasable by anyone, anywhere, irrespective of race or colour' (para. 229).

When the report was laid before the Legislative Assembly a major debate ensued. The division between the parties was absolute. Blair Ewing of the U.F.P., a member of the

[1] Second Report of the Select Committee on Resettlement of Natives (L.A.S.C. 3, 1960), Government Printer, Salisbury (para. 141).

committee, strongly defended the report. He said that the committee had discovered three vital facts. First, that the Land
Apportionment Act had not separated the races, for they were
so interdependent that total separation was impossible. Second,
that since the implementation of the Act in 1930 more than
half a million Africans had been uprooted from their homes on
land designated for Europeans. He emphasized the enormous
financial cost of this movement, but left unsaid the cost of
human misery for those forced to move. Third, he claimed that
the Act had 'stultified and retarded the economy of Southern
Rhodesia as a whole with special regard to the native areas in
particular'. These were telling criticisms, and he gave them
dramatic form by asking whether it was possible to say to
Africans:

There is 10,000,000 acres there. You cannot go there. You cannot
buy it because it is reserved for Europeans. There are no Europeans
on it and in the meantime we are going to move many of you off that
land because it is reserved for Europeans. It is going to cost the
country many millions of pounds but we think that it is worth moving
you off because one day there might be some European who might
like to come and settle on that land.[1]

Ewing's appeal found no answering chord among the opposition. The opposition's reply, given by Wynn Starling, was
clear and decisive. 'We on this side of the House regard the
Land Apportionment Act as the cornerstone of our society in
Southern Rhodesia and we wish to make it very clear to this
House and to the country that we are absolutely, utterly and
entirely opposed to any breach of the Land Apportionment Act
as suggested in this report of the Select Committee. In fact,
we find this report repugnant and cannot support it in any
way.'[2] He stated that if the Act were repealed the D.P. would
reinstate it when they came to power. For the Government,
Whitehead was, at that stage, cautious. He said that the report
would have to be studied carefully and he did not think it
would be possible to implement all its recommendations
immediately.

Amendment or repeal of the Land Apportionment Act and
the increase in the size of the Legislative Assembly were major

---

[1] S.R.L.A. Hansard, 27 October 1960.
[2] Op. cit., 27 October 1960.

issues on which a clash between the Government and the Opposition could naturally be expected. But the D.P. did not confine itself to opposition on major issues. It accepted the criterion that 'our life in this country is based on certain standards and if we lower standards in any one field we have to lower them in all other fields'.[1] Therefore it opposed the Government on issues which, for those who did not accept the D.P. philosophy, appeared trivial and petty. There was a bitter debate about the provision of communal eating, drinking, and toilet facilities at the Bulawayo Trade Fair, during which Mr. Cary of the D.P. said that seven years before, at the Rhodes Centenary celebrations: 'I never saw any discontented coloured man or Native. They were not allowed into the bars, they were not allowed into the tearooms, they were not allowed into the cafés, and most important of all they were not allowed into our public lavatories that we used at the fair ground. We have got to get right down to bedrock. They had special provision made for them and they had no objection.'[2] When Sir Edgar Whitehead suggested that the hotels in which the multiracial Monckton Commission were to stay should be opened to all races, so that members of the Commission could stay together, the accusing opposition said: 'He's all set now to show that he is a liberal of liberals and he cannot hoodwink the country into believing anything else.'[3] It was not a compliment to be called a liberal by the D.P.

With criticism from the right and left, it was obvious that, to succeed, Sir Edgar Whitehead's policy had to retain a delicate balance. Power in Southern Rhodesian politics rested upon support from a predominantly white electorate and therefore European opinion had to be watched closely. While the consciousness of the white electorate counselled caution, Sir Edgar was also convinced that more Africans must be drawn into politics. Naturally he wanted to attract them to his party. The U.F.P. therefore set out to create an image which would attract substantial numbers of blacks and whites. For the Africans the image centred around 'partnership' with its promise of increasing social and political rights. Like Lord Malvern before

[1] S.R.L.A. Hansard (Mr. Ian Maclean), 3 August 1960.
[2] Op. cit, 23 February 1960.
[3] Op. cit. (Mr. S. R. Aitken Cade), 17 February 1960.

him, Sir Edgar based his hopes upon a rising African 'middle class', who, because of their property interests, would be attracted to a party offering stability and moderation. For Europeans, the U.F.P. held out the promise of gradual and controlled political and social change, which would reflect the changing circumstances of Africa, but not permit these circumstances to control events. Emphasis was placed on the determination to ensure economic progress and the determination to maintain law and order. Sir Edgar believed that, if he succeeded in attracting substantial support from both races, he would be able to secure from Britain constitutional advance leading to independence within the Federation.

Obviously this attempt to gain support from both races had considerable difficulties. The critical decision was how far each race was prepared to co-operate with the other. Was it in European interests to grant concessions to African claims and, if so, how far should the concessions go? Was it in African interests to accept a limited role at least temporarily, and work with Europeans towards a multiracial state? During 1960 events both within and without Southern Rhodesia helped to shape the answers to these questions. The answers were not favourable to Sir Edgar Whitehead's policy of partnership.

Throughout 1960 Europeans measured their future prospects in Southern Rhodesia against the evidence of events elsewhere in Africa. To the north they saw the rapid withdrawal of European colonial power. Many white Rhodesians saw this as a series of pathetic retreats, as appeasement in the face of extremist demands. The withdrawal, they thought, could only be followed by a 'lowering of standards', both economic and political. In Kenya they were convinced that the British Government had betrayed the white minority. In Nyasaland they thought that an extremist group, supported by thugs, had blustered its way to power against British ineptitude. And then there was the Congo. Events there sent a tremor of horror and fear throughout Africa and nowhere was it more clearly felt than in Southern Rhodesia. Fear for their future in a black-dominated state seeped through Southern Rhodesian European society. Even events in South Africa held out a warning, for this was the year of Sharpeville.

Europeans did not even have to look outside the borders of the Federation for fuel to feed their growing apprehension and fears. In 1959 there had been the riots and disorders in Nyasaland. More violence followed in 1960. There was one particularly ghastly incident which personified the Europeans' fears. In May in Northern Rhodesia a European woman, Mrs. Lilian Burton, was murdered by an African mob. The car in which she was travelling with her two children was stopped by a mob coming away from a political meeting. Some of the Africans started to attack the car and, as Mrs. Burton and her children ran for safety, petrol was poured on them and they were set alight. Mrs. Burton died from her burns but the children recovered. This incident, so real, so individual, so terrifying, inevitably bred thoughts of: 'It could so easily have been me or my family.'

In Southern Rhodesia itself, 1960 saw the worst rioting and bloodshed since the early days of European settlement. On 19 July, the arrest of three leaders of the African nationalist party, the National Democratic Party, sparked off large-scale disorders and anti-Government demonstrations in Salisbury which continued for two days. Worse followed in Bulawayo where between 24 and 26 July, and, following further Government action against the N.D.P., rioters virtually took over an African township. The police in their action against the rioters shot dead eleven Africans. In October further serious rioting broke out. In Salisbury, after an incident in which a European motorist had accidentally killed an African, there was rioting, looting and arson. Stores were burnt, beerhalls attacked, and cars stoned. Seven Africans were shot dead by the police, and more than 100 were injured, seventy with gunshot wounds. Damage to property was estimated at £50,000. The disturbance spread to the provincial town of Gwelo where two Europeans' and four Coloureds' houses were burnt out, and factories and stores destroyed. The damage there was estimated at £100,000. Nobody was killed, but fourteen Africans were wounded by police guns. At Gwelo, after angry Europeans had threatened to take matters into their own hands, the army was called in to control the town.

How were Europeans to interpret these events throughout Africa? The Congo could be seen as a failure of colonialism, the tragedy of subduing and suppressing a people, and then abandoning them to their own devices without training or experience of government. Alternatively, it could be seen as proof of Africans' innate inability to rule a modern state, of their return to primitive violence and chaos when the guiding hand of Europeans was removed. The riots and disorders in Southern Rhodesia could be seen either as the outburst of a repressed and underprivileged race demonstrating in the only way open to them, or as the actions of a violent, primitive people who, inspired by outside events, had decided to overthrow all law and order and justice to seize power. For Southern Rhodesian Europeans these were no academic problems. They were the problems which were to decide their future and the future of their children. Opinion was divided, but what was clear was that these violent events had deeply disturbed the Europeans. They now realized that their relation with Africans was the principal problem they had to settle. It had become impossible to run Southern Rhodesia 'on the pretence that the native is not here'.[1]

The division of opinion among Europeans roughly coincided with the division between the political parties. In the Legislative Assembly, Wynn Starling, a D.P. member, said:

Judging by events in the Congo, the African is not interested in co-operation, he is not interested in partnership. He is interested in exterminating the European and it is no good anybody getting up and saying that the Southern Rhodesian native is different. . . . The Southern Rhodesian native, the Congo native, the Mau Mau terrorist of Kenya, the massacre plot of Africans in Nyasaland, the petrol-burning types of Northern Rhodesia, they are all the same.

'In 1896', he continued, 'the same Africans picked up little European children by their heels and bashed their brains out against the rocks.'[2] The U.F.P. approach, as expressed by Dr. M. I. Hirsch, was very different. Dr. Hirsch stated:

African nationalism, in my analysis, has an appeal to the African because it restores to him his full dignity. African nationalism in fact tells the African: 'You have a place in the world on an equal

---

[1] Statement of a Native Commissioner in 1956. Quoted by Mason, *The Birth of a Dilemma*, Oxford University Press 1958, p. 280.
[2] *The Examiner*, 30 July 1960.

basis with all other races'. . . . If we are to win this battle against African nationalism, we have to undermine its one appeal to the African. We have to make it quite clear to the African that as he emerges in the country, he will enjoy his full citizenship rights, and that is expressed in a policy of partnership. . . . The only alternative there is to that is one of warning, one of strong-arm tactics and continual attempts to maintain control by force alone, and on the other hand a continual effort to overthrow the force.'[1]

The same contrast of approaches was revealed in the newspapers. Commenting on the July riots in Southern Rhodesia, the *Sunday Mail* editorial stated: 'What happened last week at Harare once again demonstrates the appalling tendency of the Bantu to resort to violence on the slightest provocation. Atavistic repression, it seems, is part and parcel of the Bantu make-up, as it has been for centuries'.[2] By contrast, the editorial of *The Examiner*, discussing the same events, said that behind the riots, 'lies the fact that all Africans share, to a greater or lesser degree and with justification, the feeling that they have had no say in making the laws under which they are governed. Much of the present African dissatisfaction stems from personal humiliation and from poverty'.[3]

Some Europeans were so appalled at the racial divisions revealed by the events of 1960 that they attempted to build a bridge between the races by new and unorthodox methods. The clearest manifestation of this thinking came in a multiracial 'Indaba' held in Salisbury in October. The sponsors hoped that they could rekindle the mutual confidence between the races which Rhodes was said to have captured at his famous 'Indaba' with the Ndebele chiefs which ended the 1896 rising. The 1960 'Indaba' was a success for those who attended and was important in recommending an extension of the franchise with direct representation for Africans; an idea which bore fruit with the introduction of the 'B' Roll in the 1961 constitution.[4] However, it was clear that the European response would reveal itself most effectively through the existing structure of political parties. In very general terms this meant that the acceptance

---

[1] S.R.L.A. Hansard, 23 August 1960, cols. 908–9.
[2] *The Sunday Mail*, 24 July 1960.
[3] *The Examiner*, 30 July 1960.
[4] See Chapter IV of the present volume, p. 8.

of the need to compromise with African aspirations would help the U.F.P. 'partnership' policy, while an attitude resistant to change and compromise favoured the opposition. There was no election during 1960 and therefore there is no accurate method of assessing how European opinion was moving, but it seems probable that the year's events persuaded many Europeans that it was necessary to consolidate and retrench. Fear for the future built up a 'white-*laager*', a 'Do you want to give your sister to a Kaffir?' mentality. Safety lay in retrenchment, in emphasizing the distinction between the races, in a refusal to share power, in a refusal to compromise.

White fears were an inevitable and natural reaction to events in Africa during the 1960s. In a continent in revolution, the established interests, which in Southern Rhodesia were white interests, were seriously threatened. Europeans recognized this fear whatever party they supported. In the Government, the fear translated itself into a determination to preserve peace and order at all costs. No government could afford to give the impression of weakness in face of violence or civil disturbances. This determination has coloured all government actions during the 1960s. In 1959 the U.F.P. Government had introduced legislation which greatly enhanced the Government's powers and, at the same time, seriously curtailed individual rights. In 1960 the Government went much further. Yet the Government was accused by some Europeans of not going far enough, of being too weak. The accusations came from the opposition D.P. and from such people as E. V. H. Creswell who wrote:

While Sir Nero Whitehead fiddles with the Land Apportionment Act—the only safeguard the white people have for their stake in the country they have developed—agitators are permitted to roam the country inciting violence among the unemployable and criminal types.[1]

In fact the Government reacted strongly to the situation, both to satisfy their image with the white electorate, and because they as a government believed it their duty to retain order. During October and November the Government introduced three new pieces of security legislation. The first was the Vagrancy Act, which the Government argued was a social

[1] *The Rhodesia Herald*, 12 October 1960.

relief measure, but which was used as a means of collecting and restricting potential trouble-makers. Africans unemployed in the towns have always provided a strong reservoir of support for African nationalist parties, and this legislation was an attempt to mop up that reservoir. The three readings of the Bill were rushed through in one day, which is extraordinary haste for 'social' legislation, and the day after it received the Governor's approval, 22 October, 220 vagrants were arrested. By 17 November, 1,142 people had been arrested under the new Act.

The second piece of legislation was the Emergency Powers Act, which gave the Government the right to declare an emergency and rule by regulation for up to six months, whereas previously it had been for only one month. Finally, the Government passed the Law and Order Maintenance Act. This Act which has been revised regularly to increase the Government's powers, has been the chief instrument used to fight the nationalist parties. In its initial form it severely restricted rights of public assembly; a subversive statement made in the presence of three people became an offence. It gave the Minister the right to ban a publication if, in his opinion, it was 'contrary to the public's interest'. It recognized many circumstances in which arrest could be made without warrant. The new legislation also infringed the powers of the court. The Attorney-General was given the right to certify that the grant of bail in particular cases was prejudicial to public security, and the Bill specified minimum sentences for some offences, thereby removing the court's right to decide sentences on the evidence presented. The prescribed sentences were harsh: from three to ten years' imprisonment for intimidation, from five to twenty years for throwing or threatening to throw stones or other missiles at a car. Also the new legislation gave the Minister power to restrict a person without trial to a specified area, or to prevent a person entering specified areas, for a period of ninety days.[1]

---

[1] There is a distinction between 'restriction' and 'detention'. According to Mr. Justice Young, in the case of restriction 'the area must be a reasonable area, such that in it an ordinary man can support himself and his family and lead a normal life generally. It must not have the attributes of a concentration camp' (Judgment No. G.D. 31/1965, p. 13). In practice restriction orders were at first served to restrain people within their normal residential areas, such as 'within a radius of five miles from Salisbury main post office'. But later restrictions areas were set

The Prime Minister, in defending the new legislation, contended that the country was 'on the brink of a major breakdown of law and order'. But there was fierce opposition from some white as well as from many black Rhodesians. Sir Robert Tredgold, the Chief Justice of the Federation, resigned his post, because he said that the Law and Order Maintenance Act 'outrages almost every basic human right, and is, in addition, an unwarranted invasion by the Executive of the sphere of the courts'.[1] In the Legislative Assembly, Ahrn Palley, an Independent Member, fought a marathon solo battle against the Bill. He did not question the Government's motives but he did oppose the means it had chosen to implement them. He contended that the legislation represented 'the erosion of certain basic principles on which the state should be built', and emphasized that 'good government can never exist on a fettering of the civil liberties'.[2] Despite this opposition, the new legislation was approved.

The Government's discomforts and the white electorate's fears offered great opportunities for the right-wing parliamentary opposition, but during 1960 the D.P. failed to take these opportunities. The party had come so near to success at the 1958 election that the obvious course was to show itself as a united, strong party able to attract 'the floating vote' with a flexible policy. This did not happen. Under William Harper, a man with a touch of iron in his character, the policy of the territorial branch of the party hardened. It moved from cautious conservatism to outright reaction. In addition the territorial party suffered from internal disputes and weak organization. Harper was the third leader since the 1958 election,[3] and

aside in inhospitable parts of the country to which the restrictees were sent for increasingly long periods. These areas took on at least some of the attributes of concentration camps.

Powers of preventive detention without trial were contained in the Preventive Detention Act of 1959 (which expired after five years) and under Emergency Regulations authorized by the Emergency Powers Act. Detained persons were normally kept in prison and there was not even a pretence that they should be able to lead a normal life.

[1] *The Examiner*, 5 November 1960.

[2] S.R.L.A. Hansard, 8 November 1960.

[3] R. O. Stockil had led the territorial branch after the election but he resigned from the leadership because of ill health and business commitments. Stockil was followed by S. E. Aitken Cade who did not make a success of the leadership and was quickly succeeded by Harper.

among backbenchers there was equal uncertainty. Ahrn Palley had left the party shortly after the election to sit as an Independent; then during 1960 P. H. Grey and S. E. Aitken Cade, both of whom had served on the Select Committee on the Resettlement of Natives and thereby obtained a comprehensive insight into African problems, also left the party. Grey joined the U.F.P. while Aitken Cade sat as an Independent. The party's disorganization was further emphasized in June 1960 by a split between the territorial branch and the federal branch led by Winston Field. A number of reasons explain the split. First, the territorial party prompted by Harper—who had declared: 'I can only serve one master—Southern Rhodesia,'[1]—decided to oppose federation on any terms. Second, there was personal friction between the leaders, and finally the move to the right by the territorial branch was not accompanied by a similar move in the federal branch.

The divisions and disputes within the D.P. confused the Southern Rhodesian political picture. While the white electorate appeared to be moving to the right, the opposition party which could expect to benefit from this, was weak and in disarray.

While the Europeans disputed over African rights, the Africans themselves were increasingly active in forwarding their claims for a larger voice in Southern Rhodesian affairs. However, the channels open to Africans were limited and outside the established political framework. In 1960 no Africans sat in the Legislative Assembly, no Africans were in the higher grades of the Civil Service, and very few were on the voters' rolls.

There was, then, this important and basic fact that Africans were outside the mainstream of politics which led to control of the Government. African political leaders knew that however large their following might be they could never win an election, and that indeed the more successful they were in attracting mass support the more suspicious and uneasy the European Government would grow.

The African political leaders who set out in 1960 to reorganize a nationalist party faced problems similar to those of the Chartists in nineteenth-century Britain. They could appeal to

[1] *The Examiner*, 18 June 1960.

the great mass of the underprivileged. They could base this appeal upon social conditions, upon poverty, urban over-crowding, unemployment, upon rural discontent, and upon the glaring chasm which existed between the living standards and wealth of their followers and those of the privileged white minority. There was no difficulty in finding discontent in a society in which African wages were so low, in which Africans farmed a few acres, while Europeans farmed hundreds or even thousands, in which Africans could not enter many hotels and restaurants, in which society was so constructed that in any situation the white was master and the black was servant. And, like the Chartists, the underprivileged majority had no direct political power. They were ruled by a remote, alien *élite*, who had faced none of the problems of the underprivileged, and who mixed as much fear as sympathy in their attitude towards them.

The discontent was obvious, but how could it be satisfied? The African political leaders had three courses open to them. They could centre their movement around social discontent and try, without direct political power, to ameliorate the situation by influencing the Government through pressures, propaganda and public demonstrations. Secondly, they could attempt to ally their movement to existing parliamentary, political parties. But this was a difficult path, for the existing parties were predominantly European, and the aspirations of their followers were far removed from the aspirations of the great mass of the African population. A party like the U.F.P. might hope to attract African support, but it did not want to be swamped by a black mass. The Africans the U.F.P. were wooing were the 'middle class', the *élite*—the leaven not the dough. The final choice for the African leaders was to strive for constitutional change, so that they could exercise direct political power. In exercising this power they could satisfy the social and economic discontent of their followers.

Like the Chartists before them, it was this last course, the concentration on achieving political power, which the African nationalist leaders of Southern Rhodesia followed. Writing in the *Democratic Voice*, Nkomo Khumalo said:

I get sick of this talk about removing the so-called pinpricks of the

Africans. What these well-meaning people mean is that the quality and quantity of the crumbs on which the Africans feed today should be increased. What the normal and true African wants today is bread, not crumbs, and he wants to eat it at the table not under the table. In other words nothing short of sitting in Parliament and passing laws to govern the people of the country both European and African . . . The Government is what matters.[1]

As events elsewhere in Africa influenced the Europeans, so also they influenced the Africans of Southern Rhodesia, but in a very different way. While Europeans looked at these events with fear and apprehension, for Africans they were an inspiration and guide. From newspaper photographs and articles the leaders of Ghana, Nigeria, Kenya, and Tanganyika became familiar figures: men who had risen from obscurity to power in a few years. The African leaders of Southern Rhodesia could never forget that rapid, even revolutionary changes were taking place to the north. From this arose the nagging question of why the same could not be achieved in Southern Rhodesia. The slow, moderate policy of the U.F.P. was poor fare against such a lavish feast. Therefore, the hopes and ambitions of the nationalist leaders became modelled on their nationalist brothers to the north.

During 1960 African political aspirations were centred around the National Democratic Party (N.D.P.). It was a multiracial party, but drew the great mass of its support from Africans. At its inaugural meeting on New Year's Day, Michael Mawema, the first President, emphasized its political objectives. 'We believe', he said, 'in a democratic Southern Rhodesia and to that end we are committed to achieve it within as short a time as possible. We believe in one man one vote. We repudiate the evils of racialism and prejudice.'[2] The party leaders never tired of pressing for political rights, of assuring their followers that the powers of government which Africans were achieving elsewhere would soon be theirs. Yet the party continued to recognize social discontent and to call for a re-ordering of society. On 24 July Mr. Mawema listed the party's aims, which, in addition to the claim for majority rule, called for higher wages for Africans, land for people displaced by the

[1] *Democratic Voice*, Vol. I, No. 5, 18 September 1966.
[2] *Daily News*, 1 January 1960.

Land Husbandry Act, adequate educational facilities for African children, and more and better African houses in urban areas.[1]

There was no doubt about the party's popularity. It drew mass support. Its meeting-halls were filled to overflowing, its outdoor meetings drew crowds in their thousands. In July, when the party leaders were arrested, it was estimated that 25,000 supporters assembled to make their protest. In August Michael Mawema claimed that the party had 20,000 members, including 100 Europeans.[2]

The N.D.P. attracted the leaders as well as the great mass of the Africans. The Rev. Ndabaningi Sithole, Herbert Chitepo, an advocate, and Dr. Bernard T. Chidzero, a political scientist, became leading figures in the party. In his self-imposed exile in London Joshua Nkomo became the overseas representative. The movement gained in confidence and purpose. In June Mr. Chitepo told a meeting of 2,000 people at Harare:

> We come here because we are dissatisfied with the second-rate citizenship in our own country. We feel a great deal of resentment. We are tired of laws which discriminate against us in the country of our birth. We are tired of being compelled to dance to the other man's tune. We are tired of living like strangers in our own land.[3]

In the following month Robert Mugabe, the party's Publicity Secretary, the Secretary of the Harare branch declared: 'One man, one vote is not a parrot cry. It is the cry of the African will, determination and their demand for the restoration of the motherland.'[4] Mugabe appealed to the emotions. He employed emotionalism as a force to bind mass African support behind the N.D.P. leaders. Nathan Shamuyarira defended Mugabe's methods, saying: 'Nationalism is basically emotional, and has to be to succeed. At times—particularly in early years —it should be blind and blinkered if it is to establish its principles, and begin to transform or reform a decadent society.'[5]

The N.D.P. success was based upon its appeal to Africans as an underprivileged race. It translated their discontent into political terms, and emphasized that as a race they must fight

---

[1] *Daily News*, 25 July 1960.
[2] *The Examiner*, 27 August 1960.
[3] *Daily News*, 6 June 1960.
[4] *Daily News*, 5 July 1960.
[5] Shamuyarira, op. cit., p. 67.

for their rights. This appeal, and its success, was a serious threat to the established political parties. All these parties were making some attempts to attract African support, and even the Dominion Party raised two Africans for its annual conference. The most active parties pursuing African support were the ruling U.F.P., and the Central African Party, led by the ex-Premier Garfield Todd, which had no members in the Legislative Assembly. Both these parties made their appeal across racial lines. They set out to attract support for policies which, they claimed, would eliminate racial distinctions. The N.D.P. success indicated that so far this appeal had had little impact on Africans, that the division of race, which cut across Southern Rhodesian economic and social life was also the clearest political division. In the Legislative Assembly Dr. Palley warned that: 'It is only Government members and a dwindling number of persons who still believe that the expression of opinion arising from the two main racial groups in this country can be contained in the same political party.'[1]

The African nationalist movement faced two great enemies: the Government, and its own internal weaknesses. During 1960 the Whitehead Government became increasingly hostile to the N.D.P., as it became apparent that the party was preaching revolutionary changes based upon mass support, and not the gradual change within the existing constitutional framework which Sir Edgar favoured. The division between nationalist and government thinking was confirmed at the N.D.P.'s first congress in October. Before the congress there had been differences among the nationalist leaders about the means to reach their avowed aim of majority rule. Michael Mawema, the President, had said in public that he favoured participation in the next General Election which, it was then thought, would return an enlarged Legislative Assembly of fifty members, but Enos Nkala, a member of the executive, opposed this. He thought that the party should boycott the election unless Africans could be assured of twenty to twenty-five seats. This dispute was partially responsible for Mawema's resignation from the Presidency in September. Later a magazine, *Ukuru*, published by U.F.P. supporters, claimed to have discovered the minute book of the N.D.P. executive which covered the

[1] S.R.L.A. Hansard, 22 July 1960, col. 563.

period of Mawema's resignation.[1] If this is an accurate record the dispute about participation in the election continued after Mawema's resignation. According to this record, an executive meeting of 6 October decided to recommend to the Congress that the party should fight the election, but that this should be kept secret while pressure was sustained for a larger African share. But four days later the executive changed its mind, and agreed that it should not commit itself to participation.

In the event the Congress decided very firmly against fighting the next election unless it was fought on the basis of 'one man, one vote', a condition unthinkable to Sir Edgar. The Congress also called upon Britain to intervene with military forces to suspend the existing Constitution. This then was a complete rejection of the African role which the U.F.P. Government supported. It is well to remember this decision of October 1960, which was against party members registering as voters or standing for election, as it foreshadowed the opposition to the limited role provided for Africans in the 1961 Constitution.

Some months before the Congress, the Government had taken active steps against the N.D.P. The Government gave two grounds for its attack upon the party. First, it was said that the party leaders had incited hatred and discontent between the races and, second, that the N.D.P. was in fact the banned African National Congress under a new name. Early in July the police raided the N.D.P. offices. Then in the early hours of 19 July three N.D.P. leaders, Michael Mawema, Sketchley Samkange, and Leopold Takawira, were arrested and charged with offences under the Public Order and the Unlawful Organizations Acts. These arrests triggered off large-scale disturbances in Salisbury, with great crowds out in the streets proclaiming their support for the leaders. The following weekend, the Government banned an N.D.P. meeting at Bulawayo, as disturbances were feared, but the banning itself brought a violent and bloody reaction.[2] The spontaneous reactions in Salisbury and Bulawayo revealed both the strength of the N.D.P.'s support and the way in which this support had been underestimated by the Government. Sir Edgar was criticized for his handling of both the Salisbury and Bulawayo incidents. During the Salisbury demonstrations his reluctance

[1] *Ukuru*, April–May 1962.   [2] See Chapter III, p. 51.

to meet the representatives of the demonstrators was said by the press and by Africans to have prolonged and intensified the disturbances. In the Legislative Assembly the Prime Minister himself admitted that his advisers had said there would be no adverse reaction to the meeting ban in Bulawayo. Later in the year a comic incident revealed the same ignorance. In October the Prime Minister went to address a meeting in the African township of Highfields, but he was shouted down with cries of: 'Freedom now', and 'We want Mawema!' Sir Edgar was forced to flee the hall via a window.

Despite the faulty intelligence Sir Edgar was firm in his determination to contain, and if necessary suppress the nationalist movement. For periods, in the latter part of the year, Sir Edgar revealed a Charles I-like touch when he sent troops to live in the African townships, and flag marches were made through the streets. According to the Government, the troops were joyfully welcomed as the bringers of peace and order. According to the nationalists, they were bitterly resented. There was probably some truth in both claims. In some rural areas where the nationalists appeared to be gaining support more spectacular demonstrations of power were provided, with jet aircraft swooping low over the Africans' huts and light artillery blowing up trees. Again reactions were mixed. A nationalist, writing about the display given in the Zwimba reserve, maintained that the Government's attempt at intimidation had failed. He claimed that many people thought: 'They have come to frighten us; let them kill us for we can no longer be intimidated. We have seen through it all. It's the Government who are afraid and not we.'[1]

On 26 July 1960, Sir Edgar, speaking in the Legislative Assembly, explained his opposition to the N.D.P. He said that the N.D.P. had been launched with a Constitution to which no exception could be taken, and that its early activities had been reasonable, but recently it had 'given cause for grave anxiety'. Theoretically, contended Sir Edgar, the party was open to all races, but 'the doctrines put forward, the calculated distortion of history and the arguments advanced at political meetings are becoming blatantly militant and anti-European. The theme is that Africa is only for Africans and Europe is for

[1] *Democratic Voice*, Vol. I, No. 5, 18 September 1960, p. 6.

Europeans and that all Europeans should go back to Europe. This theme, plus the claim that all land belongs to Africans, and the parrot cry, "one man, one vote" is the core of this movement.' The Prime Minister said that the party had urged followers to invoke ancestral spirits rather than the Deity and preached hatred against missionaries. Then Sir Edgar made a very doubtful claim. He said that at first it had been thought that the disturbances in Salisbury had been related to the arrest of the leaders, but 'it soon became completely clear to the Government that the great bulk of the African people in Salisbury did not wish to have anything to do with any breach of the law or any disorder. There was much intimidation.' This contention, that the vast majority of Africans are politically apathetic but were intimidated into demonstrating support for the nationalist party, has been made persistently by white Rhodesians.

To contradict Sir Edgar's claim, the trial of the N.D.P. leaders gave their supporters another opportunity to demonstrate their loyalty. The crowds which assembled at the court were so great that the trials had to be moved outside Salisbury to Inkomo military camp, where the police restricted entry. The leaders were found guilty on some of the charges, but later appealed successfully. Two significant features of the trials were, first, the defence's insistence, which was not refuted, that the leaders had urged non-violence on their followers; and second, that if, as the prosecution contended, the N.D.P. was simply a continuation of the banned A.N.C., then the major African political party was illegal and should be suppressed.

These two points demonstrate the dilemma which the Whitehead Government faced. So far the N.D.P. had been wild in words rather than action, but the Government, either because it was convinced that disorder and violence would follow if no action were taken, or to satisfy its image with the white electorate, attacked the nationalist party. The Government, in attacking the nationalists, was trying to stifle the party which, for all its lack of sophistication and organization, had the support of a large number of Africans. Thus the vicious circle which had started with the banning of the A.N.C. in 1959 continued to turn. The Government, while protesting that it wanted greater African participation in politics, saw in African nationalism a wild and destructive force which could not be tolerated. Yet African nationalism was the very movement which attracted most African political support, and therefore in opposing it the Government was seen as the opponent, not the supporter, of African aspirations. As the nationalists realized that the Government distrusted them, so they became less and less inclined to trust or to co-operate with the Government. The stands grew more extreme, the conflict more bitter.

The other major problems which the nationalist movement faced were internal disputes and leadership problems. It is easy to understand how the tensions and problems arose. The leaders were inexperienced. They were faced by an actively hostile Government. There was no immediate prospect of political power to blunt the edge of dispute with ambition for high office. The leaders often had too much time and too little to do. Some of them found that, because of their political activity, employment, even if they wanted it, was difficult to find or to fit in with their political work. They had infinite time to plan, to scheme, to talk, to dispute. Then the very nature of a nationalist movement with its emphasis on mass, often emotional appeal, lent itself to tensions and over-indulgence in personality cults.

The dispute which arose between Michael Mawema and Enos Nkala has already been noted. This came to a head in September when Mawema was forced by the party executive to resign his presidency. Mr. Mawema was accused of having no original ideas, of not being tough with the Government, and of having too limited an education to lead the movement. If the N.D.P. minutes published in *Ukuru* are accurate, it was Nkala who led the revolt against Mawema. When the seven-man executive voted Mawema was defeated by four votes to three. It was agreed that Mawema should publicly state that his resignation was on health grounds but, at the same time, he was to retain a seat on the executive. When an attempt was made to fill the presidency there was deadlock, for both Mr. Silundika and Mr. Leopold Takawira obtained three votes each.[1] Takawira became acting President, but the final decision was left to the congress to be held the following month. In the days before the congress, Joshua Nkomo, who was

[1] *Ukuru,* April–May 1962.

already well known as the leader of the banned African National Congress, emerged as a strong candidate. Mr. Nkomo was still in London, uncertain whether he would be arrested on his return, but his supporters in Southern Rhodesia emphasized his experience, his stature as an international figure, and his tireless fight for freedom.

At the October congress Mr. Takawira, the acting President, called for unity and non-violence. He urged a burning determination to achieve full political rights. His speech was well received, but he did not have strong backing as a leader. When the congress voted for a new executive, only Moton Malianga of the old ruling group retained his office. The Rev. Ndabaningi Sithole became Treasurer and, most important of all, Joshua Nkomo was elected the new President. A telegram was sent to him saying: 'Congress summons you to come and lead the Nation. Whole country pledges loyalty to you.' Mr. Nkomo, who had previously dispatched Washington Malianga from London to assess the degree of support for him in Southern Rhodesia, replied: 'Grateful for country's loyalty pledges. I pledge to work for the national cause. Deeply horrified by the settlers' Government's atrocities on our people, mass arrests and intimidation.'[1] Then, after checking that he would not be arrested, he returned to Southern Rhodesia in November.

Much depended upon the new President, sometime Methodist lay preacher and trade-union official. Mr. Nkomo is a large, friendly, easygoing man, but a man dedicated to the cause of African nationalism. As a leader his greatest strengths have been his ability to identify himself with those whom he leads, to inspire great personal devotion, and to capture in his powerful speeches the mood and the hopes of his followers. These are the qualities by which he gained and retained mass support, but leadership based upon mass support inherits its own limitations. The leader can only lead as far as the crowds will follow and so he is tied to reflecting opinion as much as creating it.

When Mr. Nkomo returned to Southern Rhodesia in November 1960, he was greeted by enthusiastic crowds lauding 'The Great Son of Africa, our Great Joshua Nkomo'. Perhaps the crowds hoped for another Banda, a Messiah from overseas

[1] *Democratic Voice*, Vol I, No. 8, 5 November 1960, p. 4.

come to bring freedom. The first impressions were good, for the stay in London had given Mr. Nkomo greater confidence, poise, and maturity. Where before he had hesitated, now he was firm. Where he had shown doubt, now he was convinced.

Despite the change of leadership there were still some rumblings of discontent in the N.D.P. The new executive, which had a preponderance of Ndebele members, including the President, was attacked by some discontented Shona, who claimed that tribalism had dominated the voting.[1] This was rejected by the Reverend Sithole, one of the two Shona on the executive, who pointed out that there had been a majority of Shona at the congress. The party, he said, represented Africans not tribesmen, for 'when I was a tribalist I spoke as a tribalist, I understood as a tribalist, I thought as a tribalist, but when I became an African I put away tribalistic things'.[2]

By the end of the year many of the problems of the nationalists appeared to have been solved. Mr. Nkomo led a large, united party backed by mass African support. It was a movement built upon the contradictory emotions of hope and bitterness, ambition and frustration. It had great confidence, great certainty that it would succeed quickly in achieving political power, but it was a confidence built upon vague hopes not upon precise plans. There was still no certainty what role the party would play or be allowed to play in Southern Rhodesian politics and government.

---

[1] The two largest tribal groups in Southern Rhodesia are the Ndebele, who live in the south and west, and the Shona, who live in the north and east. Strictly speaking Mr. Nkomo is not an Ndebele but comes from an Ndebele-speaking Karanga tribe.

[2] *Daily News*, 29 November 1960.

CHAPTER IV

The 1961 Constitution

When Sir Edgar Whitehead was in London in December 1960 for the Federal Conference he also negotiated with the British Government about constitutional changes in Southern Rhodesia. Throughout 1959 and 1960 Sir Edgar had emphasized his determination to gain greater independence for his country and on several occasions had raised the subject with the British Government. Sir Edgar's ambition was shared by all Southern Rhodesian Europeans whatever their political party.

The situation was complicated by Southern Rhodesia's membership of the Federation, but, within the territorial sphere, Sir Edgar hoped to achieve greater, if not absolute, independence. The constitutional position was that Southern Rhodesia as a colony was ultimately subject to the legislation of the British Parliament, but a convention had been established that, in areas in which the Southern Rhodesian Legislative Assembly had competence, the British Parliament would not use its powers. In the years since 1923 the British Government had relinquished some of its theoretical powers to interfere in Southern Rhodesian affairs, including a substantial part of the claim to supervise the staffing and work of the Native Affairs Department. But the British Government still had reserve powers. According to Mr. Duncan Sandys, the Secretary of State, these powers were by 1961 purely negative in character: to veto discriminatory legislation, to veto amendments to the Constitution and changes in the apportionment of land between the races.[1] However, although the powers were negative they were real. Dr. Claire Palley has shown how their existence forced consultation and discussion upon the two Governments before potentially controversial legislation was introduced and how the powers acted as 'a psychological barrier' for the

[1] Hansard, 22 June 1961, col. 1809.

Southern Rhodesian Government in introducing measures which might be unpalatable in Britain. According to Dr. Palley, the existence of the reserve powers had preserved the non-racial character of the electoral roll, had hindered moves towards *apartheid*, and had helped to preserve some individual freedoms.[1]

Sir Edgar said that Southern Rhodesia's claims for greater independence were justified by her long and good record of responsible government. She could not stand still while less developed and sophisticated African states were progressing to independence. He also stressed that, while in the past Britain had honoured the convention of non-interference she was now under such international pressure that she might be tempted to intervene directly in Southern Rhodesia's internal affairs.

For the British Government the negotiations posed the difficult problem of reconciling the claims of the established white Government with the responsibilities Britain claimed for the Africans of Southern Rhodesia. Therefore, when the British Government suggested a full constitutional conference in Salisbury early in 1961, they insisted that a wide range of opinion should be represented at it. It seems probable that Sir Edgar had not originally envisaged a full-scale constitutional conference, for only a few months earlier he had introduced a substantial constitutional change (the Constitutional Amendment Act), which increased the Legislative Assembly from thirty to fifty members. Probably he had hoped to negotiate concessions from Britain without a conference but, when it became clear that a conference was the easiest route to constitutional advance and greater independence, Sir Edgar readily accepted it. The N.D.P. leaders claimed the conference as the successful outcome of their pressure on the British Government. In April 1960 an N.D.P. delegation to London had met Lord Home, then Commonwealth Secretary, to press for a constitutional conference at which the nationalists hoped to achieve adult suffrage, the end of racial discrimination by the introduction of a Bill of Rights, and the abolition of the Native Affairs Department.

Before the conference opened, there was a dispute about the representation of African nationalist interests. The N.D.P.

---

[1] Palley, *The Constitutional History and Law of Southern Rhodesia 1888–1965*, London, Oxford University Press, 1966, p. 270.

6

claimed that, as it represented the majority of Africans, it must have a strong voice at the conference, but this Sir Edgar disputed. At first he had opposed N.D.P. representation at the Federal talks but, probably under British pressure, had later relented. For the territorial conference he also started by opposing N.D.P. representation and then, much to the nationalists' anger, suggested that he should nominate which of the N.D.P. leaders attended, but eventually he again relented and the N.D.P. selected its own representatives. But this did not remove Sir Edgar's distaste for the arrangement. Later he said: 'had their claims been completely disregarded I would not have minded a bit.'[1] The nationalist leaders on their side also accepted compromise, for initially they had refused to attend preliminary talks if Sir Edgar were to be the chairman and they also said they would not attend the conference unless the detainees of the 1959 emergency had been released. However, they gave way on both points.

The friction between the Government and the N.D.P. is not surprising, for the Government regarded the N.D.P. simply as the banned A.N.C. in another guise. At the time of the constitutional talks an appeal was pending by Michael Mawema against his conviction for managing the banned party under the N.D.P. flag. Even if, because of the appeal, there was doubt about the status of the N.D.P., there was no doubt about Joshua Nkomo, its new leader. Nkomo had previously been the President of the A.N.C. and, had he been in Southern Rhodesia at the time of the banning, undoubtedly he would have been detained. It was with these thoughts in mind that the government representatives took their seats beside the nationalist leaders.

There were other interests to be represented at the conference —the D.P. opposition party, the multiracial Central Africa Party, the Indian and Coloured communities, and the chiefs, the traditional African leaders. When the full conference assembled under the chairmanship of Mr. Duncan Sandys, all these interests were represented. Inevitably they displayed a wide variety of opinion. This was reflected most clearly in relation to the controversial franchise issues. At the opening of the

[1] *The Rhodesia Herald*, 9 February 1961.

conference each delegation stated its policy. The conference report reads:

(a) The United Federal Party while recognizing that Africans must over the years play an increasing part in the affairs of the country stressed the importance of not lowering the qualifications for the franchise.

(b) The Dominion Party advocated (i) that there should be no change in so far as this would involve a lowering of existing standards; (ii) that the present Lower Roll should be eliminated; and (iii) that the monetary qualifications should be related to the value of money.

(c) The Central Africa Party advocated a simple franchise qualification of literacy in English and the inclusion of additional categories of persons holding responsible positions in public service who would not necessarily be literate in English.

(d) The National Democratic Party maintained that 'one man one vote' was the only realistic solution to the question of the franchise.[1]

In addition the Coloured community representatives asked for two reserved seats in the legislature, while the Asian members supported adult suffrage by stages.

Such catholicism was splendid, but was it practical for a constitutional conference? How could such diverse views ever be reconciled? These questions were strikingly clear but, much to everyone's surprise, the conference was a remarkable success. At the end of it, all the delegates, except the four D.P. representatives, three of whom were later to become Rhodesian Front ministers,[2] agreed to a set of proposals to be embodied in a new Southern Rhodesian constitution. The D.P. supported many of the proposals but refused to accept the new franchise and were dissatisfied with the powers retained by Britain. Obviously the conference agreement had required compromises from all sides and all but the D.P. had been prepared to make them. The nationalists had not achieved their 'one man, one vote', while the Government had accepted a much wider franchise than they had originally proposed. With compromise and agreement in the air, the conference ended on a note of high

[1] Cmnd. 1291, para. 17.
[2] Messrs. W. J. Harper, P. van Heerden and I. F. McLean. The other D.P. representative was W. J. Cary, later a R.F. backbencher.

optimism for steady constitutional development in Southern Rhodesia. It had been a great triumph for Duncan Sandys, a British Minister who at other times was viewed with suspicion and hostility by Southern Rhodesian European politicians.

The conference proposals were made public in three White Papers. The first one, which gave the proposals in general terms, was followed by two others giving greater detail.[1] The proposals were then incorporated in the 1961 Constitution,[2] under which Southern Rhodesia was governed until the Unilateral Declaration of Independence in November 1965. The major constitutional changes introduced by the proposals were a new franchise, a recomposition of the Legislative Assembly, and a reduction in British reserve powers, which were replaced by checking devices.

In the second White Paper the British Government, after being threatened by Sir Edgar Whitehead that he would reject the whole constitutional arrangement unless the point were made,[3] formally acknowledged the convention of non-interference. The White Paper stated:

> The constitution of 1923 conferred responsible government on Southern Rhodesia. Since then it has become an established convention for Parliament at Westminster not to legislate for Southern Rhodesia on matters within the competence of the Legislative Assembly of Southern Rhodesia except with the agreement of the Southern Rhodesian Government.

The British Government also agreed to relinquish its theoretical right to veto certain Bills passed by the Southern Rhodesian Legislative Assembly, except for those involving international obligations or stock issued under the Colonial Stock Act. Thereby Britain had lost its power of disallowance over discriminatory legislation, and she also relinquished her theoretical control of the Native Department. As British powers diminished, so those of the Southern Rhodesian Government increased. In future the Southern Rhodesian Legislative Assembly could pass laws having extra-territorial power, while the Governor became a 'constitutional Governor'. He was to be appointed by the Queen after consultation with the Southern

---

[1] Cmnd. 1291, 1399, and 1400.
[2] Order in Council No. 2313 of 6 December 1961.
[3] Palley, op. cit., p. 317.

Rhodesian Prime Minister. In carrying out his duties the Governor would be advised by the Cabinet, and would act in accordance with that advice except in dissolving the Legislative Assembly or appointing the Prime Minister, when he was to observe the constitutional conventions followed by the British monarch.

To replace the old British powers checks were written into the Constitution. A Constitutional Council was established to examine new laws in order to ascertain whether they were discriminatory and in accordance with a new Declaration of Rights. However, the Council's powers were limited, for it could be overruled by a two-thirds' vote of the Legislative Assembly or after a six-months' delay by a simple majority of the Assembly. The Council's power did not apply to a money Bill, nor could it delay a Bill which the Prime Minister certified was urgent and against the public interest to delay. The Council could draw attention to discrimination in existing legislation, but had no powers to initiate action. The other main checking device was a lengthy Declaration of Rights, which was intended to secure individual rights, irrespective of race, creed, or political opinion, for all people of Southern Rhodesia. Any person who believed that his rights under the Declaration had been denied him could take his complaint to the High Court with a right of appeal to the Privy Council. But again the Declaration had its limitations. It did not apply to existing laws at the time of the introduction of the new Constitution, and therefore legislation such as the Land Apportionment Act was unaffected by it.

The other major changes introduced by the new Constitution were the new franchise and the re-composition of the Legislative Assembly. Two voters' rolls were established—an 'A' or Upper Roll, and a 'B' or Lower Roll. Both the Rolls were based upon property and educational qualifications, with the exception that chiefs, headmen, kraal heads, and ministers of religion were given the vote *ex officio*.[1] The educational and property qualifications were such that, at least at the time of their introduction and for some years to come, the 'A' Roll, which had the same qualifications as those already existing for 'ordinary' voters, would be dominated by European voters,

[1] For details of the franchise, see Appendix III.

while the 'B' Roll would be African-dominated. Again, land held by Africans in the communal tribal areas was not recognized as a property qualification. The country was to be divided into fifty constituencies and fifteen electoral districts, each returning one member to a new enlarged House of sixty-five members. The boundaries of the constituencies were to be drawn to give an even distribution of 'A' Roll voters, while the electoral district boundaries were to contain approximately equal numbers of 'B' Roll voters. There was a system of cross-voting whereby every voter had two votes—one in a constituency and one in an electoral district, but in the constituencies, if the 'B' Roll votes exceeded one-quarter of the votes cast by 'A' Roll voters, they were devalued to equal a quarter. Similarly 'A' Roll votes in an electoral district could count only for a maximum of one-quarter of the 'B' Roll votes. What this meant was that the candidates for the fifty constituencies would have to look for their main support from the 'A' Roll, although the 'B' Roll had some influence, while candidates for the fifteen electoral districts would have to direct their main appeal to the 'B' Roll. Constituencies were commonly called 'A' Roll seats, and districts 'B' Roll seats.[1]

The new franchise contained important breaks with the past. The franchise, being entrenched in the Constitution, was not, as in the past, subject to amendment by a simple parliamentary

---

[1] An example of the way cross-voting worked was given as an annexure to Cmnd. 1291:

'A' Roll Constituency
The following example illustrates the effect of the proposed new electoral system in an 'A' Roll constituency where the 'B' Roll votes amount to more than 25 per cent of the 'A' Roll votes cast:

	Total	Candidate W	Candidate X
'A' Roll votes cast	1,000	550	450
'B' Roll votes cast	500	100	400
'A' Roll votes (reckoned in full)	1,000	550	450
'B' Roll votes (devalued to 25 per cent of 'A' Roll votes)	250	50	200
Total		600	650

Candidate X is elected.
A similar example was given for a 'B' Roll district.

majority. Also the common roll had been abandoned. Traditionally, voting in Southern Rhodesia had been confined to an *élite* who could satisfy high qualifications. In theory the roll had been non-racial. In fact it had been dominated by Europeans. Voting had been regarded as a measurable skill not as a natural right. The exclusiveness of the franchise had been partially challenged by the amendment in 1957 which introduced voters with 'special qualifications'.[1] However, in the new franchise direct representation was accepted for voting groups with different qualifications. The underlying principle remained that the right to vote was a measurable skill, but candidates were no longer to be returned from a single roll dominated by those who satisfied the higher qualifications. Because of the different racial composition of the rolls, if votes were cast on racial grounds the new Legislative Assembly could be expected to contain fifty Europeans ('A' Roll constituencies) and fifteen Africans ('B' Roll electoral districts).

To amend any part of the Constitution required a two-thirds' majority vote of the Legislative Assembly. But, in addition, there were entrenched clauses which could only be amended by a two-thirds' majority plus either a majority vote by each of the four main races (African, European, Asian, and Coloured)[2] voting separately in a referendum or, alternatively with the approval of the British Government. These entrenched clauses covered the franchise qualifications, the appointment and terms of service of High Court judges, the Declaration of Rights, the Constitutional Council, the Tribal Trust Lands, the responsibility of trustees, and the amendment of the Constitution. But neither the composition of the Legislative Assembly nor the proportion of 'A' and 'B' Roll seats were entrenched.

Under Section 111 of the Constitution full powers were reserved for the Queen to amend, add, or revoke certain sections by Order in Council. The Queen would, if she used these powers, act on the advice of the British Government. The sections were said in the White Papers to be related to the position and 'formal functions' of the Sovereign and the

---

[1] See Ch. I of the present books, pp. 12.
[2] Until 50,000 Africans were on the voters' rolls, all Africans over 21 years with Primary education could vote in a referendum to amend the Constitution.

Governor, colonial stock holding, and international treaties and agreements.[1] Accusations were later made that the British Government had acted dishonestly and deceitfully by inserting Section 111. It was said that the provisions of the section had not been contained in the White Papers and were unknown to the Southern Rhodesian electorate when they voted for the Constitution.[2] This was advanced as one of the reasons for Southern Rhodesians' lack of faith in Britain which led to the U.D.I.

Although superficially the accusations about Section 111 appear to have substance they do not stand up to close examination. In the White Papers it was stated quite clearly that the United Kingdom would reserve some powers. Section 50 of Cmnd. 1399 reads:

Under the new proposals Southern Rhodesia will be free to make amendments to any sections of the Constitution without reference to the United Kingdom, with the exception of amendments which would affect:

(a) the position of the Sovereign and Governor;
(b) the right of the United Kingdom to safeguard the position regarding:
    (i) internal obligations
    (ii) undertakings given by the Government of Southern Rhodesia in respect of loans under the Colonial Stock Acts.

Clearly one of the chief intentions of the reserve powers was to protect foreign interests, but when the constitution was published Section 111 appeared to contain much more than the 'trifling', 'entirely formal' powers which Mr. Duncan Sandys had said Britain would retain. In particular, Section 2 (one of the sections reserved for the Queen under Section 111) stated that: 'The Governor shall have such power and duties as are conferred or imposed on him by or under this Constitution or any other law, and such other powers (not being powers to be exercised in his personal discretion) as Her Majesty may from time to time be pleased to assign to him.' However, while theoretically the British Government had these powers to interfere in Southern Rhodesian affairs, the powers were limited by the other clauses of the Constitution and—what was even more

[1] Cmnd. 1399, paras. 49 and 50; Cmnd. 1400, paras. 36 and 78.
[2] See A. J. Peck, *Rhodesia Accuses*, Salisbury, The Three Sisters, 1966, Ch. 6.

important—by the British Government's acceptance that with regard to internal affairs it was bound by the convention of non-interference which embraced the powers exercisable under Section 111. Sir Edgar Whitehead emphasized this when he said: 'We believe that the convention also covers these clauses [Section 111] with regard to interference in our internal affairs: we believe that firmly as a result of experience and discussion.'[1]

In the United Nations the British Government consistently maintained the all-embracing nature of the convention to resist the persistent demands of African and Asian countries for direct British intervention. British ministers never deviated from this. For example, on 15 November 1963, the Secretary of State told the Commons:

Southern Rhodesia, we must remember, has for over forty years enjoyed complete internal self-government. Up to the creation of the Federation she was responsible for her own defence and was represented by a High Commissioner in London. I hope that those outside who always tell us that we ought to interfere and do this or that in Southern Rhodesia will realize that there is not a single official or soldier in Southern Rhodesia responsible to the British Government. We have long ago accepted the principle that Parliament at Westminster does not legislate for Southern Rhodesia except at its request.[2]

In the independence negotiations with the Rhodesian Front Government, Mr. Butler, for the Conservative Government,[3] and Mr. Wilson, for the Labour Government,[4] accepted the binding nature of the convention.

The constitutional complexities surrounding Section 111 were discussed in a long and able debate in the Legislative Assembly in March 1964. Mr. Lardner-Burke introduced a motion requesting the Queen to use her powers under Section 111 only with the advice and consent of the Southern Rhodesian Government. Mr. Lardner-Burke's motion was in fact an attempt to remove Britain's constitutional power to prevent Southern Rhodesia making a legal Unilateral Declaration of Independence. The debate underlined the purpose, other than

[1] S.R.L.A. Hansard, 11 March 1964, col. 686.
[2] Hansard, 15 November 1963, col. 585.
[3] Cmnd. 2073, Butler-Field (2 May 1963).
[4] Cmnd. 2807, Wilson-Smith (29 March 1965).

the protection of foreign interests, of Section 111 which was to give Britain a negative vetoing power. Sir Edgar Whitehead explained that: 'These clauses were inserted to protect Britain against unilateral action by the House without their approval—that is why they were put in there. They were not put in to give Britain power to act here.[1]

In the debate on Mr. Lardner-Burke's motion, there was a division of opinion about whether the convention legally covered Section 111, but, even if there were doubts about the legal extent of the convention, there was no accusation by Ministers or ex-Ministers that Section 111 was a 'despicable hoax'. Sir Edgar Whitehead was quite clear that the section was covered by the convention and stated:

I want to do a very unpopular thing now, and that is to pay a tribute . . . to the scrupulous way in which Her Majesty's Government have exactly carried out the bargains we made. . . . And from that day to this they have adhered to it. Even when their trusted representative at the United Nations resigned from Government service because of his disapproval of their policy in supporting Southern Rhodesia in the United Nations, what was their action? They did not rat on us. They did not depart from that agreement. They did not break it, despite the tremendous pressures that I know were applied.[2]

For the Rhodesian Front Government Mr. Harper commented: 'Of course we accept the views expressed by the leader of the Opposition [Whitehead] that in his dealings with Her Majesty's Government at the time of the formation of our existing constitution they abided by their agreement with him, and I believe that there is no reason to anticipate they will not continue to abide by it.'[3]

In practice, the British Government acted as though the powers relating to internal affairs under Section 111 were covered by the convention, and it is practice not precise legal definition which underpins a convention. When Mr. Lardner-Burke's motion was debated there was considerable concern in the British Government—concern which rapidly spread to the Southern Rhodesian Government—that Britain's whole case

---

[1] S.R.L.A. Hansard, 11 March 1964, col. 686.
[2] Op. cit., cols. 682–3.
[3] Op. cit., 18 March 1964, col. 1003.

at the United Nations would be undermined. This concern became so great that although the substance of Mr. Lardner-Burke's motion passed the Legislative Assembly the request was not, to the best of my knowledge, forwarded to the Queen. If it had been, it would have implied that Britain could and would legislate directly for Southern Rhodesia.

To summarize the position in relation to Section 111: theoretically, the British Government could have exercised direct powers in Southern Rhodesia by using it. In practice they did not do so, because they accepted that for internal affairs Section 111 was covered by the convention of non-interference. What in practice Section 111 did imply was that legally Southern Rhodesia could not unilaterally break off her final ties with Britain. The accusation of deceit against the British Government could only be sustained had that Government used Section 111 to interfere in Southern Rhodesia's internal affairs, which it did not, but the accusation again revealed a lack of trust in the British Government. At least some of this distrust was based upon the change of British policy over the Federation.

At the constitutional conference there had been a large measure of agreement. Only the delegates of the right-wing European D.P. had opposed the final proposals. But once the proposals became public the agreement disappeared. Right-wing European opinion remained recalcitrant. *The Citizen*, a right-wing newspaper, called the franchise proposals a 'farce'. It was ridiculous, the editor thought, to estimate how many Africans would be eligible, as they would not want to register because 'they do not give a damn for a vote'. However, *The Citizen* agreed with the D.P. objections that the new franchise was a 'setback in a country which has so far prided itself on the complete absence of parliamentary race politics', by following a policy which 'has saved us from the horrible spectre of Colonial Office radicalism'.[1]

Opposition from the right was anticipated, but there was also mounting criticism from the 'liberals' and nationalists. Liberal opinion criticized the ineffectiveness of the safeguards provided in the Constitution. It was pointed out that the Declaration of

[1] *The Citizen*, 17 February 1961.

Rights was not retrospective and therefore could not alter the established structure of racial discrimination. It was pointed out that the powers of the Constitutional Council could easily be overridden by a determined Government. Unhappily these fears proved well-founded, but the weaknesses were not only in the drafting of the Constitution, for however firmly individual rights or racial equality had been written into the Southern Rhodesian Constitution it would require a Government committed in spirit as well as word to implement them. This point was made in 1965 by the Director of Housing and Amenities in Bulawayo. He wrote: 'Ostensibly the Government stands by the terms of the 1961 Constitution which envisaged African political advancement, but whether it also stands by its spirit is not so clear.'[1]

Much more serious than the liberal doubts was the growth of opposition by the African nationalists. The attendance of four N.D.P. leaders, including Joshua Nkomo and Ndabaningi Sithole, at the conference had marked an important step forward for the nationalist movement. It marked an acceptance, however reluctant, that the nationalist leaders were genuine representatives of the African people. However, for the leaders it posed new problems. It created a new mood, a new environment. Previously the leaders' tasks had been to retain the allegiance and maintain the emotional fervour of a large, unwieldy mass party. The field of operations had been large meetings, where simple, uncomplicated slogans and general appeals to rights had had the greatest effect. The leaders had caught the emotions, hopes, and desires of the African crowds. They could throw out the challenge of 'one man' knowing that it would produce a thunderous response of 'one vote'. The invitation to the conference was a measure of the N.D.P.'s success, but it created its own dangers. The leaders left the great crowds to face the clinical atmosphere of the conference room. The cheering followers were replaced by experienced, sceptical politicians. The general slogans were abandoned for discussions of precise constitutional details. The leaders realized the dangers inherent in their changed roles. They went to the conference preaching universal suffrage, but T. G. Silundika warned their followers not to expect miracles.

[1] Report, Director of Housing and Amenities, Bulawayo, 1964-5.

At the conference the nationalist leaders obtained much less than their avowed aim of universal suffrage, but they did initially agree to the proposals. Following the conference, the N.D.P. leaders called a Press conference at which they said:

We feel that the new provisions have given us a certain amount of assurance that the country will not pursue policies which mean that Africans would perpetually be unable to control their country. Several new features of the constitution have fallen in line with the demands that have been made by the N.D.P since its inception. These have been the enshrinement of a Declaration of Rights, the outlawing of discrimination and the protection of rights by the courts. Above all, we are to have a new constitution which is an achievement resulting from the pressure of the N.D.P., a thing never before thought of in this country. If we did not go as far as universal suffrage we prevented the settlers from getting the independence they wanted.

But on the franchise proposals the nationalist leaders were clearly on the defensive. They came from the conference not boasting of what they had achieved, but apologizing for what they had not achieved. At the Press conference Mr. Nkomo said: 'We do not stand in the way of this plan, but we do not accept it at all . . . We shall continue to fight for "one man one vote".' Also he emphasized Britain's ultimate responsibility. Southern Rhodesia, he declared 'remains a colony and we shall continue to look upon Britain as the overriding authority over the settler Government here.'[1]

At the Press conference the nationalists' reservations about the franchise were so strong that there were doubts expressed about whether they had in fact accepted the conference proposals. Mr. Silundika on behalf of the N.D.P. confirmed that the proposals had been accepted, but that the N.D.P. would fight for further extensions of the franchise. He asked Mr. Sandys to issue a Press statement which said:

The statement that was made by the President, Mr. Nkomo, at his Press Conference today does not imply any repudiation of the report of the conclusions of the Constitutional Conference. He only wishes to correct the impression conveyed in the local press regarding the N.D.P. attitude to the franchise and representation proposals outlined in the report and to make it clear, as stated in

[1] *The Daily News*, 8 February 1961.

Paragraph 18 of the report, that the N.D.P. maintains its position and intends to continue the campaign for its objective of 'one man one vote'.[1]

Mr. Sandys commented that applying pressure in the Legislative Assembly for extensions of the franchise was the right course for the N.D.P. to take, and he hoped that they would succeed in doing this rather than waiting for more conferences.

Immediately the proposals were known, Mr. Nkomo came under attack from fellow-nationalists. The attack was based on the franchise, which it was said gave Africans a façade of representation but no real power or the prospect of power in the future. Mr. Takawira, who was then representing N.D.P. interests in London, cabled: 'We totally reject Southern Rhodesian constitutional arrangements as treacherous to future of three million Africans. Agreements diabolical and disastrous. Outside world shocked by N.D.P. docile agreement.'[2] In Southern Rhodesia Mr. Mawema supported Takawira, and stated that the N.D.P. leaders at the conference had 'completely failed to present the views of the African people'. Takawira and Mawema, who had both recently been deposed in the leadership contest, could be accused of jealousy and bitterness, but criticism came from other nationalists and continued to mount. Soon the critics within the N.D.P. ranks were joined in their chorus of denunciation by the nationalists of other African states. Kenneth Kaunda in Northern Rhodesia was critical, Dr. Banda called Mr. Nkomo 'weak-kneed'. As the criticism mounted, Mr. Nkomo was faced with a clear choice of fighting back or of repudiating his agreement to the proposals. At first it appeared that he was prepared to fight. Messrs. Mawema and Takawira were suspended from the party. Mr. Nkomo flew to London to discipline Mr. Takawira, but in London his attitude changed.

It is not clear why. A variety of reasons have been suggested. Mr. Takawira was said to have represented the unanimous opinion of nationalists in London and to have convinced Mr.

---

[1] Hansard, 23 March 1961, col. 737. Mr. Silundika gained notoriety for having issued this statement, although it appears that he was only performing his party function, and stating what had been agreed. Later, when he was excluded from the Z.A.P.U. executive, the exclusion was said to have stemmed from his having issued the statement.

[2] *The Daily News*, 11 February 1961.

Nkomo of this unanimity. It has been suggested that Mr. Nkomo had never been keen on the constitutional proposals and had only reluctantly accepted them on the insistence of the other nationalist leaders who attended the conference, but with the change of perspective and context in London Mr. Nkomo had seen the error of acceptance. Another suggestion was that Mr. Nkomo resented the change in his Press image from an unrelenting champion of nationalism to a compromiser. Finally, it has been suggested that other African states and foreign agencies which were supplying funds for the N.D.P. threatened to withdraw support unless the proposals were rejected.

Perhaps there was no one reason, perhaps it was a combination of some of these possibilities, but whatever influenced Mr. Nkomo there was a clear change. Lord Alport wrote: 'I do not know what happened but Mr. Nkomo, when he came to have a cup of tea with me at the C.R.O., gave the impression of being a very worried man, inexplicably ill at ease in the presence of a British Minister.'[1] When Joshua Nkomo returned to Southern Rhodesia, it was he who had been disciplined. The rebels, Mawema and Takawira, were permitted back into the party, and immediately the shortcomings of the conference proposals were stressed. For the nationalists the path was leading away from the 1961 compromise.

African nationalist criticism of the constitutional proposals was based both upon the immediate failure to obtain manhood suffrage and upon the poor prospects which the new franchise offered Africans for the future. The nationalists assumed that race would be the main political division in Southern Rhodesia and therefore asked the question: how long would it be before Africans could form a parliamentary majority on the basis of the 1961 franchise? This question was still causing furious debate when Southern Rhodesia unilaterally declared independence. There have been a series of guesses at the answer, but no certainty that any were accurate. In 1962 Sir Edgar Whitehead estimated fifteen years. In 1963 Mr. Duncan Sandys said it would take twelve years, but Mr. Garfield Todd replied by affirming that Africans would still not have a majority after

[1] Lord Alport, *The Sudden Assignment*, London, Hodder and Stoughton, 1965, p. 52.

twenty-five years. In 1964 Mr. Ian Smith said he did not foresee an African nationalist government in his life-time, and in
London in 1965 he said he had heard various estimates ranging
from fifteen to fifty years.

The calculations which have to be made centre on the 'A'
Roll qualifications. Based simply upon racial divisions, and
assuming that Africans win all the 'B' Roll seats (15) and that
the number of 'B' Roll seats is not changed, the problem to be
decided is when there will be sufficient Africans on the 'A' Roll
to control eighteen constituencies and thereby create an African
parliamentary majority. It is impossible to answer this in any
precise terms, for it depends upon a series of imponderables: the
future structure of education, the economic development of the
country as a whole, the wage structure for Africans, Africans'
opportunity to acquire recognized property rights, the future of
African agriculture. The answer to the question lies not just in
mathematical calculations, but in how the future society will be
ordered. As soon as detailed predictions are examined, it becomes apparent that a change in the political power in the
country will require a social revolution but, to complete the
circle, the timing and nature of the revolution, if it occurs at
all, depends largely upon who holds political power. In the past
Southern Rhodesian society has been organized on the assumption that Europeans are a well-paid *élite*, claiming high rewards both for their skill and so that they can retain their
European standards of living. The Africans have formed the
great mass of the workers, the proletariat of the towns, and the
peasants of the country, drawing low wages because of their
restricted skills and their assumed limited needs. Thus in 1960
the average wage for all Europeans in employment was £1,134
per annum, while for Africans it was £94 per annum. In 1964
the average European wage was £1,241 per annum, the
average African £121 per annum.[1]

The relationship between the social order and political power
can be seen clearly in relation to education which, in itself, is a
standard set for the franchise, and is also the means to higher

[1] *Monthly Digest of Statistics*, Salisbury, Government Printer, December 1965.
The range of African incomes in 1964 extended from £67 per annum in 'Agriculture, Forestry, and Fishing' to £292 per annum in 'Transport and Communications'.

salaries and the achievement of other franchise qualifications. With the exception of a few private schools, European and African education is separated. For Europeans ten years' education is compulsory. For Africans, education is not compulsory but is widely sought. The European population is small, and demands the same facilities as it would expect in the 'home' country. The African population is expanding at an enormous rate. Every two years more African babies are born than the total European population. This expanding society demands education, but it has no past standard to which it can appeal, and in sheer numbers it presents enormous problems of finance and staffing. There simply is not enough money or trained staff to offer full educational facilities for all the African children. Similar problems face most underdeveloped countries and create the dilemma of how the limited funds can best be spent. Should they be used to educate as many as possible to a low level; should they be concentrated upon an *élite*, or should some compromise be achieved? In Southern Rhodesia the answer to these questions helps to determine the composition of the electorate, and thereby the seat of political power.

During the 1960s Southern Rhodesian Governments have spent large sums of money on African education. In 1949 just over £½ million were spent, in 1960 the figure had risen to almost £3 million, and by 1964 to over £6 million. The number of African children in the schools and the number of schools, both government and mission, have risen sharply. In 1959 there were 467,567 African children enrolled in schools. By 1964 there were 642,596. Despite these efforts the rapidly increasing African population and the popularity of education have created a series of financial crises and enormous pressure on school places. In 1962 there was a crisis which threatened a wholesale discharge of teachers and which was only prevented by a British Government loan of £355,000. In 1963 the financial problems were greater than ever. The Government was forced to withdraw boarding and equipment grants to Primary schools, to defer paid leave for staff, and to declare 200 African teachers redundant. In 1964 the Government introduced school fees in all government schools, whereas previously they had been charged only in mission schools. This set off a strong reaction from African parents and became a point of great

7

political friction. The problem of finding money and staff continues, with many African schools underequipped, overcrowded, and understaffed.

Accepting that resources are limited, successive Southern Rhodesian Governments have decided as the first priority to concentrate upon providing five years' Primary education for as many African children as possible. In his report for 1961 the Secretary for African Education wrote: 'The first immediate aim of African education is five years of Primary school for all, and a steady extension of as many schools as possible (within the finances available) to the full Primary course of eight years. . . . The next priority is post-Primary education.' At a meeting with the Msengezi Council late in 1965 the Secretary for Education confirmed that the priorities were at that time unchanged.[1]

Because of the concentration on Primary education for the mass, Southern Rhodesia has been able to boast a higher percentage of children attending school than many other African countries, although publication, in 1964, of an African census has thrown doubts upon the boast.[2] Examination of the statistics reveals how broad the African educational system is at its base, but how very narrow it is at the apex. In 1963 there were 590,795 African children in Primary schools. In each of the lowest three standards (sub-Standard A, sub-Standard B, and Standard I) there were more than 100,000 children. In Standard 3 (i.e. the fifth year of schooling) there were 80,065, but then came a major blockage. Less than half the children who reached Standard 3 could go on to Standard 4. In 1963 there were 35,825 children in Standard 4. Similar blockages occurred between Primary and Secondary school, and in reaching the top of the Secondary ladder. In 1963 there were only 7,045 African children in Secondary schools and, of these, only 36 were in the upper sixth form.

The education system reflects Southern Rhodesia's social structure, with a great gulf dividing Africans and Europeans.

---

[1] I attended this meeting.

[2] The Government used to claim that about 90 per cent of African children receive Primary education, whereas the 1962 Census (published June 1964) revealed that only about 60 per cent were attending schools (1962 Census, para. 86). In 1962 46·6 per cent of all African adult males and 58·7 per cent of all adult females (i.e. persons born before 1946) had never been to school (para. 90).

This is clearly revealed in education expenditure and the availability of Secondary school places. For a European school population of about 50,000 £6,000,000 is spent. For an African school population of about 620,000 £6,600,000 is spent. The contrast in Secondary school opportunities is revealed in the following table:

TABLE IV

PRIMARY AND SECONDARY SCHOOL ATTENDANCE,

BY RACES

	European children at school			African children at school		
	Primary	Secondary	Sixth Form	Primary	Secondary	Sixth Form
1960	33,937	17,640	1,058	484,299	4,139	67
1964	30,834	19,488	1,150	610,298	8,846	93

Strong arguments are put forward to defend the existing education system. It is argued that for the African population it is only fair that as many children as possible should be given an education, and that, by building on a broad base, a strong foundation will be laid for future Secondary-school expansion. However, the provision of five years' Primary education for a large number creates serious social problems, especially in finding employment for youths with so limited an education. The arguments in favour of the existing European educational structure are very strong. It is rightly argued that the standards are no higher than would be found in most Western European countries, that if expenditure on European education was drastically reduced and therefore school standards lowered many Europeans would leave the country and it would be impossible to persuade other skilled expatriates, who are needed for future development, to emigrate to Rhodesia.[1]

After U.D.I., in April 1966, Mr. Arthur Smith, the Minister of Education, announced a complete revision of the African educational system. The Minister explained that, although in

[1] See *Progress in African Education*, Rhodesian Information Service, February 1965.

the past the main emphasis had been on Primary education, the R.F. Government had initiated Secondary expansion. In the three years following the R.F.'s first election victory, forty-five African Secondary schools had been established, the number of Africans at Secondary schools had almost doubled, and the number of sixth-formers almost trebled. For the future, the Minister announced that the Primary course would be reduced from eight to seven years and that by 1974 it was hoped to place $37\frac{1}{2}$ per cent of those leaving Primary school into a new type of Secondary school which would give a two-year course combining academic work and vocational training. In addition, roughly $12\frac{1}{2}$ per cent of the most academically gifted Primary school-leavers would go into conventional Secondary schools offering four-year courses, with the opportunity for those who were suited to continue into sixth-form and university education.

However, the Minister also announced that expenditure on African education would not be allowed to exceed its present level of 2 per cent per annum of the gross national income. The new policy therefore implied a shift of direction and not a dramatic expansion in the Government's African education expenditure. Confirming this Mr. Arthur Smith said: 'Our immediate problem is to curtail the amount spent by Government on ever-increasing costs of Primary education in order to devote more money to Secondary education.' He warned that school fees might have to be increased and greater dependence in Primary education laid on local effort.[1]

Any Rhodesian Government faces enormous problems in education and it would be pointless to minimize them, but education policy cannot be divorced from the country's political and constitutional development. Given certain conditions educational development could dictate political development. If the 1961 franchise is retained it is Africans who enjoy four years' Secondary education and more who are likely to qualify for the 'A' Roll, the roll which largely determines the composition of the legislature and therefore the government. It is difficult to make precise predictions about the significance of the educational changes announced in April 1966, but, again assuming that the 1961 franchise is retained, they are not likely to create

[1] S.R.L.A. Hansard, 20 April 1966, cols. 1847–60.

a dramatic change in the number of Africans who qualify for the 'A' roll, for only $12\frac{1}{2}$ per cent of the Primary school-leavers are to be channelled into the four-years' Secondary stream. For the more immediate future the figures of the recent past are more important. In 1964 the total of all Africans who had received four years' Secondary education was only 5,701.[1] It is safe to say, therefore, that for many years to come control of the 'A' Roll will remain with Europeans.

The 1961 Constitution was attacked from both sides of the political spectrum and, amid the clamour of opposition, it is easy to underrate the achievement—for achievement it was. For the first time black and white had negotiated together about the future of their country. For the first time there was a clear acceptance that Africans would sit in the Legislative Assembly. For the first time the franchise was entrenched in the Constitution. For the first time there was a legal acknowledgement that all races should enjoy individual equal rights.

The Constitution was, however, no more than a skeleton. The flesh, the form, even the lifeblood of the body politic, would depend upon the political parties which worked within and around it. Depending upon the nature of these parties there were a variety of directions open to Southern Rhodesian politics. Sir Edgar Whitehead might realize his ambition of leading a strong and successful multiracial party which in exercising power would largely invalidate a racial conflict within the society. Alternatively strong racial parties might contest for power. These racial parties, African and European alike, would be dissatisfied with the restrictions of the new Constitution. A powerful African party, the party of 'the have-nots' would see the new Constitution as no more than the first step in a series of steps to change the political and social order by obtaining quick majority rule. It would therefore agitate for a wider franchise with increased African representation. In contrast a powerful European party, the party of 'the haves', would aim at preserving the existing order by holding back African participation in government. The European party would abhor the concessions already made to Africans and aim to reverse the trends of the new Constitution. The Constitution,

[1] Palley, op. cit., p. 790 (Appendix Table J).

far from being the first step in a series of reforms, would be seen by the European party as an excessively liberal measure, the implications of which would largely have to be invalidated.

The future course of Southern Rhodesian politics would therefore depend in the main upon who was prepared to contest for power within the new Constitution and who among the contestants was successful enough to form the Government. But there was a complication which added another dimension. Some groups might refuse to work within the Constitution and agitate for a new conference at which their demands might meet a greater response. Failing this, they might aim at revolutionary change. The struggle for power could therefore be contained within the Constitution, or alternatively it could be a struggle of those who exercised the powers of government against those who refused to accept the constitutional framework in which that government was set.

CHAPTER V

The Constitutional Referendum: 1961

Sir Edgar Whitehead had stipulated that acceptance of the new Constitution must be confirmed by a referendum of the existing electorate. This had two important effects. First it had meant that the new Constitution had been framed in the knowledge that its acceptance depended upon a predominantly European electorate. The Southern Rhodesian Government had therefore been prepared to accept only a degree of change which they could defend before this electorate. There could be no hint of a 'sell-out'. The second important effect was that, between the conference in February and the referendum in July, the political parties had time to define their attitudes before the implementation of the Constitution. The referendum gave the opportunity to campaign about Southern Rhodesia's future structure of government.

As the campaign developed, the resemblance to early British nineteenth-century politics became striking. There were many parallels in the situations. Both societies were undergoing rapid economic and social change, moving from a large degree of dependence on agriculture to an increasing dependence on industry. In both societies there were rapid growths in populations, populations which contained a small *élite* and an unprivileged mass. Political power was the preserve of the *élite*. Both societies were subjected to new, revolutionary ideas. In nineteenth-century Europe the egalitarianism of the French Revolution and the growth of socialism; in twentieth-century Africa the racial equality preached by nationalists and the fear of international Communism. But Southern Rhodesia faced one major problem, which nineteenth-century Britain did not even envisage: the division of race.

If one allows the imagination to run across the 1961 political scene, the U.F.P. becomes the Whigs, a party from the *élite* but convinced that revolution can be avoided only by sharing power, at least with a section of the great unenfranchised mass. The D.P. are the Tories, so afraid of revolution that they oppose all change. They consolidate and dig in, while the U.F.P. fraternize with the potential revolutionaries. Then there is the N.D.P., or the Chartists of Southern Rhodesia, backed by the great unenfranchised majority and determined to obtain political rights for that majority. There are even Radicals, men like Ahrn Palley and Garfield Todd, who as individuals make great contributions to politics but do not fit easily into a party. The temptation is to let the imagination run on, to picture some future Rhodesian Tory emulating Disraeli by introducing a Reform Bill to out-liberalize the Liberals, but a glance at the ranks of the present Rhodesian Front quickly stifles imagination.

The main onus of persuading the electorate to accept the new constitution fell on the U.F.P. Government. Two possible lines of persuasion could be used and both were invoked, sometimes separately, sometimes together. The first argument was that the constitutional proposals were a clear step towards bringing Africans into Southern Rhodesian politics and thereby fulfilling the promises of 'partnership'. The second line of persuasion was that the fifteen 'B' Roll seats were a bargain made to obtain greater independence from Britain, and did not imply any lowering of standards because control still lay with the 'A' Roll.

Sir Edgar Whitehead genuinely believed that the proposals were the foundation upon which a non-racial society could be built. In supporting them Sir Edgar accepted compromises, for he had not achieved the full independence he had sought and, in agreeing to the fifteen 'B' Roll seats, he had gone much further than his recent decision to enlarge the Legislative Assembly to fifty members. There can be no doubt of Sir Edgar's enthusiasm for the new Constitution. He staked his career on having the proposals accepted. He defended them on the radio, in the Press, at public meetings, and in the Legislative Assembly. He told the Legislative Assembly that:

however excellent the intentions of the members of one race, however excellent their practice . . . there is no real substitute for people having some voice in the decisions that are taken. This Constitution gives the 'A' Roll full control but it also means that the voice of those who will only aspire to the 'B' Roll will be heard inside this House at an early date.[1]

It has been suggested that Sir Edgar's enthusiasm for the proposals was based upon the advantage which he thought they would give to his party.[2] The accusation is that his own multiracial party would be able to win African 'B' Roll seats while the D.P. would not, and therefore the D.P. would have no chance of defeating the government at any forthcoming election. It would be unrealistic to imagine that Sir Edgar did not hope that his party would gain an advantage from the new arrangements, but to select this as the only cause or even the main cause for Sir Edgar's support is to distort his motives. Sir Edgar would not have led and fostered a multiracial party unless he thought that the races could and should share political power. By supporting the new constitutional proposals, he thought that he was helping to achieve this end.

As the campaign developed, the need to reassure the European voters began to predominate. Members of the Government such as Mr. A. R. W. Stumbles, the Minister of Roads, emphasized that control of government would remain in the responsible hands of the 'A' Roll voters. Sir Edgar himself joined the chorus. Shortly before the referendum he mentioned the future possibility of increasing the number of 'A' Roll seats as the 'A' Roll electorate increased. He described as 'political claptrap' the suggestion that the new franchise would mean an African majority in the Assembly in five to ten years' time. He estimated that it would require 100,000 Africans on the 'A' Roll to achieve this, which, because of the educational barrier, was impossible in a short time.

Also with the European electorate in mind, the U.F.P. stressed that if the proposals were rejected the dangers of direct British interference in Southern Rhodesia's internal affairs would be increased, and it would be impossible to negotiate other terms with the British Government without making even greater concessions to the African nationalists. Another U.F.P. argument was that by Southern Rhodesia making a concession to African political aspirations there was a much greater chance of holding together the Federation on which the country's economic prosperity rested.

[1] S.R.L.A. Hansard, 20 June 1961.   [2] See Peck, op. cit., Chapter IX, p. 11.

The most controversial issue of the campaign was a dispute about the degree of independence the new Constitution would confer. The controversy, which outlasted the campaign, was still raging when U.D.I. was declared. The U.F.P. leaders were so keen to have the proposals accepted, so keen to emphasize the advantages of the new arrangements that, in speaking about independence, they sometimes indulged in double-talk. Sir Edgar explained that the new proposals did not mean full independence in an international sense, but did mean freedom from interference in internal affairs. However, in the heat of the campaign the U.F.P. slipped into talking of independence without qualifications. In speaking of future discussions on the Federation Sir Edgar said that Southern Rhodesia would have a much stronger voice if 'she goes there having voted for her independence and obtained it'.[1] A U.F.P. advertisement urging the electorate to approve the new constitutional proposals read: ' "Yes" the key to independence. Independence is a sign of maturity. Independence for our country means that we hold up our heads among the nations of the world without glancing over our shoulders. The Reserve Powers of the United Kingdom over Southern Rhodesia are removed in the New Constitution. This makes our independence real.'[2]

Doubtless, from the U.F.P. statements and from the sheer complexity of the constitutional position, some of the electorate were misled into thinking that they were genuinely voting for independence. In the years following the referendum campaign there have been accusations of dishonesty and deceit about this issue. One accusation is that the electorate were deceived into thinking that they were voting for full independence; another that the British Government promised independence on this Constitution if the Federation broke up; another that the British Government permitted Sir Edgar to mislead the electorate for his and their ends.[3] There probably has been a genuine degree of misunderstanding, but allied to this has been the growing distrust and suspicion of the British Government. The accusations are believed not because they can be supported by accurate evidence, but because they reflect a mood; a mood

[1] S.R.L.A. Hansard, 20 June 1960.
[2] The Citizen, 21 July 1961.
[3] See Peck, op. cit., Chapter II, p. 12, and Chapter VI, p. 38.

created by the deep-seated belief that Southern Rhodesian Europeans have been misunderstood, misjudged, and sacrificed to the needs of British appeasement. The accusations are believed because many of the Europeans of Southern Rhodesia want to believe them.

In fact during the 1961 referendum campaign there was ample evidence for those who wanted to hear that acceptance of the proposals gave neither a promise of immediate independence nor the terms for future independence. On several occasions Sir Edgar himself explained the degree of independence he thought Southern Rhodesia would obtain under the new Constitution. For example, on 22 February he told the U.F.P. Congress:

Now, I do want to make this absolutely clear—I know there has been considerable objection and a feeling that what we are getting is not complete independence. Well, of course, the country that will ultimately get complete independence is the Federation because External Affairs and Defence are the Ministries which can make treaties of alliance and go to U.N.O. and so on. These are not Southern Rhodesian subjects, and of course we cannot get complete independence while the Federal Government holds these powers. It is up to us to help the Federal Government to get that complete independence and at the earliest possible moment.[1]

In a broadcast on 8 February, he said: 'Southern Rhodesia will, of course, not have achieved complete independence in the international sense, but the United Kingdom participation in our internal affairs will have ceased.'

Even if the electorate could justifiably complain that the U.F.P. clouded the independence issue in vague, misleading, and optimistic phrases, there could be no such complaint levelled at the D.P. Shortly after the conference a statement was issued stating:

The Dominion Party have attended the Southern Rhodesian Constitutional talks with the express hope of gaining from these talks the independence of Southern Rhodesia. The party draws the attention of the Conference to the fact that agreement by the United Kingdom to the removal of certain clauses in the Southern Rhodesian Constitution will not give Southern Rhodesia independence. . . . The party cannot accept the situation safeguarding rights whereby

[1] Congress speech, 22 February 1961, Central African Archives.

the United Kingdom still retains the power to legislate for Southern Rhodesia thereby destroying any real form of independence.[1]

Mr. Harper told the Legislative Assembly: 'I do not believe that it is possible to achieve independence under these proposals. I do not believe it is right that in gaining our independence, in gaining dominion status, that we should go about it by taking two bites of the cherry as this involves. This is merely the first bite of the cherry and hon. members opposite have to admit it.'[2] One of the main planks in the D.P. referendum campaign was that the proposals did not give independence, and in this they were supported by the two future Rhodesia Front Prime Ministers: Winston Field and Ian Smith.

There appears to be no substance in the accusation that Britain promised independence based upon the new Constitution if the Federation broke up. At the time of the referendum there was little discussion of the issue. The Federation was still in existence, both the British and Southern Rhodesian Governments were publicly committed to supporting its survival, and therefore did not speculate about its collapse. However, at a press conference on 7 December 1961, Sir Edgar was directly questioned on this issue. He was asked: 'This is a somewhat hypothetical question, Sir, as regards the new Constitution; if the Federation were to break up or if the ties linking the countries together were to be substantially loosened, would the progress of Southern Rhodesia towards full independence within the Commonwealth be entirely automatic?' Sir Edgar replied:

I think that—as you say, this is a hypothetical question—if the ties were loosened, of course the international figure would still be the Federation. If the very worst came to the very worst and the Federation were to break up, then I think Southern Rhodesia would probably have the few formal matters taken out of their Constitution that now remain. But they are formal, as the Secretary of State told you in this room last June, at the end of our conference. I think that you'd find that in those circumstances we'd have to paddle our own canoe. Actually, internal independence is a thing that I've always been keen to have. I've never been quite so enthusiastic about having to appoint embassies all over the world and

[1] S. R. L. A. Hansard, 20 June 1961, cols. 5915-6 (quoted by Mr. McLean).
[2] Op. cit., 21 June 1961, cols. 6001-2.

that sort of thing; I've been in one in Washington, and they're darned expensive.[1]

While Sir Edgar was clearly very optimistic about the chances of independence if the Federation were dissolved, this answer cannot be interpreted in any way to imply that there was a formal undertaking with Britain. In the answer Sir Edgar had again laid stress on the importance of internal, not international, independence. It was this which he claimed to have achieved in 1961.

The imprecise use of 'independence' was the product of the confused constitutional situation and the eagerness of the U.F.P. to have the proposals accepted, but clearly Southern Rhodesia as a member of a dependent Federation could not have full independence. Furthermore, Southern Rhodesia was still a colony and, although by the terms of the Constitution and the convention the British Government had accepted that they would not interfere in internal affairs, the British Government never conceded its right to ultimate authority through the Colonial Laws Validity Act of 1865. In the first White Paper it was noted that the Southern Rhodesian Government had requested that in future no legislation within the competence of the Legislative Assembly of Southern Rhodesia should be initiated unless the Southern Rhodesian Government asked for it. 'The Secretary of State for Commonwealth Relations took note of this request without commitment.'[2] In the Commons debate of March 1961 Mr. Sandys said: 'As I have explained . . . nothing we can do, no assurance I can give in regard to any Act of Parliament here, can remove the inalienable power of this Parliament to legislate [for Southern Rhodesia]. At the same time provision is made to ensure that basic safeguards, including the Declaration of Rights, may not be amended without specific agreement.'[3] But in a later debate he explained the practical situation:

In theory . . . they [the reserve powers] could be taken back, but in practice the possibility of the Parliament at Westminster upsetting a constitution once given was nil. That is broadly true. Once

---

[1] Record of Press Conference, 7 December 1961, Central African Archives.
[2] Cmnd. 1291 (para. 34).
[3] Hansard, 23 March 1961, col. 729.

this Parliament has given a constitution which represents an advance towards self-government to any territory in Her Majesty's Dominions, in practice it is broadly not possible to go backwards and to take back those powers.[1]

Behind the confusion of whether it was or whether it was not 'independence' for which the electorate voted at the referendum, the reality was that if Southern Rhodesia accepted the proposals she still remained a colony within a dependent Federation. Within Southern Rhodesia the functions and administration of government would still be divided between the federal and territorial Governments. Within its areas of competence the Southern Rhodesia Government would enjoy virtual independence of action. However, the new Constitution gave the Southern Rhodesian Government no legal power unilaterally to declare full independence. But equally, because the British Government accepted the impracticability of direct interference in Southern Rhodesia, it bound itself by a convention which precluded a unilateral solution by Britain. Full legal independence for Southern Rhodesia required the agreement and concurrence of both Governments.

Although the U.F.P. had projected the main part of its campaign towards the European electorate Sir Edgar continued to affirm that his policy was a *via media*, a rejection of extremism by either white or black. 'There is', he declared, 'no future for Southern Rhodesia on the basis of a struggle for power between all European parties advocating white supremacy for all time on the one hand and African nationalist parties advocating a black supremacy for all time on the other.'[2] He believed that, if extremism by either race were successful, it could only lead to tyannical government, leaving the opposing race with no political rights and violence as the sole means of opposition.

Whitehead had no difficulty in carrying the great bulk of his party with him. At a party conference late in February all the delegates but one voted for the new constitutional proposals. The exception was an important one. It was Ian Smith. Mr. Smith criticized two main aspects of the constitutional

---

[1] Op. cit., 22 June 1961, col. 1109.   [2] *The Rhodesia Herald*, 9 February 1961.

proposals—the failure to achieve independence from Britain and the new franchise arrangements, which he thought were making provision for Africans on a racial basis. At the conference Whitehead accused Smith of inflexibility and not moving with the times, but Smith continued to attack the proposals and outside the conference gained support from a few right-wing U.F.P. members. Such a major policy division could not be ignored. In April Ian Smith and his small group of supporters were called before the party standing committee and, when they were told that their attitude was unacceptable, they resigned. Ian Smith decided to continue to sit in the Federal House as an Independent, but in territorial matters he expressed sympathy with the D.P. opposition for, he said, he was committed to a single voters' roll which did not entrench racialism. He did not, however, join the D.P. Instead he formed a strange triumvirate with Winston Field, the leader of the Federal D.P., and Sir Robert Tredgold, the former Chief Justice, to campaign, on non-party lines, against the new Constitution. It is a striking irony of Rhodesian affairs that the future Prime Minister left the U.F.P. in opposition to a Constitution which he later used as the basis for Southern Rhodesia's claim to independence.

At that time Mr. Smith's opposition had seemed of little importance. The opposition of the European D.P. and the African N.D.P. were of much greater moment. The D.P. had opposed the proposals from the beginning and organized a campaign for their rejection. The D.P. concentrated their attack upon the two issues raised by Ian Smith—Britain's remaining powers and the new franchise. They rightly pointed out that Southern Rhodesia was not gaining independence and, as they explained this point, so their distrust of the British Government and its attitude towards African advancement was clearly revealed. Ian McLean said that the very fact that the United Kingdom Government was enthusiastic about the proposals warranted their rejection, for British policy was 'the orderly hand-over of these possessions to the indigenous inhabitants.'[1] McLean's statement emphasized the gulf which existed between British thinking and right-wing European thinking. A policy advocating an orderly hand-over of power to the indigenous

[1] S.R.L.A. Hansard, 20 June 1961.

inhabitants would draw support from all sides in the Commons; it sent a thrill of fear and horror through the D.P. ranks. McLean went on to claim that British policy was based upon political and economic expediency with no thoughts for the interests of Southern Rhodesia. So convinced were the D.P. of the evils of British interference that immediately after the February Conference William Harper, the leader, spoke of resorting to force to gain independence 'if the people demanded it'. He said that he was 'no longer prepared to recommend to the people of Southern Rhodesia that independence can be gained through discussions such as this nature'.[1] A small cloud was gathering on the horizon which was soon to grow into the storm of U.D.I.

The D.P. case was that the future welfare and prosperity of the country rested upon their narrow interpretation of who had the right to rule. British interference was resented, African nationalism was rejected, and, according to the D.P., the U.F.P. policy of partnership could only open the flood-gates to the black masses. In a radio broadcast Harper said: 'I recommend that the only safeguard for the foreseeable future is if we keep control of this country in European hands and let us make no bones about it.' He saw the new franchise as 'a sell-out of the heritage we must hand to our children', and concluded by saying that 'white leadership by precept and example by the proved ability which we have shown and by fair play for all the people, is a far better approach than by using misleading words like supremacy and domination'.[2] The D.P. contended that there could be no security in a Constitutional Council or Bill of Rights; only continued European rule could ensure the future. At a meeting at Greendale, William Cary took a piece of paper and tore it in two, declaring that 'a Bill of Rights in the hands of Joshua Nkomo would mean just that'.[3] William Harper, unconscious at that time of his own potential as a destroyer of Constitutions, warned that 'African Governments are notoriously arbitrary and it will probably not be long before the Constitution is, in any event, torn up and a dictatorship formed.'[4]

[1] *The Rhodesia Herald*, 8 February 1961.   [3] Op. cit., 25 April 1961.
[2] Op. cit., 11 February 1961.   [4] Op. cit., 14 July 1961.

The D.P. appeal was intended primarily for Europeans, if for no other reason than their conviction that Africans were apathetic towards politics and incapable of understanding it. When they spoke of 'the public' or 'the people' they meant Europeans. When they spoke of 'our heritage' or 'our future security and way of life', they were thinking of these in terms of the Europeans. Yet they believed that what they offered would benefit all Southern Rhodesians. They could see no middle way.

It was either white rule or black rule, and white rule was better for everybody. William Harper believed that Africans should have some say within their own areas, but were incapable of participating in central government. He told the Legislative Assembly that: 'The blacks will have justice and humanitarianism under the whites but the whites will not necessarily experience it under the blacks.'[1]

The D.P. concentrated their main attack upon the new franchise. It was, they claimed, the end of voting by merit on a non-racial basis. They emphasized the dangers of the fifteen 'B' Roll members combining with Africans or African sympathizers returned by the 'A' Roll to put government in 'racial African hands'. With obvious disapproval Ian McLean estimated that with the new franchise there might be an African-dominated government in twenty-five years' time. The D.P. opposed automatic voting rights to be given to chiefs and headmen, 'irrespective of whether they can read or write or whether they possess any more than they can get from collection of taxes'.[2] This was an attitude markedly inconsistent with future right-wing policy. Far from accepting the need to extend the franchise, the D.P. proposed to restrict it even further than the existing one. They wanted to abolish the 'special qualifications' and to make the upper-roll qualifications even more stringent, which would have excluded most of the small number of Africans already registered. For example, the existing upper-roll qualifications gave the vote to a person with an income of £480 per annum or immovable property worth £1,000 plus full Primary education. The D.P. wanted to change this to an

---

[1] S.R.L.A. Hansard, 21 June 1961.
[2] Op. cit., 18 April 1967 (William Cary).

income of £640 per annum, or property worth £1,800 plus two years' Secondary education.[1]

The D.P. coupled their views on African participation in government with another of their favourite schemes, large-scale European immigration. Harper repeated persistently that he could envisage equality of political rights only when European and African population numbers were roughly equal. This revealed not only a fear of the sheer weight of African numbers but also a profound ignorance of population statistics and trends. In 1961 there were 3,520,000 Africans and 221,000 Europeans in Southern Rhodesia. The African population was expanding at a rapid rate, with a natural increase of 3·5 per cent per annum, which means that it is doubling itself every twenty years. But even this is probably a conservative estimate for the future, because a large proportion of the African population consists of children and, as the population bulge moves up into the child-producing age groups, so the rate of increase can be expected to rise. In 1962 21 per cent of Southern Rhodesia's African population were aged four years or under; 51 per cent were aged fourteen years or under.[2] Even accepting the 3·5 per cent rate of increase, there will be 7 million Africans in 1981 and 14 million by 2001.

No European immigration scheme could keep pace with this. The European population trends are very difficult to assess with any accuracy for they are closely related to political and economic conditions. In 1954 there were 158,000 Europeans in Southern Rhodesia but this figure rose quickly to 224,000 in 1963. Since then, however, the population has fallen and in 1965 there were only 219,000. This trend is discernible even more clearly in migration figures. In 1956 there was a net gain of 13,000 Europeans, but in 1963 a loss of 5,430 and in 1964 a loss of 6,733. The European natural increase was 2 per

[1] The full proposals were (existing upper-roll 1957 qualifications in parentheses):
    (1) Income £920 p.a. (£720) or property £2,400 (£1,500) + full Primary education (literacy).
    (2) Income £640 p.a. (£480) or property £1,800 (£1,000) + 2 years' Secondary education (Primary education).
    (3) Income £420 (£300) or property £1,200 (£500) + 4 years' Secondary education (same).
These qualifications were coupled with literacy in English and the future introduction of 'a worthiness test' (*The Rhodesia Herald*, 24 February 1961).
[2] Central Statistical Office, 1962 African Census.

cent per annum in 1954, but had fallen to 1·2 per cent in 1964, compared with a fairly consistent African increase of 3·5 per cent.[1] If Africans were to wait for political rights until the European numbers equal their own, they would wait for ever.

The D.P. then stood firmly against the constitutional proposals. Although they welcomed the reduction of British powers, they thought that more should have been achieved, and that the bargain of extending the franchise was completely unacceptable. Vote 'No', proclaimed the D.P. posters. Oppose the new proposals, declared the D.P. leaders, for acceptance could only lead to a lowering of standards, a loss of confidence in Rhodesia's future, and the disappearance of outside investment and business enterprise. Mass unemployment and emigration of Europeans would follow. The future of all races depended upon rejection of the 1961 Constitution.

The opposition for the right-wing European party was matched by African nationalist opposition. Immediately after the conference the leaders who had attended it were caught between their initial acceptance of its proposals and the open hostility of other nationalists. Nkomo and his fellow-delegates gradually moved from a position of doubtful acceptance to one of unmitigated opposition. At an N.D.P. conference in March 1961, Nkomo still made some show of defending his earlier stand and offered to resign from the leadership. His resignation was refused, the party rallied behind him, but to ensure future support he diverted attention from the unpopular franchise proposals to issues on which the party was agreed. He then related the two together and the N.D.P. conference agreed that the constitutional proposals could be accepted only if certain agreed conditions were fulfilled. The conditions included the release of all detainees; the settlement of the land question, which implied the repeal of the Land Apportionment Act; clarification of the membership and function of the Constitutional Council and the lifting of the ban on political meetings in rural areas. The N.D.P. leaders complained that the ban on meetings prevented them from consulting their followers. As the referendum campaign progressed, emphasis was placed

[1] Central Statistical Office, *Monthly Digest*, July 1965.

more and more on the need to obtain the conditions rather than to accept the new franchise. It was evident that the conditions would not be accepted by the Government.

The N.D.P. began to adopt a more militant policy, issuing threats rather than offering negotiations. In April Moton Malianga, the N.D.P. Vice-President, said that the British Government had taken advantage of 'our reasonableness', but could only 'impose a Constitution over our dead bodies. We are prepared to leave our country to the sweet music of the winds that come in the wake of devastation. From the All Africa People's Conference we shall secure all the support we require, moral and otherwise to smash once and for all imperialism and colonialism not only in Southern Rhodesia but in the whole of Africa.'[1] Whitehead replied to this wild threat by saying that violence would be crushed by all the forces available to the Government and that any attempt to call in foreign powers would be treason. In May the N.D.P. leaders walked out of renewed constitutional talks, called to examine the detailed implementation of the agreed proposals, because, said the nationalists, their conditions had not been met.

Pressure on the N.D.P. leaders to reject the new Constitution continued. On 10 June 1961, Michael Mawema and Patrick Matimba announced the formation of a new party, the Zimbabwe National Party (Z.N.P.), claiming that acceptance of the constitutional proposals had shown that the N.D.P. leaders had been 'politically inconsistent, unreliable and even dishonest . . . treacherously leading us into a gas chamber.'[2] The new party had a bad start, for at its first press conference the leaders had to be rescued by the police after being assaulted by members of the militant N.D.P. Youth Wing. Although the new party failed to attract popular support, either at its inauguration or in its subsequent career, it was another warning to Nkomo that signs of moderation would lose him support.

Eventually, at a special N.D.P. congress in June, any remaining pretence of support for the Constitutional proposals was abandoned. Nkomo assured the congress that none of their conditions had been met and he was now convinced that Britain was prepared to accept long-term rule by a white minority. The new Constitution was branded as 'a whitemen

---

[1] *The Examiner*, May 1961.   [2] Op. cit., July 1961.

to whitemen agreement that could not be made binding on the millions of Africans'.[1] Later Sithole and Nkomo gave their reasons for rejecting the franchise and the constitution. Sithole said that the new franchise proposals were not based so much upon qualifications which some men had, but upon qualifications which the majority of Africans did not have; universal education, high wages, and property qualifications. 'To expect a man to qualify on what he hasn't is really to expect him not to qualify at all.' Sithole said that the new franchise was in reality 'one man, one vote for the white man'.[2]

Nkomo said that the franchise was intended to reserve power for Europeans and only allow a few Africans across 'the holy line'. He said that 'any changes in education, wages, systems of property ownership and all those factors that enable one to qualify for membership in the "electorate club" are strictly controlled and jealously guarded by the club. . . . As far as we are concerned the whole thing is inhuman, uncivilized, uncultured, stupid, selfish, and above all un-Christian.' Nkomo said that he had rejected the 1961 Constitution for political and moral reasons:

> Politically we could not accept a constitution and sit in a Parliament created by that Constitution and justifiably reject a motion by that House requesting Britain to grant a Smith type of independence. If we had done that we would have committed national political suicide. . . . Morally we could not have accepted a Constitution which implied that the white minority section of our population was superior to the African majority.[3]

Although these comments were written some years later, they represent the feelings of the N.D.P. Congress of June 1961.

The Congress's rejection of the constitutional proposals was followed by a marked increase in N.D.P. militancy. It was decided to take 'positive' but unspecified action to achieve the party's objectives. Sithole declared that it was noble to go to jail for one's convictions. The party leaders urged any of their followers who were registered voters to boycott the government referendum, and instead decided to organize a separate referendum in which all adults, of any race, could vote.

The rejection of the new Constitution was an important

[1] *Daily News*, 19 June 1961.   [3] Op cit., 25 June 1964.
[2] Op. cit., 4 April 1962.

turning-point for the African nationalist movement. It marks the rejection of compromise and left the movement outside the constitutional framework. Previously the nationalists had had no voice in the Government. In 1961 they were offered a restricted voice but rejected it as insufficient. This led them to seek power by unconstitutional means and in time led them to violence, which brought misery and suffering to many fellow-Africans and a strong reaction from the Europeans.

It is easy to understand why the nationalists rejected the proposals. They were offered much less than they had hoped for; they saw dangers that the Constitution might be misused to entrench white rule; they were opposed by many of their own followers and by nationalists in other countries. Mr. Nkomo and his executive probably decided that if they continued to support the proposals they would lose the leadership of the movement. They decided that the price was too great to pay for proposals to which they had never given their unqualified support. Mr. Nkomo later gave a very narrow definition of leadership, saying that the leader's task was simply to reflect the opinion of his followers. But, in addition to this local pressure, the success of nationalism elsewhere in Africa, and the pressure which foreign nationalist movements put on the N.D.P. told heavily in the decision to withdraw agreement.

The N.D.P. leaders concluded that African nationalism was an irresistible force which no white government could defeat. Success was only a matter of time, and maintaining the pressure. What had been achieved in Guinea, in Ghana, in Kenya would be emulated in Southern Rhodesia. It was inevitable that such a lesson would be absorbed, but it was the wrong lesson. In territories where nationalism had been so successful, it had faced colonial governments which accepted that independence for African governments, backed by a majority of the population, was a desirable aim. The colonial régimes became geared to the task of handing over power, and disputes with the nationalists centred around how and when this should be done. These were ideal conditions for the use of the boycott, the threat of non-co-operation and intransigence, but these conditions did not exist in Southern Rhodesia. There the Government was in the hands of a white minority, who, far from showing anxiety to hand over power, were determined to 'retain standards', to keep control in 'civilized hands', which many of them translated to mean continued white rule. What threat was it to boycott an election when it left the field open for the white voters? What threat was it to refuse to negotiate when the Government was prepared to make decisions in the absence of the nationalists?

Had the nationalists worked within the 1961 Constitution, they would probably have won most, if not all, the 'B' Roll seats. They would have formed the 'African Party' in opposition to the ruling 'European Party'. A racial political struggle would have developed in the Legislative Assembly, thereby destroying Sir Edgar Whitehead's dream of non-racial political parties. However, accepting—as the nationalists did—that race was the main political division, there would have been an immense advantage for the nationalists in participating. In the Legislative Assembly they would have had a platform from which their ideas would have received wide national and international publicity. They could not have formed an administration, but they could have revealed the strength of their support and have exerted pressure on the Government of the day. This pressure could have been concentrated on achieving further constitutional changes and greater African political advancement. The onus of holding back constitutional advances or even breaking constitutional arrangements would have rested on the Government, not the nationalists, but, by refusing to participate, the nationalists were accused of rejecting peaceful constitutional development and aiming at violent revolution. By channelling their energies through a parliamentary party, the nationalists may well have avoided the violence and destruction with which their movement became associated. In refusing to participate they made a grave tactical error and, for the future, one of the greatest weaknesses in the African claim for more political rights was the nationalists' refusal to abide by the 1961 arrangements.

After rejecting the proposals the nationalists renewed their emotional but impractical appeal for 'one man, one vote now'. No Southern Rhodesian Government, with its foundation of European support, could or would accept such a proposal. Nor, in relation to the organization of government, was the nationalist appeal practical. Whatever the justice of the nationalist

claim that Africans had been denied their rights, the reality
was that Europeans had controlled all the processes of government. To attempt to change this overnight by the introduction
of what was for Southern Rhodesia a revolutionary franchise
was to invite chaos similar to that which had overtaken the
Congo. The African ambition to acquire an increasing and
eventually decisive role in the Government had to be balanced
against the stability of the Government and society. Without
inviting confusion and disorder, African advancement would
have to be phased, with Africans moving into the higher
branches of the civil service and armed forces, with Africans
acquiring parliamentary and ministerial experience, with
Africans enjoying greater responsibility in local government.
This process would take time and no accurate assessment was
possible of how quickly it could be implemented while retaining
a stable society in which eventually all men could enjoy a say
in their own government. The important point in 1961 was to
set the process moving, and however imperfect the new constitutional proposals may have appeared to the nationalists, they
did give an opportunity for the process to begin. Success
depended upon whether Africans were prepared to work within
the new constitutional framework, but the nationalists were not.

As the referendum drew near, the U.F.P.'s political isolation
became striking. The D.P. and N.D.P. were joined in their
opposition to the constitutional proposals by the Field-Smith-
Tredgold group who thought that the common roll should not
be abandoned, and by the members of Garfield Todd's Central
Africa Party who thought that the franchise was too restricted.
Eventually only the U.F.P. supported the proposals. But this
isolation reflected political reality, for although the proposals
had emerged from an all-party conference and although initially other groups had supported the proposals, the new Constitution was moulded in the image of the U.F.P. It was the
Constitution of 'partnership', a partnership which was rejected by the right-wing Europeans because it gave the Africans
too much, and rejected by the nationalists because it gave
them too little.

Late July was a time of great activity. The N.D.P. arranged

their referendum for 23 July, the Government's was set for 26 July, while sandwiched in between, on 24 July, the N.D.P. called for a strike to demonstrate their opposition to the new constitutional proposals. The Government moved with great decision. There was no direct interference with the N.D.P. referendum, but on 19 July police and troops moved into the African townships of Salisbury and Bulawayo, 'to protect people and property'. This time the Government did not make the mistake of arresting the N.D.P. leaders, which had set off the troubles of the previous year. The leaders remained free but were followed and watched wherever they went. To counter the N.D.P. call for demonstrations on referendum day, the Government placed a ban on all meetings of more than twelve people for that day.

The N.D.P. referendum naturally ran into administrative difficulties and by the standards of the official referendum it had serious deficiencies but, if nothing else, it confirmed the strength of the movement. In a predominantly African vote, it was claimed that 372,546 votes were cast against the new Constitution and 471 in favour and, even if it is accepted that these numbers were inflated, the popular backing of the movement was confirmed. The N.D.P. referendum passed peacefully but there was some trouble the following day, strike day. The strike was a failure. The Government gave protection to workers, in some places using armoured cars to protect the main routes. Most men accepted that for that day at least the government was stronger than the N.D.P. but in Highfields in Salisbury there was trouble, with clashes between workers and strikers which resulted in police intervention. The police opened fire on strikers who were stoning blacklegs, killing one man and wounding four others.

With their own referendum over, the N.D.P. leaders called on their supporters to stay at home on the official referendum day. Joshua Nkomo issued a statement saying:

Tomorrow, Wednesday, 26 July, the settlers in our country are carrying out a referendum amongst themselves to approve proposals which entrench them into power permanently and at the same time sealing off any possible chance for further constitutional settlement. Following on our previous announcements, and taking into account the deliberate cold-blooded shooting of our people yesterday in

Highfields, we are calling on all our people to refrain from all forms of work and spend the whole of this day in prayer and re-dedication to the struggle for the liberation of our country.[1]

Whitehead replied by threatening that violence would be put down with 'a rod of iron'. The 'rod of iron' was not required immediately. In Bulawayo the police used tear gas to disperse a crowd of nationalist supporters, but otherwise the referendum took place without incident and again the N.D.P. strike call was a failure.

On 27 July the referendum result was announced. It was a great triumph for Whitehead. 41,949 had voted 'Yes' and only 21,846 'No'. 'Extremism is dead', proclaimed the Prime Minister. The result of the referendum 'marks the birth of a Rhodesian nation' in which 'African people can play their part fully in the political life of the country'.[2]

The referendum success made the U.F.P. Government's future look secure, but this was deceptive. The referendum result was a diversion, an exception from the swing of European Rhodesian politics. This was not clear in 1961. There had been a right-wing swing in the 1958 election, but the picture then had been confused by the disorder and division in the U.F.P. ranks. The two elections which followed, in 1962 and 1965, left no doubt about the swing to the right, and therefore posed the question of why the 1961 referendum result went against the political trend.

A number of reasons account for this apparent contradiction. Although the new Constitution would not mean full independence from Britain, it did have the attraction for the European voters of reducing British powers and making it exceedingly difficult for Britain to interfere in Southern Rhodesia's internal affairs. The constitutional changes, with their acceptance of African representation in the Legislative Assembly, were seen as a means of preserving some form of federation, which most Europeans thought was essential for continued economic prosperity. Also there must be a strong suspicion that the opposition of the African nationalists convinced many Europeans that it was safe to vote 'Yes'. They reasoned that if

---

[1] S.R.L.A. Hansard, 13 September 1961, cols. 1216–7 (quoted by Mr. A. R. W. Stumbles).
[2] *Daily News*, 27 July 1961.

the nationalists were so opposed to it, then the new Constitution could not be capitulation to African extremism, as the D.P. claimed. Finally, Whitehead and his Government had gained the confidence of Europeans by their firm handling of the nationalists during the referendum period, while by mid-1961 the right-wing party, the D.P., was divided and badly organized. The federal and territorial branches had split, there were rumours of personal clashes, and the territorial party had been losing members.

The paradox of the 1961 referendum result is that the very motives which were responsible for an affirmative vote—the desire for freedom from British interference; the attempt to entrench economic advantages; the aversion to African nationalism; the support for a Government willing to wield a 'rod of iron'—were the same motives which were moving the European electorate away from the compromise solution which the U.F.P. thought it was creating in the new Constitution. The result was a contradiction, but the main reasons for it were consistent with the swing to the right.

None of this was realized after the referendum. It appeared that European moderation had succeeded. The Chief Native Commissioner wrote: 'We feel that the new provisions have given us a certain amount of assurance that this country will not pursue politics which mean that Africans would perpetually be unable to control this country.'[1] The South African solution of racial separation appeared to have been discarded, and for those who believed that the races could share political power the land ahead looked bright.

[1] Chief Native Commissioner's report for 1961.

CHAPTER VI

The U. F. P. Government and African Support

Success in the referendum convinced the U.F.P. Government that it had the confidence and support of a sizeable majority of the predominantly European electorate. Working on this assumption the government party, eager to implement its policy of partnership, turned its attention to gaining support from Africans. The Government believed that, if the new Constitution were carefully explained, if it could be shown that Africans would play an increasing part in government, if nationalist violence and intimidation could be suppressed, then many Africans would support the moderate non-racial U.F.P. policy. This confidence rested on the belief that there was a strong and increasing 'middle class' of Africans. These Africans, who would be eligible for the 'B' Roll, would favour a policy of moderation and security, and reject the wild extremism of the nationalists. The Prime Minister thought that the new Constitution would attract members of all races who had a stake in the existing order: the property-owners, the established farmers, the businessmen, the better-educated, the professional men and civil servants, the mature and settled. 'Control', he said, 'would be in the hands of those who have something to lose, who had assets, who had education and had made a success of life and we even put in for certain categories of voters that they should be over thirty years of age so that we could add maturity to the other qualifications.'[1] It was these responsible elements among the Africans that Sir Edgar set out to win and, perhaps unwittingly, staked his future political career on its success or failure.

The U.F.P. was the first major political party to appeal

[1] S.R.L.A. Hansard, 8 December 1961.

directly to Africans. Previously, policy towards Africans had been an important issue, but Africans had been the subjects, not the makers, of decisions. The new constitution was intended to change this. The U.F.P. launched two campaigns: 'Build a Nation' and 'Claim a Vote'. The 'Build a Nation' campaign was to be the fulfilment of the party's policy of a racial partnership, eliminating the racial, 'two nations', division of the past. 'I am perfectly certain,' said Sir Edgar:

that we can get the participation of those of the African people who are eligible for the Roll to take a really active part under the Constitution provided that intimidation is not allowed to prevent them from doing so . . . It is our firm intention in the interests of all races in this country—but probably more in the interests of the European than anyone else because he is the one who has the most to lose—that any discrimination that remains in this country shall be removed as soon as it can be done. Secondly that equality of opportunity shall be made a reality, and I believe that there is a real prospect of getting long-range peace along these lines.

After stressing that political advance should follow economic and social advances, the Prime Minister continued: 'I believe that it is quite impossible to maintain—if we are going to have a happy future in this country—that artificial separation of the races by law can continue.'[1]

The 'Claim a Vote' campaign was an organized attempt to ensure that all people who had the necessary qualifications registered for a vote. The campaign concentrated upon 'B' Roll African voters, who previously had not enjoyed the franchise. They were urged by government officials and campaign-organizers to exercise their new rights.

The two campaigns presented a problem of communication between the U.F.P. Government and Africans. The Government was attempting to create a new relationship, and therefore the old administrative channel of contact via the Department of Native Affairs and Native Commissioners was inadequate. The Prime Minister undertook a nation-wide tour in which he spoke to predominantly African audiences, a rare if not unique gesture. He told them of the new political rights and urged those who were eligible to use them. The U.F.P. also called upon active support from its African party members, and

[1] S.R.L.A. Hansard, 13 December 1961, cols. 503 and 513.

opened new branches in urban and rural African areas. Paid
and voluntary assistants were employed, and a 'Build a Nation'
secretariat created, which initially was attached to the party
but later existed in its own right.

Despite these efforts there remained an obvious and large
gulf between the European Government and the great mass of
Africans. It was a gulf which the African nationalists had exploited and were not anxious to see bridged. The nationalists
considered that the 'partnership' of the U.F.P. was a sham, that
it would compromise African interests, and therefore they
opposed the Government's campaign. Faced with nationalist
opposition and the inadequacy of conventional party techniques, the U.F.P. was forced to look more closely at the existing
relations between the Government and Africans.

The U.F.P. gave some attention to urban areas, where they
encouraged the municipal and town authorities to devise
means by which urban Africans could be directly represented
in the local governments. New party branches were opened in
African townships and meetings of the party and the campaign
organizers were held. But the main focus of attention was the
rural areas where the majority of Africans lived. There was, and
to some extent still is, an air of neglect hanging over the African
rural areas. This is the product not so much of sinister motives
but of the fact that Southern Rhodesia has been built upon
European enterprise and settlement. European farming,
mining, industry, and commercial activity have been the
foundation of the country's economic development and of the
Government's revenue. There has therefore been no great incentive to develop African rural areas. Over long years the
Government's main aims in these rural areas has been to maintain peace and order, to ensure that sufficient food was grown,
to preserve rather than develop.

In the past the administration and control of rural areas had
been left almost exclusively to the Native Commissioners, but
with rapidly changing circumstances the old system was under
great pressure. There was deep-seated discontent, a discontent
which the nationalists had used to gain widespread support.
The U.F.P. Government set itself two interrelated tasks: to
alleviate the discontent and to gain active political support.

A map showing the geographical divisions of the races in

Southern Rhodesia looks like a patchwork quilt. Diagonally across it, from south-west to north-east, is a band of white marking the main European settlement. Alongside this band and sometimes isolated in it, are the African areas: imperial red for the Tribal Trust Lands, and purple for the Native Purchase Areas. To complete the pattern there are patches of green for the National Lands, yellow for the unreserved land, in which people of any race may live, and other patches of white where European settlement is isolated from the main band. The Tribal Trust Lands are settled by Africans on a communal tribal basis, while in the Native Purchase Areas more advanced African farmers have individual holdings. In 1962 the rough distribution of the African population was 51 per cent in the Tribal Trust Lands, 7 per cent in the Native Purchase Areas, 23 per cent in the European areas (rural and urban) and 18 per cent in the African urban areas.

Rural discontent took many forms. There was dissatisfaction with the educational bottlenecks and the payment of education fees to mission bodies, while in the towns there were free government schools; dissatisfaction with a lower price for crops than was paid to European farmers (the difference went in higher collection and transport charges, and a cess paid to an African development fund). However, the main cause of discontent was the allocation and use of land. In the early 1960s this was identified with two pieces of legislation; the Land Apportionment Act of 1930 and the Native Land Husbandry Act of 1951. While the Tribal Trust lands are guaranteed in the constitution, and, together with the Native Purchase Areas, now cover 44,240,000 acres, from a total land area of about 96,600,000 acres, the growth of the African population and its increased stock holdings continue to put enormous pressures on many sections of these lands. While the Africans are pressed into their areas they can see the wide acres of the European land, some of it unoccupied, some of it underworked, and they ask: 'Is the Land Apportionment Act fair to Africans?' It was the same question which the Select Committee on the Resettlement of Natives had asked, and that committee came to the conclusion that the Act was against the interests not only of Africans but of all Southern Rhodesians.[1]

[1] See Chapter III of the present volume, pp. 46-8.

Added to the traditional problem of land shortage had come the Native Land Husbandry Act. The Act aimed at converting the communally held tribal lands into individual titled holdings. From an agricultural and economic point of view the step was absolutely logical and right. It aimed at soil preservation, at introducing better farming methods, at giving African farmers an individual stake in the land. But however logical and right it might have seemed to Europeans, it met strong African opposition. There were a variety of reasons for this opposition. First, the Act introduced a concept of individual land ownership alien to African belief that the land belongs to the tribe even though it is allocated to an individual's use. Second, the Act aimed at cattle destocking to prevent soil erosion, but cattle are a major form of African wealth and are valued for their numbers as well as their quality. Third, the allocation of land was sometimes done hastily without consideration for the feelings or rights of the individual farmers. Finally, and the most basic cause of opposition, is the fundamental role which land plays in African society. In a society with few social-security services, in which many people live at a bare subsistence level, in which employment opportunities are strictly limited, land is the one certain security.

This is as true for many of the urban Africans of Southern Rhodesias as it is for their rural brothers. In the urban areas few Africans have property rights, there are no provisions for unemployment or old-age pensions, and therefore many urban dwellers look to the land for security. The line between African rural and urban society is often difficult to draw, for many men have a foot in each camp, and divide their working life between the two. There is a dual economy, with the urban areas providing the cash, and the rural areas food and a place of refuge in times of distress or unemployment or old age. Even before the introduction of the Land Husbandry Act, it was becoming increasingly difficult for urban workers to find land, but it became even more difficult after the implementation of the Act. For the Land Husbandry Act to have worked effectively it would have required an urban as well as a rural revolution; a revolution in which full provisions would have been made for a large, permanent African urban population. This was not done and therefore the importance of land as security remained.

Ian Smith

Harold Wilson and Joshua Nkomo, October 1965

The Reverend Ndabaningi Sithole in Restriction

Sir Edgar Whitehead and Sir Roy Welensky

The Land Husbandry Act gave greater security for some Africans, but for others it cut away their chance of becoming land-holders. The Act was implemented by giving land rights to all people farming in the African reserves on a set date. This gave rise to immediate problems. In some areas it was discovered that, although the plots were designed to provide little more than subsistence farming, there were more claimants than plots. For example, in the Gutu Reserve it was reported that there were 3,000 families on the land 'in excess of the assessed sound carrying capacity and thus the Reserve is over-populated by 40 per cent. In addition, there are 4,000 people surplus from the Gutu area, with at present no land right but for whom land has to be found.'[1] In some cases the plots were reduced in size, in others people were told to seek land elsewhere. Then other claims started to come in from Africans, who on the set date had been working in the towns, from sons of farmers who each wanted their own land, and from Africans who were being moved from European areas. All those Africans wanted land. Obviously it was impossible to satisfy them all but, without an alternative form of security, the search would go on and the frustrations increase.

Added to these particular discontents was the general discontent of a wretchedly poor rural society living alongside an affluent minority. The Government had made efforts to improve the standards of African farming but, partially because the resources and effort directed to it had been insufficient, partially because of the deep-seated resistance to change of a rural peasantry, there had been no substantial breakthrough. African farming techniques remained backward; the cash rewards remained small. The Government, which was conscious of this problem, had appointed in late 1960 an advisory committee (the Phillips Committee) to study the country's economic resources with particular reference to African agriculture. The Committee reported in 1962, drawing up a five-year development plan. The main themes of the report were that self-help must be encouraged among Africans by such means as local government, education co-operatives, improved credit facilities, and marketing; that there must be greater co-operation

---

[1] Phillips' Committee Report, C.S.R. 15–1962, Ch. XIV, p. 204.

9

between the races; and that African support and confidence in a development programme must be won. The Committee, which emphasized that agriculture would remain the major industry, reported:

A reduction in the poverty—relatively widely spread in the Tribal Trust areas—depends largely upon the raising of the productive efficiency of the pastoralists, the cultivators and those engaged in simple mixed farming. It is imperative that this improvement should be brought about as rapidly as possible because otherwise the migration of rural inhabitants to the towns will be accelerated, the level of wages in urban and related activities will remain depressed, there will be a continuance of a social structure slowing down an expansion in the demand for consumer goods except of the simplest and cheapest kinds, and finally the market will not be sufficiently widened and varied.[1]

In August 1961 H. J. Quinton, the Minister of Native Affairs, gave the Legislative Assembly the average annual cash incomes of African farmers, above their subsistence production. For a master-farmer it was £40 per annum (there were 600 master-farmers), for a plot-holder and member of a co-operative it was £6 per annum, for an ordinary farmer it was £3 10s. per annum, and for a woman cultivating alone it was £1 per annum.[2] The members of the Legislative Assembly were divided about the reasons for what Dr. Burrows of the U.F.P. called, these 'appalling figures'. Dr. Burrows thought that a much greater effort must be made to put capital and technical knowledge into African farming, while Mr. Cary, the D.P. stalwart, thought that low production was 'due to laziness . . . reverting back to type'. The Committee on the Resettlement of Natives had examined the same problem. It gave comparative figures for African and European farming which showed how efficiently European farming was organized for cash-crop production while African farming was inefficient, wasteful, and concentrated largely on subsistence production (para. 308). The tabulated figures for 1958 were:

---

[1] Non-Technical Summary of Phillips' Report, Salisbury, Government Printer, 1962, p. 6.
[2] S.R.L.A. Hansard, 29 August 1961. Clearly many African farmers produced no cash crops and depended for their cash needs on money which found its way to the Reserves from wages paid in European rural and urban areas.

TABLE V

COMPARATIVE FIGURES FOR AFRICAN
AND EUROPEAN FARMING

	Cultivated acreage	Cattle holding	Total value of produce	Value of produce sold
European	853,400	1,500,000	£52,400,000	£49,900,000
African	3,291,600	1,389,000	£14,700,000	£3,400,000

The Committee noted that there had been a substantial increase in capital investment in African rural areas 'rising from £2,300,000 for the nine years, 1940–41 to 1948–49 to more than £15,000,000 for the nine years 1950–51 to 1957–58'; but 'this sixfold increase has not been paralleled by anything like a corresponding increase in output even allowing for some time lag for the expenditure to take effect' (para. 298). The Committee found that:

(a) Shortage of land is not one of the factors militating against increased agricultural output in Southern Rhodesia.

(b) The African labourer is not technically proficient; nor is he diligent—he requires incentive to overcome his high leisure preferences.

(c) Management is lacking owing to the limited extension services available and to the fact that available advice is not fully utilized.

(d) Lack of knowledge tends to lead to dissipation of effort and, consequently to loss of capital.

(e) Capital is wasted unless expenditure is directly related to sound management.

(f) The Africans' lack of capital—their inability to borrow—is one of the reasons for the lack of development in the native areas.[1]

Whatever the reasons, the sheer poverty of the African rural areas was in itself a major source of discontent and was a great obstacle to any form of development emanating from the Africans. There was no easy or quick solution to a problem which still taxes the Rhodesian Government.

The nationalists' success in voicing and using rural discontent had brought strong pressures on the government administration and particularly the Native Commissioners (the title was

[1] Para. 299.

changed to District Commissioner at the beginning of 1963).
The District Commissioner is still the key figure of the administration. It is he who is responsible for good order and government in his district. From him radiate the Government's
activities; he supervises the chiefs, he guides the councils, he
co-ordinates departmental work, he collects revenue, and he still
hears some cases. Until recently it was accepted that his was a
paternal role, that he ruled fairly but firmly, listening to advice
but making the decisions. The chiefs were his assistants, not he
their guide. By the early 1960s it was clear that this was no
longer a satisfactory relationship, for the Native Commissioners
were losing African sympathy and confidence. To the Africans
they had become the personification of the Government's unpopular policies, especially the land policy. In the late 1950s,
the African National Congress had fostered this unpopularity
by deliberately challenging and discrediting the Native Commissioners' authority.[1] In 1961 the Mangwende Commission
reported:

The problem is aggravated by the fact that so much of this legislation [i.e. related to African administration] is of a restrictive
character, imposed from above. Since the Native Commissioner is
held responsible both for the implementation and the subsequent
enforcement of these measures, he is placed in the anomalous position of first having to persuade the people to accept his instructions,
then to initiate prosecution in cases of default, and finally to sit in
judgment upon the cases. This multiplicity of inherently conflicting
roles can but have a detrimental effect upon his relations with the
people. As he perforce becomes more remote and estranged from
them, his traditional image of a stern but often helpful and understanding 'father' is fading from the public eye. Instead, he tends to
become regarded as the local symbol of a restrictive if not 'oppressive' White Government, and therefore unavoidably the target of
mounting resentment.[2]

The pressures upon the Native Department led to dissatisfaction
and loss of morale among its members. In some European
circles it was advocated that the Department should be abolished and its functions distributed among technical officers.
The dissatisfaction and uncertainty resulted in resignations and

[1] Shamuyarira, op. cit., pp. 42-3.
[2] Report of the Mangwende Reserve Commission, 1961, para. 107.

difficulty in finding new recruits. In 1959 the Chief Native Commissioner reported that 'the administration is on the verge of breakdown'. In 1960 he wrote:

In previous reports since 1956, I have sounded warnings that the Department had not the qualified and experienced staff that it should have and that this was likely to continue for some years . . . The staff position has deteriorated still further during the year; the number of resignations, retirements, and transfers out of the Division has exceeded the intake of recruits—this applies to both the administrative and agricultural departments.[1]

The difficulties facing the Native Commissioners revealed the vulnerability of the rural administration. Authority had been concentrated in their hands and a threat to them was a threat to the whole structure. Tribal chiefs had been recognized and paid small subsidies but they had not enjoyed the same prestige or power given to chiefs under the British Colonial Office's system of 'indirect rule'. The Land Husbandry Act had dealt another blow to the chiefs, for it had removed from them one of their greatest remaining strengths—the right to allocate land in the tribal areas. Before the government administrative reorganization the chiefs, even more than the Native Commissioners, were criticized as an anachronism with little remaining purpose and no future.

One possible road for African advancement lay in local councils, which are composed of a majority of elected members plus chiefs and headmen who sit *ex officio*. (In Native Purchase Areas, there are no chiefs and therefore all the councillors are elected.) A new Council's Act had been introduced in 1957 to rejuvenate existing councils and introduce councils where none had previously existed. However, the councils had not flourished. They were opposed by the nationalists. They were given too few responsibilities. The Native Commissioners were often too involved in other work to give support and guidance, and when the Native Commissioners did turn their attention to the councils, too frequently they dominated them instead of advising them. This was partly the result of the old 'paternal' attitude, and partly because the Native Commissioners were made council chairmen. But the greatest weakness of the councils was

[1] Chief Native Commissioner's Reports, 1959 and 1960.

lack of finance and because of this they were severely limited in the services they could offer. The weakness stemmed partially from the difficulty of collecting rates, but even more from the fact that the rural Africans whom the councils served and from whom they derived their strength were very poor. The councils relied heavily upon small central government grants. In 1961 the total revenue of the fifty-nine councils in existence was £129,026. In 1962 four of these councils had collapsed and the total revenue for the remaining fifty-five was £124,726. In 1962 twenty-three of the fifty-five councils failed to collect £100 in rates and only three councils collected £1,000 or more. Councils, because of their limited funds, because of the central Government's paternalistic embrace, failed to flourish or to show results. The Chief Native Commissioner wrote in his 1961 report: ' "The Council does nothing for me" is the almost universal reaction and when the opinion is examined it is found to be due to absence of adequate schooling and health facilities or failure of the council to influence government plans.' He further commented that:

Council rates dropped very considerably; four councils were abolished at their own request; several councils, unable to decide whether to keep going or give up, just coasted along on accumulated financial reserves; and at many annual elections so few voters turned up or no one would stand for election that the very basis of a council's existence was paralysed.

Obviously a major overhaul and reorientation of rural African administration was required. The need was spelt out in detail in the reports of two Commissions: the Robinson Commission[1] and the Mangwende Reserve Commission, both of which reported in 1961. The Robinson Commission dealt in general with the role and functions of the Native Affairs Department, while the Mangwende Commission examined the breakdown of administration in a particular area. Both Commissions revealed sufficient common ground to become the basis for an administrative reorganization.

No doubt this reorganization would have come in any case, but it became particularly important at a time when the U.F.P. Government was searching for new channels of contact and

---

[1] Salisbury, Government Printer, Command Southern Rhodesia, 22, 1961.

sympathy with Africans. It was decided that in future government officials should endeavour to persuade and advise rather than order. The Native Commissioners became District Commissioners and were relieved of some of their functions, including much judicial work, so that they could concentrate on advising and keeping contact with Africans. The Native Affairs Department became the Department of Internal Affairs and lost functions concerned with farming and cattle-keeping. Sir Edgar Whitehead told the Legislative Assembly that the administrative reorganization was:

almost a new science . . . the science of Community Development in which the District Commissioners were to be the spearhead. . . . I am absolutely certain that the change will have the effect of mobilizing a tremendous amount of local enthusiasm. . . . [the people] will learn to appreciate that progress depends primarily on their own efforts, that the Government can help with advice, they can help with technical advice, they can help with grants, but the initiative must come from the people themselves, and the Government will not try to overrule them if what the people feel to be their greatest need is not what the Government thinks is their greatest need.[1]

If the new policy were to succeed it would require more than an administrative reorganization. It would also require African co-operation, which would mean removing some of the existing grievances and creating opportunities for Africans to play a more prominent role in local affairs. The land grievances obviously had to be confronted. Although the Land Husbandry Act was not repealed modifications were rapidly introduced. The demarcation of farms was slowed down so that greater attention could be given to the needs of the individual farmers, and so that the chiefs' advice could be sought. Landless people were permitted to settle on areas previously allocated to grazing. These specific steps were soon followed by a general reversal of policy. By 1962 the whole spirit of the original legislation had been changed. The compulsive element was removed; in future demarcations and allocation of land were only to be undertaken in areas where the tribesmen requested it; and the opposition to the Act was so deep-seated that few requests were made. In reality the Land Husbandry Act had been abandoned.

[1] S.R.L.A. Hansard, 28 June 1962.

Of even greater significance was the U.F.P. Government's attitude to the Land Apportionment Act. In June 1961 the Government, inspired by the recommendations of the Select Committee on the Resettlement of Natives, introduced amendments to the Act. The particular recommendations on which the Government acted were that no good purpose would be served by moving Africans from land they were 'illegally' occupying, and that the 10,000,000 acres of European Crown Land as yet unsurveyed and unalienated should be made available for purchase by Africans as well as Europeans. The results of the amendments was that 45,000 African families living communally on land previously allocated for European occupation or as Native Purchase Areas did not have to move, that 2,500,000 million acres were added to the Tribal Trust Lands, and that more than 5,000,000 acres were categorized as 'unreserved', and thereby could be acquired by members of any race. In the following year more changes were introduced, including the addition of about 450,000 acres to the Native Purchase Area from the Wiltshire and Lancashire Estates in the Charter District.

These were substantial changes, but even more revolutionary was the U.F.P. decision, confirmed at the Party's 1961 Congress, that if the party won the next election it would repeal the Land Apportionment Act. In terms of land the repeal could only benefit Africans, for their main areas, the Tribal Trust Lands, were already protected by the Constitution, whereas if the Act were repealed they could extend themselves into areas previously reserved for Europeans.

In local government in African rural areas, the Government decided that new life should be put into the almost moribund councils. The Chief Native Commissioner thought it essential that 'the people can, with external financial and technical aid from Central Government, run their own affairs. . . . The present Native Council system is to be rebuilt into this organization of local government.'[1] The councils were to be given more responsibilities and where possible the District Commissioners would hand over the chairmanship to a council member.

New wine was to be poured into the relatively new council bottle, but it was also to be poured into the ancient bottles

[1] Chief Native Commissioner's Report, 1962.

of the chieftainships. It was decided that the chiefs should be given wider powers and larger rewards and that they should be used as a channel of contact and consultation with Africans. There are more than 200 chiefs recognized by the Government in Rhodesia. In 1962 they ranged in number of followers from the small Zambezi chiefs, one of whom had only thirty-one followers, to Chief Gutu, who had over 16,000 followers. There are differences between the chiefs of the two main tribes: the Ndebele and Shona. The Ndebele, because their structure of chieftainship was largely destroyed at the European conquest, have relied more upon government support than have the Shona, whose structure of small, independent chiefs largely survived. The Ndebele have a simple primogeniture system of succession and their chiefs tend to be considerably younger and more physically able than the Shona, who are burdened with a system of succession which lends itself to long-drawn-out disputes and feuds, with lengthy interregnums and, even when a new chief emerges, as often as not he is an old man long past his physical and mental prime.

However, neither set of chiefs had previously been given onerous tasks by the Government. They had assisted the Native Commissioners, and had settled civil cases within the tribe, but their main function had been as a centre of loyalty and respect for the tribal groups. Efficiency and ability had been desirable but not essential. Chiefs received subsidies based upon the number of taxpayers in their area and, in addition, personal allowances were paid on the recommendation of the Chief Native Commissioner, 'who shall have regard to such factors as personal attributes of the chief concerned, his administrative ability, co-operation with the administration, tribal importance, control and authority over the people'.[1] In 1961 the maximum chief's subsidy was £240 per annum and the maximum allowance £360 per annum.

Although in the past individual chiefs had gained the respect of government officials, the opinion of chiefs in general, and in particular of the Shona, was not high. When, therefore, the Government decided to give greater prominence to the chiefs, there were many questions to be answered. What powers

---

[1] S.R. Government Gazette, Notice No. 249, 1961.

should be granted to them? What powers were they in fact capable of exercising? Would there be a clash between their traditional role and the new functions they were asked to perform? Were the chiefs representative of a wide section of African opinion? What would be the relations between chiefs and Africans elected to the Legislative Assembly or the local councils?

All these questions and more had to be faced, but, despite the difficulties and despite their personal inadequacies, the chiefs did provide one channel of contact between the Government and Africans. The U.F.P. Government decided to use this channel. In May 1961 the first national congress of chiefs was held at Gwelo. Representatives who had come from all over Southern Rhodesia showed their independence by asking government officials to leave while they managed their own business. The chiefs were firm against the Land Husbandry Act; declaiming that 'the land is the chief's and the chief is the people'. They voiced rural discontent and made a plea for more land. They decided that they would not involve themselves with any political party but that the ' "Freedom Now" gentlemen should leave us alone to settle our own rural problems'. After this conference it was decided to establish a permanent council to meet regularly and advise the Government. In October the chiefs were promised greater legal powers over civil cases and the establishment of appeal courts of three chiefs sitting together. In November the Government introduced the Council of Chiefs Bill.

When the Minister of Native Affairs, H. J. Quinton, introduced the Bill, he said: 'It is a matter of urgency to establish direct contact with the African people through their own tribal authority'; and this would be done through the Chiefs' Council which would be advisory and consultative, but not 'a state within a state'.[1] The debate which followed gave an insight into

---

[1] S.R.L.A. Hansard, 21 November 1961. The functions of the Council are prescribed in the Council of Chiefs and Provincial Assemblies Act, 1961, and are:

    (a) to make representations to the Minister of Internal Affairs in regard to the needs and wishes of the tribesmen living on Tribal Trust land;

    (b) to consider any representations made to it by a provincial assembly (of chiefs); and

    (c) to consider and report on any matter referred to it by the Minister of the Tribal Trust Land Board of Trustees.

the European parties' philosophies on the future political role
of Africans. John Pittman, who was on the left of the U.F.P.,
accepted the measure but had doubts about how representative
chiefs were of African opinion. 'We must', he said, 'treat it as
experimental and transitional. This is an anachronism in a
modern community. A homogeneous community could not
have anything like this. We are tending towards homogeneity
in our affairs and what we want is modern machinery in our
politics, but at this stage I accept that something on these lines
is necessary and that is why I accept the Bill.'

In sharp contrast to Pittman's doubts, the D.P. opposition
was so enthusiastic that it wanted to go further in extending the
functions and powers of chiefs. In a speech which had under-
tones of separate racial development, W. J. Harper welcomed
the Bill, but said that the Government had to decide whether
Africans were to be represented by parliamentarians or by
chiefs. 'I have', he admitted, 'been one who for a long time
has doubted the wisdom of parliamentary representation or the
democratic system such as we practise it for Africans.' He believed that tribalism was strong and would continue far into the
future. Mr. Cary, who supported him, thought it a tragedy that
chiefs' powers and authority had been reduced by Europeans.
'In the tribal areas they [the Africans] are not concerned with
the modern state . . . The people in the reserves are still the
backward people and I am wondering whether we, in our
wisdom, are doing the wise thing in trying to change this.'

The most incisive criticism of the Government's policy came
from neither of the main parties, but from Ahrn Palley, the
radical Independent. He contended that, although the Chiefs'
Council had restricted functions, it created an extra-parliamentary channel of consultation, and could be used to by-pass
Parliament. He thought that it was a step into the past rather
than the future and contended that if the Government increased the official functions of chiefs they would be no better
than civil servants and would be useless as a truly consultative
body. With growing industrialization, and growing claims for
individual rights and property among Africans, the chiefs'
position was growing less and less powerful, and more remote
from modern needs. There was nothing the Government could
do to stop this, but by its actions the Government was trying to

establish contact with Africans via a body of men who were themselves losing contact with their fellows.

The U.F.P. Government went ahead with the Council, but there was no implication that the chiefs were the sole or even the main voice of African opinion. The rejuvenation of the chiefs' prestige was just one aspect of the Government's determination to establish contact with Africans and to give Africans a larger share in the country's affairs. The thinking of the Government at that time was captured by the Chief Native Commissioner, who stated that there had been criticism 'largely under the misapprehension that Government intends to accept the chiefs' Council as the only voice of the African people'. This, he said, was an entirely wrong view:

There is no intention of turning chiefs into politicians nor of establishing the Chief's Council as a political body . . . In the political field chiefs should be able to express their views and Government should attach as much importance to their views as it does to any other responsible and organized representative group such as a Chamber of Mines or Commerce, but in no way a substitute for or to exclude normal political expression and other representative organs of African thinking.[1]

The Government was confident that with the steps it was taking to reorganize African administration; with the prospect of direct African representation in the Legislative Assembly; with the legislation it had passed against racial discrimination; and with the future promise of more non-discriminatory legislation, including the repeal of the Land Apportionment Act—that with all these measures it could attract large-scale support from African moderate opinion. Africans would come forward in increasing numbers to demonstrate the practicability of racial partnerships and so undermine the support of black and white extremists.

The chief opponents of the Government among Africans continued to be the nationalists. Although they had strongly opposed the new constitutional proposals, the acceptance of these proposals by the electorate gave the nationalists another opportunity to participate within the Constitution. They could,

[1] Chief Native Commissioner's Report, 1961, p. 2.

like the European D.P. Party, which had also opposed the Constitution, have decided to work within it after its acceptance.
The nationalists did not choose to do this. They repudiated all
the Government's attempts to make the new constitution work.
While the Government organized its 'Claim a Vote' campaign,
Mr. Nkomo said: 'No African should register as a voter under a
system which discriminates against him . . . we must have
nothing to do with these elections.'[1] Africans who were already
on the voters' rolls were urged to return their voting cards.

Equally the nationalists opposed the 'Build a Nation' campaign, which they criticized as a façade behind which white
supremacy was to remain entrenched. Joshua Nkomo said:
'We don't want to swim with them in the pools—we want to
swim with them in Parliament.'[2] On another occasion he said:
'The N.D.P. does not accept multiracialism and these people of
other races who want to remain here must identify themselves
with the African people.'[3] The proposals of the U.F.P. Congress, including the repeal of the Land Apportionment Act,
were scorned. 'The concessions might have been acceptable
some fifteen years ago,' said J. B. Msika, 'but certainly not today
as the African people were no longer talking minor changes but
of changes which will enable them to run their own country.'
J. Z. Moyo said that Africans were not interested in the U.F.P.
proposals, for 'we want to rule ourselves'; while T. G. Silundika
called the land proposals 'propaganda'.[4]

As nationalist claims became more extreme, as their actions
became wilder and more violent, what European understanding and sympathy there was for the movement largely disappeared. Europeans found it difficult to understand how the
majority of Africans could support such extremists. The puzzled
Chief Native Commissioner wondered 'for how long and to
what extent the mass of tribal people will allow themselves to
be duped by these false tenets'.[5] Europeans concluded that the
movement reflected no more than the aspirations of a small,
power-hungry group of African 'city slickers', who by wild

[1] *Daily News*, 25 October 1961.
[2] *The Examiner*, December 1961.
[3] *Daily News*, 21 October 1961.
[4] Op. cit., 9 October 1961.
[5] Chief Native Commissioner's Report, 1960, p. 2.

assertions, and by stimulating racial hate, misled the great mass of the people who were taken in because they had no understanding of politics or even their own long-term interests. The movement, with 'its political exuberance and racial animosity with all its accompanying impertinences and its wild disdain of the truth', was not representative of African opinion, 'but rather represents the feelings of the rabid, fanatical power-seeking elements. The parrot-cry of "one man, one vote", "freedom" and "self-government in 1961" were the tactics to influence the masses of these rabble-rousers.' So wrote the Chief Native Commissioner.[1]

Among Europeans there was a widely held belief that nationalism flourished on ignorance, apathy and the stimulation of illogical emotionalism, but that where these failed physical and social intimidation was used. These contentions are inadequate. For all their oratorical abilities, for all their wild assertions, and for all their use of intimidation, the nationalist leaders, who have always been opposed in Rhodesia by powerful government forces, could never have achieved their success without awakening deeply felt emotions and needs. To argue that Africans are politically apathetic and ignorant is to underrate their ability and understanding. If political apathy implies that a large majority of a particular society do not wish to participate as political leaders, or even as active, paid-up members of a political party, then Southern Rhodesian Africans, like their European counterparts, *are* politically apathetic. If political ignorance implies a lack of knowledge and understanding of Constitutions, political processes, and international affairs, then most Africans are less well equipped than Europeans.

But if an interest in and understanding of Southern Rhodesian politics implies knowledge of and interest in such questions as how one's children are educated, how much land a man can have, and on what terms he can hold it, what wages will be paid for one's labour, where a man or his family can live, how government will spend its funds and who will benefit from them, how one is treated in relation to fellow-men, and what opportunities are open for people of one's race; if Rhodesian politics implies these things, and it does—then Africans are

[1] Chief Native Commissioner's Report, 1960, p. 1.

passionately interested in politics, and have a very clear under-standing of where their own interests lie. When Enoch Dumbut-shena returned to Southern Rhodesia after three years' absence, he wrote: 'What impressed me most after being away from this country . . . is the growing interest Africans are showing in politics. School children and old men and women speak the language of Z.A.P.U., they know Nkomo.'[1]

African political aspirations in Southern Rhodesia, as in the rest of the continent, have found their outlet in the nationalist movement. The movement has been fed by the 'bread and butter' issues of education, wages, and land, but it has wider implications and appeal than any particular grievance. It has as its foundation the claim of black people to rights and treat-ment which previously had been denied to them. There is probably no African in Southern Rhodesia who has come into regular contact with Europeans, and who has not at some time been personally humiliated because of his race. Because of the size and nature of the movement, nationalism has great variety. There *are* deplorable aspects, some of which have been promi-nent in Southern Rhodesia: intolerance, intimidation of opponents, mass hysteria, corruption, the growth of personality cults, race hatred, bullying by thugs who have used the move-ment as a cover for their personal sadism. This is the one side which opponents of nationalism have seen but, while it cannot be ignored, it is far from being the only side, and certainly does not explain the strength and popularity of the movement.

African nationalism has created a strong emotional appeal by offering rights and dignity to Africans. In Southern Rhodesia, while Europeans have preached that direct participation in politics is a measurable skill, the nationalists have preached that it is a natural right. While Europeans have urged Africans to emulate European achievements, the nationalists have urged their followers to take pride in being Africans. While many Europeans have contended that, at least for the present, it is in the interests of all races to develop separately, the nationalists have replied that this is only a means of suppressing African aspirations, of keeping them as second-class citizens. While some Europeans have forecast that it will take decades, perhaps even generations, for Africans to acquire the skill and

[1] *The Examiner*, September 1962.

sense of responsibility to organize a modern state, the nationalists have claimed that Africans can do so now.

The case for African nationalism has been clearly and forcibly stated by one of Southern Rhodesia's leading nationalists, the Reverend Ndabaningi Sithole. In his book *African Nationalism*,[1] he states that 'African Nationalism is directed against European domination and not against the white man' (p. 24) but that nationalist aspirations are opposed because 'the average white man in Africa equates his existence with white domination'. White supremacy, Sithole argues, is based upon a 'chosen people' concept, or expressed in another way, a 'keep-down-the-nigger policy' (p. 29). 'The overall European policy in Africa may be summed up in two words—white supremacy . . . That is they have a mania to rule Africa' (p. 36). He claimed that multiracialism and partnership as had been practised in East and Central Africa at the time of writing (1959) 'means that other races are allowed to participate in government affairs so long as they are satisfied with a secondary place in the whole scheme, while the first place is reserved for whites only' (p. 124). African nationalism was a challenge to this acceptance of white superiority and its necessary corollary that blacks were inferior. 'The victory of African nationalism', wrote Sithole, 'will therefore be the triumph of human personality and dignity' (p. 38).

In making an appeal to personality and dignity, Mr. Sithole had captured the greatest strength of African nationalism. It is an idealistic appeal which underlies the empirical demands for better education, more land and the vote. It offers equality where there has been discrimination, dignity where there has been humiliation, power where there has been servitude.

Joshua Nkomo repeated and re-emphasized many of Sithole's points in a series of articles he wrote for *The Daily News* in 1964.[2] Nkomo wrote that the whole pattern of Southern Rhodesian life had been dictated by the separation of the races through the division of land. 'We lived', he wrote, 'in one country only in theory. But for all practical purposes we lived in two separate worlds.' He claimed that 'the Government has been and is still concerned mainly about European progress.

---

[1] *African Nationalism*, London and Cape Town, Oxford University Press, 1959.
[2] *Daily News*, 24–26 June 1964.

It can be safely said, therefore, that whatever progress has been made by the African people in this country has come as a by-product and almost an accident.' He denied that the nationalists' aims were to drive away Europeans. 'What we are fighting to crush in Zimbabwe [the nationalist name for Southern Rhodesia] is not the white man, but white domination.' Majority rule would not result in the expulsion of Europeans, but it would mean the opening-up of political and administrative posts for Africans. Majority rule would bring national confidence and economic expansion with excellent prospects for Africans and Europeans alike.

With this great force behind them, Joshua Nkomo and his fellow-nationalist leaders were faced with the decision of how it should be deployed to achieve their aim of rapid majority rule. As the N.D.P. had rejected participation in the new Constitution, the leaders had to devise extra-constitutional methods. They took some passive and symbolic steps such as demonstrating their opposition to European standards by persuading their followers to take off shoes and ties at public meetings, and urging African women to abandon lipstick and high-heeled shoes. On 'Occupation Day' 1961, the day which commemorated the Pioneer Column's arrival at Salisbury, Joshua Nkomo called for a fast, because the day was 'a very sad reminder to us of the establishment of the evil system under whose oppressive yoke the African population has groaned for seventy years'.[1]

These passive demonstrations had only a limited appeal for the nationalist leaders. Increasingly they turned to violence. Before the 1961 referendum nationalist followers had taken part in violent acts, but this appears to have been more the natural offshoot of an ill-organized and frustrated mass movement than a centrally directed campaign. After the referendum it is almost certain, despite their public denials, that violence became one of the weapons advocated by the leaders. Their thinking was probably based upon the old assumption that nationalism was an irresistible force and a morally right movement, and therefore that any action to stimulate its success was permissible. The leaders reasoned that if there was a breakdown of internal order, if European confidence was undermined,

[1] *Daily News*, 9 September 1961.

if capital investments and industry were threatened, if the Government was publicly forced to take repressive measures, it could only work in African interests. It would be clear to Southern Rhodesians and to the world in general that the new Constitution could not work, that the Government could survive only by repression, and therefore new arrangements would have to be made giving Africans a much larger and even the dominant share in the Government.

It was also said that Mr. Nkomo had been influenced by discussions with the Duke of Devonshire, a junior British Minister, during a London visit in July 1961. The Duke told Mr. Nkomo that with such heavy capital investment involved Britain would never risk handing over power to Africans, because of the threat of instability. Mr. Nkomo wanted to show that instability would come because power was not given to Africans. At the N.D.P. Bulawayo Congress in October 1961 it was decided that in addition to boycotting the election the industrial basis of 'the settler economy' would be attacked and at a suitable time violence would be used.[1]

The increased use of violence stemmed both from a change of policy by the nationalist leaders and from their acceptance that strong pressures in the movement must be given their head. As a leader Joshua Nkomo usually moved by consultation, by taking his executive along with him, by sounding opinion, and by restricting his decisions and actions to those which were acceptable to the majority of his followers. When in late 1961 a strong militant element emerged in the N.D.P. Mr. Nkomo and his fellow-executives were not prepared to stand against it. In October *The Daily News* reported that the N.D.P. executive had given greater freedom to the party's Youth Wing to deal with Africans who were opponents or politically apathetic; the 'stooges', 'Tshombes', and 'sell-outs'.[2]

The Youth Wing interpreted this as the right to extend and intensify their existing campaign against rival parties, and to disrupt week-end public meetings, such as sports meetings or church services, which were drawing Africans away from N.D.P. meetings. On 11 November 1961, Robert Mugabe, the N.D.P. Publicity Secretary, outlined the party's new 'positive action' plans. He said that the party would take over the Government

[1] Shamuyarira, op. cit., p. 201.   [2] *Daily News*, 1 October 1961.

within a year. This would be achieved by a campaign directed against industry and external capital investment, and by wrecking the working of the new Constitution. He claimed that unless Europeans accepted African nationalism a racial clash was inevitable, and, in any case, the immigration flow of Europeans into the country must be reversed. He announced that the N.D.P. would concentrate more of its attention on rural areas.[1] Early in December Dr. Terence Ranger, a European university lecturer and N.D.P. supporter, urged a large party meeting to unite but to avoid violence. Yet from the same platform John Noko, the Chairman of the Harare Youth Council, declared that violence paid.[2]

A wave of violence spread across African townships and African rural areas. The violence was confined chiefly to African society, and attacks upon Europeans or European property were relatively rare. In some African rural areas the houses of chiefs and political opponents were fired, schools and cattle-dipping sheds were damaged or burnt down, government property, agricultural and conservation works were destroyed, government orders were ignored or disobeyed. In his report for 1961 the Chief Native Commissioner wrote:

Meetings of any kind were disrupted and defiance, incitement and intimidation were spread by a motley collection of political agents who seemed to have all the time and money in the world to make their presence felt in particular districts. Owners of cattle attending cattle markets were prevented from selling their animals. Some Women's Clubs were stopped from meeting. Some Councils were brought to a standstill. Dip tanks were found to be easily set alight to or filled with stones and poles by gangs who disappeared into the night. Arson—the immemorial fear of the African under a grass roof and the equally ancient remedy of the coward in African society— became a word on everybody's lips as threats of arson backed up by actual occurrences disturbed their lives.

N.D.P. membership cards and subscriptions were said to guarantee immunity from arrest, from paying tax, from interference by gangs who accosted you on the path or in the store, and to license you to plough where you wished, to have as much land or as many cattle as you wished, or to free you from dipping cattle. Health campaigns against tuberculosis and vaccinations were shouted down by allegations of causing sterility or even that people were being

[1] *Daily News*, 11 November 1961.   [2] Op. cit., 4 December 1961.

marked so that they could be turned into tinned meat. 'Freedom farming' became a slogan which incited people to plough up and down the hillsides, to plough in the drainage strips and violate every principle of land use. Some Chiefs and Headmen took to not wearing their badges of office for fear of being molested and found the performance of their duties deliberately made impossible by unknown youngsters of such a defiant, truculent and hostile manner that old people lamented that they were possessed by an evil spirit.[1]

In the main African townships a similar pattern emerged. On 23 October, after the opening of the N.D.P. Congress in Bulawayo, rioting mobs rampaged through the African townships of Makokoba and Mzilikazi, firing buildings, stoning police, attacking U.F.P. supporters, and looting.[2] In the last weekend of November there were more riots in Bulawayo in which police and European cars were stoned, buildings were attacked, and the congregation driven from a Salvation Army service. Early in December a mass march to protest against the new constitution was organized by women supporters of the N.D.P. Although there was little violence connected with this incident, the police used tear gas to disperse the demonstrators and almost 700 arrests were made. The pattern of violence and boycotts continued in the towns, sometimes in large-scale demonstrations, more often in isolated incidents against individuals, small groups, or property. 'There has been civil commotion and unrest in our African areas bordering on anarchy,' wrote the Director of African Administration in Salisbury.[3]

The N.D.P. had lost its way. As a political movement it had degenerated so that violence and intimidation had become its main weapons. The decision to reject the new Constitution without even a trial had led the nationalist leaders into the false belief that only violence could achieve their ends. On 9 December 1961, the Government banned the party and seized its assets under the Unlawful Organizations Act. The leaders were prohibited from addressing public meetings for four months. Explaining the Government's action, Reginald Knight, the Minister of Justice, referred to the intimidation, the threat to industry, the danger of large-scale bloodshed, and

---

[1] Chief Native Commissioner's Report, 1961, p. 3.
[2] *Daily News*, 23 October 1961.
[3] Report of Director, 1 July 1960– 30 June 1962, para. 4.

the nationalist claim that the established Government would be overthrown within a year. This, he said, 'clearly indicated that it [the N.D.P.] had rejected completely any form of compromise. There was a complete disregard for established authority.'[1]

The D.P. opposition agreed with the Government's action as far as it went, but wanted even firmer action against the nationalists. They wanted legislation which would prevent the creation of any future nationalist party. What, they asked, was the value of destroying one party if a phoenix were to arise from the ashes? Wynn Starling suggested that N.D.P. leaders should be prohibited from political activity and, if necessary, deprived of civil liberties. William Harper took the opportunity to voice again his ideas of separate development. He stated that while the experimental process of educating African people was being explored, the only satisfactory policy was 'to retain power in your hands completely and fully and to have a *modus vivendi* if you like, of some form of separate autonomy for African people in their own area'.[2] The Prime Minister's approach was very different. He had no doubts about banning the N.D.P. and, for a time at least, restricting the activities of its leaders, but he accepted that another nationalist party would appear and, provided it behaved as a political party and stayed within the law, he thought that this would be a healthy growth. However, he warned the nationalists that the old violent formula in a new guise would be treated harshly by the government. Even among his own supporters, many Europeans thought that Sir Edgar was too lenient towards the nationalists.

After the banning of the N.D.P., the Government showed its determination to dictate events by moving troops and police into the worst-affected rural areas, where they were used to help with tax collections and to ensure that government orders were obeyed. But, while the Government was revealing its strength, a new nationalist party was announced, the Zimbabwe African People's Union (Z.A.P.U.). The Prime Minister said that the new party was so similar to the banned N.D.P. that he had doubts about its legality, but he decided that 'if it is not going to intimidate people who belong to other parties and

---

[1] S.R.L.A. Hansard, 12 December 1961.
[2] Op. cit., 13 December 1961, col. 502.

. . . not going to force people to join . . . we will respect such a party'.[1] The new party contained many of the old N.D.P. leaders, with Joshua Nkomo again the President, but there were some new names among the executive, including George Nyandoro and James Chikerema, who were still in detention from the banning of the African National Congress in 1959. It was inevitable that the new party would have many of the old leaders. In any society the number of people prepared or even capable of undertaking political leadership is limited, and in underdeveloped African societies this is even more the case. The same faces, the same names, keep reappearing. As the new party inherited many of the N.D.P. leaders, so it inherited N.D.P. policies. Again this was inevitable, for the aims of African nationalism were common and well established. The greatest room for flexibility was in the methods the new party adopted to achieve its ends. Could it, without turning to violence, devise extra-parliamentary pressures which would achieve nationalist aims?

The Z.A.P.U. policy statement said that the party opposed the new constitution, that it would abolish economic exploitation, that it was determined to eliminate imperialism and colonialism, and to establish in their place a democratic state, based upon 'one man, one vote'. It supported Pan-Africanism and declared that African culture would be fostered. Africans were told not to register for a vote. Dr. Parirenyatwa,[2] the Z.A.P.U. Deputy President and a widely respected figure in the new party, announced that any party member who registered would be expelled and reminded his audience that the voters' lists were published for inspection.[3] Emphasis was again placed on the rapid achievement of majority rule. Parirenyatwa called for majority rule by December 1962, saying that 'God created the world and gave Africa to the Africans.'[4] The U.F.P. 'partnership' policy was rejected as a fraud.

The public image of the new party was therefore very similar to that of the N.D.P. but, in the early months, the use of

[1] S.R.L.A. Hansard, 19 December 1961.

[2] Dr. Parirenyatwa was killed in a car crash in July 1962. Before his death, many nationalists thought that he might become the leading figure in the movement.

[3] *Daily News*, 22 January 1962.

[4] Op. cit., 15 January 1962.

violence as a means of achieving its aims was much less pronounced. Nkomo and Parirenyatwa both spoke against violence, although some did continue despite the leaders' opposition. The Government took no chances. Restrictions were placed on ex-N.D.P. leaders addressing meetings; from time to time complete bans were placed on political meetings; the Z.A.P.U. leaders were watched and followed; and the police were no longer content simply to attend party meetings, but on occasion arrested speakers on the platform, when they were thought to be contravening the law. The Government's attitude was generally more aggressive and determined.

The most significant change in the early life of Z.A.P.U. was that greater concentration was placed on stimulating international support. The nationalist movement in Southern Rhodesia had always been responsive to external influences, and had drawn substantial funds from foreign sources. During 1962 the international aspect of the movement became more pronounced, with frequent visits overseas by Mr. Nkomo and appearances by him at the United Nations. Among the Afro-Asian states, he had a ready audience which was naturally sympathetic to the nationalist cause. Mr. Nkomo hoped that from this sympathy would come sufficient international pressure on Britain to convince her that fresh constitutional arrangements, more favourable to the nationalists, would have to be made. In March, at the United Nations, Mr. Nkomo demanded immediate majority rule and independence for Southern Rhodesia. 'We need no further preparation,' he claimed, and condemned the new constitution as racist. He voiced the hope that the then Mr. R. A. Butler, who had recently been appointed to supervise Central African affairs would be the 'liquidator of British imperialism'. He felt safe to reject Britain's role as a potential protector of African interest, and claimed that the British Government had formed an alliance with the Whitehead settler government to keep down the Africans.

In London in April, he warned the British Government that, if it did not heed the United Nations' call for early majority rule and independence, it would 'shortly have to move when there are thousands of dead bodies in Southern Rhodesia. There must either be a settlement along the United Nations

line or the natural result will be bloodshed'.[1] In Accra, Nkomo,
at a party given for his birthday, said: 'We have done the best
for our country; if Britain won't listen then the people will act
for themselves. I pledge myself that I will not celebrate another
birthday as a slave.'[2] Obviously the trips abroad had filled
Mr. Nkomo with new heart. In mid-April he returned from one
of these trips saying that, as far as his party was concerned,
there was nothing left but 'taking over the country', which was
just a matter of 'straightening up the papers before the Africans
are in power . . . I am not interested in the fifteen lower seats
whether they be contested on the basis of one man one vote or
not . . . I am interested in all the seats, and they must be contested on one man one vote'.[3] When Mr. Butler visited the
Federation, the Z.A.P.U. executive, after a heated dispute,
decided not to accept his invitation to a meeting. Instead
Mr. Butler was greeted at the Airport by Z.A.P.U. youths
carrying posters which read: 'We don't want you, Butler.'

In June Nkomo was in New York again when Afro-Asian
countries forced a debate on Southern Rhodesia in the General
Assembly. The British and Southern Rhodesian Governments
strongly resented this interference, especially as some wild accusations were made, the Russian representative speaking of
'slavery' in Southern Rhodesia. At the end of the debate the
Assembly passed a resolution demanding that a new Southern
Rhodesian Constitution be negotiated by all races. Z.A.P.U.
saw this as a resounding victory and said that the British
Government was bound to implement the resolution.

Joshua Nkomo returned from this second United Nations
visit more confident and militant than ever. The nationalist
movement has always worked in waves of activity and enthusiasm. The nationalist leaders have never doubted, at least publicly, that their cause would triumph, but at times there has
been lack of purpose and drive, while at others victory has
seemed imminent and there has been great spirit and life in the
movement. Nkomo's return in July 1962 produced a period of
high tension and excitement. Inspired by international support, and by the huge crowds of Southern Rhodesian Africans
who always gravitated to him, Nkomo threw out his demands

---

[1] *Daily News*, 12 April 1962.   [3] Op. cit.,. 30 July 1962.
[2] Op. cit., 9 June 1962.

and terms: that those who did not support the United Nations' resolution 'initiated by Z.A.P.U.'s 3 million supporters' must leave the country; that no elections would be held under the new Constitution 'while we live'; that a party congress would be held in sixty days and that he would 'quit the present form and nature of politics in the country if self-government and independence on the basis of universal suffrage were not attained within a time to be given at the Congress'.[1] On the following day he challenged Whitehead to produce proof that he, Nkomo, had ever signed the 1961 constitutional agreement, and added that 'the time has come for the settler community to be shaken from the deluding Rip van Winkle slumber in which they have visualized themselves as demi-gods with the masses of the Africans as mere serfs'.[2]

From Nkomo's return late in July, either by design or because of the excitement created by his apparent success abroad, the pattern of violence and intimidation reasserted itself. In the early months of the year there had been some violent incidents, with attacks on schools and dipping tanks in rural areas and a serious strike in Salisbury during May, but the incidents were irregular and infrequent. From August onwards the number and intensity of the incidents increased sharply. They had the same character as in the past—attempts to disrupt government activities, to suppress opposition and rival groups among Africans, and they continued to provide a cover to satisfy personal feuds and animosities, but also about this time Z.A.P.U. started to send young supporters overseas for sabotage training.[3]

The Government's reaction was almost inevitable. It granted itself greater powers to suppress disorders and violence. In August both the Unlawful Organizations Act and the Law and Order (Maintenance) Act were amended. The amendment to the Unlawful Organizations Act was designed to prevent a banned party or its leaders from forming a similar organization. The amendments to the Law and Order (Maintenance) Act increased the severity of already severe legislation. The definition of a 'public gathering' was changed to include twelve or more people meeting in a public place or 100 or more, even

---

[1] *Daily News*, 30 July 1962. [3] Shamuyarira, op. cit., p. 202.
[2] Op. cit., 31 July 1962.

if the meeting were in private. Permission to hold such meetings was required. There was a new section relating to intimidation with penalties of up to ten years' imprisonment for such offences as following a person about from place to place, acting in a manner likely to make another person apprehensive for himself, his family or his property, or demanding that any person should join or refrain from joining a political party.

Another section set a maximum sentence of twenty years' imprisonment for setting fire or attempting to set fire to a building which contained people. Another had a maximum of seven years' imprisonment for trying to persuade another person to stop work illegally. In some sections of the new legislation the onus of proof lay with the accused. For example, it would not be necessary for the prosecution to prove that the accused knew somebody was in a building when he fired it or attempted to fire it, and in attempting to persuade another person to stop work the onus would be on the accused to show that the statements he had made were lawful.

On 20 September 1962, Z.A.P.U. was banned and the leaders were restricted to specified rural areas for three months. The Prime Minister said that Z.A.P.U. 'was not banned because of its political opinions. It was banned because its members adopted terrorism as a weapon to force people to support its cause',[1] but Sir Edgar made conflicting statements about whether the leaders would be permitted to form a new party. At the time of the banning the government issued a white paper in which it was stated that Z.A.P.U. is the N.D.P. 'with a new face on it'. Then, after listing Z.A.P.U.'s official aims, the paper continued: 'In brief its manifesto was neo-Communist and Pan-African in character and it fostered racialism.' Nkomo was quoted as saying that 'one man, one vote' was essential and that 'this could be achieved either by negotiation, by bringing about a complete economic breakdown or by bloody revolution'. The incidents which it was alleged that Z.A.P.U. had initiated during August and September were listed; and included thirty-three petrol bomb attacks and eighteen cases of arson and damage to rural schools. The White Paper presented

[1] *The Rhodesia Herald*, 11 October 1962. Mr Nkomo was out of the country at the time of the banning, and according to his African rivals it was with great reluctance that he agreed to return to face restriction with his fellow-nationalist leaders.

no evidence whatsoever to substantiate its accusations that Z.A.P.U. was neo-Communist.

Relations between the U.F.P. Government and the nationalist movement had deteriorated to a position where both sides were trying to achieve victory over the other by force and intimidation. The Government naturally claimed that it had responsibilities for law and order which meant that firm action had to be taken or the Government would be forced to abdicate its power. The tragedy was that such a position had ever been reached, and this had its roots in the country's social, economic, and political order. The frustration among Africans had misguidedly turned to violence and the Government had little choice but to answer in the same terms. Once the pattern had started there seemed to be no end: violence bred violence. Both sides attempted to out-intimidate the other. For example, on 14 May 1962, the Southern Rhodesian African Trade Union Congress called a general strike for higher wages for Africans. The strike, which was said to have a political foundation, was a partial success; blacklegs were attacked and their houses stoned. The Government replied by sending in the troops, and they used their guns to disperse the rioting crowds. Two Africans were shot dead and five were wounded. Two days later the African employees of the Salisbury City Council refused to work, and many of them remained in their hostel rooms. This time the Government took the initiative and the police drove the men out of their rooms and to work by use of tear gas and police dogs.

During the second half of 1961 and throughout 1962 the Government and the nationalists fought for African support. In numerical terms there is no doubt who won. The U.F.P.'s 'Build a Nation' and 'Claim a Vote' campaigns were failures. In the registration period 5,961 Europeans, 230 Asians, 402 Coloureds, and 8,249 Africans claimed their vote. The high hopes of Sir Edgar Whitehead that 50,000 new African voters might register for the 'B' Roll were dashed.

It is extremely difficult to estimate how many Africans were eligible to register, but Dr. Claire Palley has made an analysis based upon education, income, and property statistics. She estimates that in September 1962 a maximum of 5,500 Africans were eligible for the 'A' Roll and 55,000–60,250 for the 'B' Roll. The actual numbers of Africans on the roll at that date were 1,920 on the 'A' Roll and 9,585 on the 'B' Roll.[1]

Of the Africans who did register a fair proportion were chiefs, headmen, and government employees who felt obliged to do so. The Government claimed that Africans had not registered because of nationalist intimidation. No doubt intimidation counted for part of the failure, but it could not account for more than a part. The great crowds that followed Mr. Nkomo did not follow him and listen to him because they were afraid but because they believed and accepted what he said. The U.F.P.'s failure with Africans did not spring principally from apathy or ignorance or intimidation but from distrust. The wide gulf which had divided the races in the past continued to divide them politically. It is true that the U.F.P. preached 'partnership', that as a Government it started to take down racial barriers, but this was something new, something to be distrusted and was incomprehensible to many Africans. In the past Europeans had not been prepared to share their privileged position, it was easy for the nationalist leaders to persuade their followers that the Europeans had no real intention of doing so now.

The greatest miscalculation by the U.F.P. was that there was a substantial and growing African middle class, which was pre-pared to follow the Government's lead. There were some Africans who did, but they were few and eventually politically ineffective. In a society in which distinction and discrimina-tion had been built upon race, the African 'middle class' felt much more in common with the mass of their fellow Africans than they did with any section of the European *élite*. They might imitate European society, they might receive a European-type education, but they had never crossed or been allowed to cross the gulf which separated them from the European *élite*. Europeans were deceiving themselves about African moderates, wrote S. G. Gozo. 'If an African claims for a fair deal in the country of his birth he is labelled an extremist. The opposite view is one of a moderate, namely to be subservient and agree to stay a second-rate citizen. The truth is that moderates do

---

[1] Palley, op. cit., Appendix Tables O and P and p. 421. Also see Appendix IV.

not exist for either a man claims his rights as a human being or else he is as good as dead.'[1] As the debate and conflict over Southern Rhodesia's future intensified, Africans, far from moving towards the Government's multiracial approach, grew increasingly suspicious and the suspicion drove them towards their own racial camp. Enoch Dumbutshena wrote: 'The average white person thinks that there are moderate Africans. They do not exist. It is true that there are African mercenaries in the U.F.P. but they have no followers.'[2]

One of the severest blows for the U.F.P. was the resignation in August 1962 of Mr. Jasper Savanhu from his post as Parliamentary Secretary of the Ministry of Home Affairs in the Federal Government. Mr. Savanhu had been the first African political appointment to the Federal Government and had frequently been held up as an example of what an African could achieve under a policy of partnership. He said that he had resigned because the Federal Government had failed to implement a policy of partnership and because affairs in Southern Rhodesia had reached a point where he felt his duty was to identify himself with his own people. 'The situation in Southern Rhodesia is, in my view, explosive and no African can afford to hob-nob with European-dominated parties.' As an example of the failure of partnership he cited the Federal Civil Service where, in nine years, only nine Africans had been appointed to Branch I of the administrative and clerical grades while 20,000 Europeans were employed in the same category. 'I feel', he said, 'that my presence among an all-white civil service is just tolerated and I am a mere piece of window dressing and completely frustrated.'[3]

The African attitude to partnership may have been mistaken. They may have miscalculated the implications of rejecting it and been far too suspicious of European motives. But while some Africans were prepared to work in co-operation with the U.F.P. to search for a non-racial society, for most Africans, whether middle-class or peasant, the nationalist message was much more comprehensible: that distinction had always been and continued to be based upon race; that the European-dominated Government intended to retain power for the racial

[1] *Daily News*, 24 April 1962.   [3] *Daily News*, 15 August 1962.
[2] *The Examiner*, September 1962.

minority; that the only way to overcome the inferior position
granted to Africans was to pit their strength as a majority
movement against the existing Government, as had been done
successfully elsewhere in Africa.

CHAPTER VII

The 1962 Election:
The Triumph of the Right

The Government's resounding victory at the 1961 referendum had dealt a sharp blow to the already weakened D.P. but, in the Legislative Assembly, the opposition continued its attack upon the Government's changes in the social order. When the Government introduced an amendment to the Immorality Bill, whereby in future it would not be illegal for a consenting adult European woman to have sexual intercourse with an African male,[1] Ian MacLean declared that 'many African rapists of European women will in effect get a new lease of life should the Bill go through'.[2] When Mrs. Watson introduced a Private Member's Bill to remove restrictions on Africans drinking spirits, William Cary concluded that 'the native by habit has been used to having a large quantity of Kaffir beer and he is only satisfied, to put it crudely, when his tummy is full. . . . Is the African going to be satisfied with two tots of brandy?'[3] The same member, when debating an amendment to the Land Apportionment Act in November 1961, said: 'It is my humble submission that any white man who will lower himself to marry an African woman at this stage is not a fit and proper person to associate with the average European.'[4]

There was one point of agreement between Government and opposition in relation to Africans, and that was the attack upon the nationalists, but even here the opposition wanted to go further. In an adjourned debate calling for measures to stamp out riots, violence, and destruction, Mr. Harper said: 'Let us

[1] Sexual intercourse between a European male and an African female was not an offence.
[2] S.R.L.A. Hansard, 18 August 1961.
[3] Op. cit., 23 August 1961.
[4] Op. cit., 11 November 1961, col. 385.

see once and for all this rod of iron that we have heard so much about . . . Government must stop this ridiculous policy of theirs, this policy of appeasement, masquerading under the name of partnership', for to African nationalists it simply revealed weakness. 'British Liberalism is all very well behind the English Channel, but we have got to be more realistic . . . we have got to be a great deal firmer and a great deal harder and take a lesson or two from those down south [i.e. South Africa].'[1]

The opposition's policy was sterile and unimaginative. It appeared to offer little threat to the Government. Meanwhile the U.F.P. Government was trying to implement its dual policy of firm measures to retain law and order and the introduction of 'partnership'. Blair Ewing described it as 'social justice combined with national discipline'. He claimed that this twin policy was the only way to succeed; 'and in neither field will you ever find an African nationalist ever admitting that the Government has ever done anything right, because they know perfectly well that if we succeed in our policy, their basic philosophy is lost and any natural appeal they might have to the masses of this country can no longer exist.'[2] As the Government continued with gradual reform, 'in the spirit of the new Constitution . . . to repeal all laws imposing racial discrimination',[3] there seemed to be no political force capable of stopping them. Late in 1961 and early in 1962 some political commentators feared that after the next elections there would be no parliamentary opposition to face the U.F.P., and that the only opposing force would be the extra-parliamentary nationalist movement. Gordon Collins thought that the D.P. was finished as a strong opposition; it was 'virtually a museum piece'.[4]

The declining strength of the D.P. was misleading, for it failed to reflect the growing if disorganized dissatisfaction of many Europeans with Whitehead's 'partnership' policy. The policy, they thought, smacked of appeasement; it was too revolutionary; it was placing power in irresponsible hands; Whitehead was 'too soft'. This opposition had revealed itself unsuccessfully at the referendum but, despite this setback, fresh

---

[1] S.R.L.A. Hansard, 8 December 1961.
[2] Op. cit., 21 June 1962, cols. 95–6.
[3] Op. cit., Speech from Throne, 8 June 1961.
[4] *Daily News*, 2 January 1962.

efforts were made early in 1962 to give it coherence. The Rhodesia Reform Party was formed with Ian Smith and John Gaunt as leaders, and it boasted among its followers I. H. Samuriwo, a conservative African politician, and D. C. ('Boss') Lilford, a wealthy farmer, and shadowy background figure. The party claimed to follow a 'middle-of-the-road' policy, which implied setting a course between the U.F.P. and the D.P., not between Africans and Europeans, but its policy statement laid the main emphasis on opposition to the Government. It was opposed to 'forced integration', it was against the 'Build a Nation' campaign, and it favoured a united opposition to the U.F.P. Before the party could test its strength, an important development reorientated the right wing. Early in February 1962 William Harper resigned as leader of the Dominion Party. He stated that his action was intended as a catalyst in the creation of a united opposition, and was 'in the interests of the country, so that there is no issue of personality conflict and because I am no longer able to give as much time as I have done in the past to party matters'.[1] Harper's resignation was said to be partly for personal reasons, but its importance was that it removed from the leadership a man who, for all his ability, had failed to attract any strong personal following and was distrusted and disliked by some colleagues. William Cary became the interim leader of the D.P. while negotiations took place to establish a united opposition.

The task of uniting the right wing was no easy one, for it contained men who had opposed each other on personal and policy grounds, but, in 1962, they had two strong common bonds: their unsuccessful opposition to the 1961 Constitution, and their dread of Whitehead's policy. They had lost the referendum but now they fought to prevent the implementation of the new Constitution in Whitehead's terms. Although the right wing always gave prominence to its economic ambitions, initially at least it was these negative forces which kept the right wing together. By mid-March the framework of a new party, the Rhodesian Front (R.F.), had been formed, with Mr. Winston Field, the Federal M.P., as its leader. Mr. Cary, who had support from those who favoured a Southern Rhodesian M.P. rather than a Federal M.P. to lead the party, decided in

[1] *The Rhodesia Herald*, 3 February 1962.

the interests of unity not to contest the leadership. It was a wise decision, for Winston Field was an important focal point in the early days. He had great personal prestige, based upon his charm and honesty, he was trusted by the divergent forces of the right and gave the new party an air of respectability. The R.F. quickly decided that it would ignore the forthcoming Federal elections—a decision which reflected the decreasing importance of the Federation; but instead concentrate its strength on opposing Whitehead in Southern Rhodesia. It issued an interim policy statement which declared that the party would fight to retain the Land Apportionment Act, to reject 'forced integration', to provide equality of opportunity and justice, to stimulate the economy, and to retain those aspects of the Federation which were mutually beneficial.

The danger of right-wing divisions was still apparent at the first R.F. congress in September 1962. Field had to appeal for unity and for the members to have confidence in the leaders. His call was answered and perhaps it was the greatest achievement of the early R.F. days that he led a united party to the hustings. Another outstanding party achievement was its excellent organization and its success in collecting funds. It was particularly strong at grass-roots level. Enthusiastic, efficient branches were quickly formed throughout the country, canvassing was widespread, and so, when the election was fought, the Government faced a new but well-organized and efficient opponent.

The 1962 election was originally scheduled for October, but in May the Prime Minister announced that it would have to be postponed because of delays in delimiting the new electoral constituencies and districts. He was criticized from both sides for the delay. The R.F. claimed that the postponement was directed against them, with the Prime Minister 'playing party politics at its worst and . . . he is quite prepared to sacrifice Southern Rhodesia's future for possible party gain and the implementation of measures for which he has no mandate'.[1] The R.F. argued that the delay would give the Government more time to accustom the white electorate to the idea of abolishing the Land Apportionment Act and racial discrimination, more

[1] *The Rhodesia Herald*, 17 May 1962.

time to register new African voters, and finally more time to make a federal settlement which would benefit the U.F.P. In fact the postponement was probably advantageous to the R.F., as it gave them much-needed time to organize their new party. The nationalists were equally certain that the delay was directed against them, for it gave the opportunity 'to intimidate the Africans into participating'.[1] The election was eventually held on 14 December 1962.

Because the African nationalists were not fighting the election, there was no purely African party competing for power. It became a direct contest between the multiracial U.F.P. and the R.F., the European party (the Central Africa Party also put up candidates but without success). But nationalist influence was important. The nationalists had had considerable success in persuading Africans not to register, but, at the time of the election, there were 9,708 Africans on the 'B' Roll from a total roll of 10,632 and 1,915 Africans registered on the 'A' Roll from a total of 90,785. If European support for the main parties was closely divided, then the African voters could have a decisive influence, particularly with the cross-voting system. The nationalists told Africans not to vote. The Government, which was confident that, in the absence of the nationalists, it could attract most of the African voters, urged them to use their voting rights.

The Government campaigned for the African vote, but the main concentration had, as in the past, to be on the Europeans who formed the bulk of the electorate. Both the R.F. and the U.F.P. set out to demonstrate how their policies would benefit Europeans in a rapidly changing Africa. The U.F.P. said that change must be accepted, that reconciliation between the races was essential, that Africans must be given rights to avoid frustration and revolt against European rule. The R.F. said that the pace of the change must be slow, that appeasement and revolution had to be halted to preserve the existing satisfactory structure of society.

As the Europeans weighed these policies they continued to be strongly influenced by events inside their own country and elsewhere in Africa. Fear of African rule continued to grow. The violence of nationalism in Southern Rhodesia was matched

[1] *Daily News*, 12 June 1962 (Joshua Nkomo speaking in New York).

by the continuing chaos of the Congo. At periods of extreme crisis, Congo European refugees passed through Southern Rhodesia to give, in the eyes of many Europeans, a living warning of the danger of handing over government to Africans. Events in British colonial and ex-colonial territories were less spectacular but no less disturbing. Dr. Banda, regarded by many Europeans as no better than a terrorist leader, was moving into power in Nyasaland, while in Kenya the white settlers were being 'sold out' to Jomo Kenyatta, the 'leader to darkness and death'.[1] There was a widespread European belief that the old colonial powers, their strength exhausted by the war efforts, their spirit sapped by the growth of the affluent society and a misguided liberalism, had decided to abandon their African territories with no thought for the future. They had lost 'the will to rule'.

During 1961 and 1962 no formal constitutional changes had been made in the Federation, but there had been significant changes in the individual territories. After the release of Dr. Banda, Nyasaland had made steady progress towards self-government with majority rule. In the month before the Southern Rhodesian elections, this was confirmed at a constitutional conference in London. In Northern Rhodesia constitutional change had been much less smooth. A long and often bitter struggle, involving the British Government, the nationalists, the Northern Rhodesian Europeans, and the Federal Government, had taken place over the pace of development and the size of African parliamentary representation. But even this struggle had resolved itself before the Southern Rhodesian elections. In Northern Rhodesia, as in Nyasaland, a majority of Africans sat in the Legislative Assembly and they were nationalist supporters.

What was clear from these changes was that the two northern states were moving to self-government under predominantly black government and these governments would be hostile to the existing Federation. Despite the protests of Sir Roy Welensky, despite the absence of formal constitutional changes, the Federation was dying fast. By March 1962 even Sir Edgar Whitehead had abandoned hope of retaining the Federation in its

---

[1] Sir Patrick Renison's description, quoted by G. Bennett, *Kenya: A Political History*, London, Oxford University Press, 1963, p. 153.

existing form. He proposed a scheme that was suspiciously like the old Federal D.P.'s Central African Alliance.[1] Even clearer evidence that the Federation was dying came when Sir Roy Welensky called a snap election for April 1962. Measured in parliamentary seats the U.F.P. scored a great triumph, winning fifty-four out of fifty-seven, but it was a hollow victory. No other major party thought it worthwhile to contest the election. Thirty-nine members were returned unopposed and, where contests did take place, only 47 per cent of the electorate voted. Two specially elected African members, who were returned in Northern Rhodesia, acquired only forty-seven votes between them, a 1·37 per cent poll. 'Hallelujah', said Harry Nkumbula, 'Sir Roy has killed the Federation himself.'

In Southern Rhodesia European opinion about the future of the Federation was confused. There was increasing acceptance that it could not continue in its existing form, but the dire economic consequences of a complete break-up, which the U.F.P. and some prominent economists had forecast, persuaded most Europeans that some form of association should be retained. But, unknown to the Southern Rhodesian electorate, the break-up of the Federation was virtually certain at the time of the December election. At the Nyasaland conference in November the British Government had conceded the right of secession from the Federation. At the request of Sir Edgar Whitehead this decision was not made public until after the election.[2] Even though this decision was unknown, the general trend of events which indicated that the Federation was breaking up was reinforced in the days immediately before the election by specific developments. In Northern Rhodesia election results were announced by which Kenneth Kaunda's United National Independence Party and Harry Nkumbula's African National Congress were able to form a coalition Government, the first African Government of Northern Rhodesia. Both these African leaders were committed to breaking up the Federation. Meanwhile, in London Ministers of the Federal Government were conducting long, acrimonious negotiations with British Ministers. Although the negotiations were confidential, it was strongly rumoured in the Southern Rhodesian

[1] *The Rhodesia Herald*, 9 March 1962.
[2] Lord Alport, *The Sudden Assignment*, p. 209.

Press that they were concerned with the dissolution of the Federation and that the British Government had already accepted Nyasaland's right to secede.[1]

In an atmosphere of suspicion and uncertainty the Europeans' distrust of the British Government intensified. Perhaps the distrust was inevitable because of the different angles from which the problems of Central Africa were seen, but without doubt the British change of policy in relation to the Federation, from full-blooded support, through vacillation to acceptance of its dissolution, cemented the distrust. However justified and logical the change may have appeared to British and African politicians, the Europeans of Southern Rhodesia saw it as a betrayal.

The distrust which developed between the Federal and British Governments provoked clashes of personality as well as policy. This is reflected in books which two of the principal characters, Sir Roy Welensky and Lord Alport, the British High Commissioner, have subsequently written.[2] The degree of suspicion was so intense that on occasions both sides suspected that the other would use force to impose a solution. Sir Edgar Whitehead personally avoided most of this acrimony but it affected the European electorate. They believed that they were fighting a battle on two fronts, against African extremists and against a British Government which, because of self-interest, was prepared to abandon all her responsibilities in Africa.

The suspicion of Britain, the doubts about the future of the Federation were components of a general air of uncertainty which has been endemic in Southern Rhodesian politics throughout the 1960s. All political parties have stated their determination to remove this uncertainty, but it still persists. It is an uncertainty which asks such questions as: can political change be achieved without sacrificing economic progress? Can the interests of the races be reconciled or must they inevitably conflict? Must individual rights be subordinated to those of the state? It is an uncertainty not only about who or which party will rule but about the future structure of government, and upon this structure hangs the fabric of the society. At the

---

[1] *The Rhodesia Herald*, 11 December 1962.

[2] Sir Roy Welensky, *4,000 Days* (London, Collins), and Lord Alport, *Sudden Assignment* (op. cit.).

time of the 1962 election there was uncertainty about the Federation's future, and there was uncertainty about which of the political alternatives would triumph within Southern Rhodesia. Would it be the nationalists with immediate majority rule, or the U.F.P. with their multiracial solution, or would the R.F. succeed in preserving white minority rule?

In this general atmosphere the two political parties fought their 1962 election campaign. Neither side doubted the importance of the occasion. Clifford Dupont told the R.F. Congress that the issue was whether the whites of Southern Rhodesia were prepared to be dominated within the next ten years by an African government. 'I call on all Southern Rhodesians who wish to see this African domination prevented to unite and fight. We have a war to win—a war of survival.'[1] The campaign was fought with an intensity and a bitterness which was new to Southern Rhodesian politics. Meetings were well attended, leaders and candidates were closely questioned, heckling became common, especially at U.F.P. meetings.

In their policy statements the parties shared some general objectives—economic prosperity, political stability, and internal security—but even within these general objectives there were differences of emphasis and method. Both parties stressed the need for internal order and security, but the R.F. advocated tougher measures than the Government had used. Both hoped to retain some links with the northern territories, but the U.F.P. was more committed to retaining a political link. Both wanted independence for Southern Rhodesia but the R.F. was more insistent upon this. In its party principles the R.F. affirmed loyalty to the Queen, but the party 'rejects the principle of subordination to any external government', and was prepared to seek independence either inside or outside the Commonwealth.

The great division between the parties was, of course, the dispute about race relations. The R.F. was not simply the D.P. in another guise, although it absorbed the old party and its members. The new party was better led and organized, appealed to a much larger section of the population and offered more positive policies for the future, but it inherited

[1] *The Rhodesia Herald*, 29 September 1962.

the D.P.'s reactionary attitude to African advancement. Therefore the long-drawn-out dispute which had been fought in the Legislative Assembly was transferred to the hustings.

The division became all the more obvious because of Sir Edgar Whitehead's personal convictions. As Sir Edgar mounted his party's appeal to Africans, so increasingly he became convinced of the justice and need for reform, and convinced that the future of the country depended on successful partnership. Even his failure to persuade Africans to register in large numbers did not deter him. He still believed that African political advancement must be gradual, but during 1962 he accepted that the pace should be quicker than he had previously estimated. He moved steadily to the left of his party. He emphasized that Africans who had supported the party must never be deserted, especially as their support had often involved them in physical and social intimidation. In October 1962 Sir Edgar told a United Nations Committee in New York that within fifteen years Africans would form a majority of the voters, but claimed that 'politics will quite depart from racial lines in my country'. A. D. Butler, another U.F.P. leader, expressed similar views when he spoke at the United Nations. In November Sir Edgar urged the U.F.P. Congress to have 'no reservations, no hold-backs', for maintaining standards did not imply suppressing Africans. The Congress, at which one-third of the members were Africans, took the U.F.P. further along the road to reform. It confirmed that all racial discrimination must be abolished, that the Land Apportionment Act should be repealed, and further it agreed that, if the U.F.P. won the election and discovered 'that certain responsible, civilized, and educated groups were inadvertently omitted' from the franchise, amendments could be made without reference back to the electorate. The terms of this extension were small but the principle of the Government's accepting direct responsibility for a franchise amendment was important. On one point, schooling at Primary and Junior Secondary level, Sir Edgar was not prepared to advocate integration, and the Congress agreed with him.

The U.F.P. attacked the R.F. as an anachronism. A U.F.P. poster showed a white man with his head buried deep in the sand: he was an R.F. supporter. Sir Edgar said that, if the R.F.

won the election, it would be 'utter and complete disaster. I am satisfied that if Southern Rhodesia returns the Rhodesian Front, the country will lose every sympathizer we have outside our borders—apart from two.'[1] In contrast to the R.F.'s reactionary policy Sir Edgar told an audience at Marandellas that, if the U.F.P. were returned, he would appoint Southern Rhodesia's first African Minister, and he predicted that after the following election there would be anything between three and six African Ministers.[2]

Sir Edgar's policy caused alarm in his own party. The right-wing European section had increasing doubts about the wisdom of the policy, both in itself and as a means of capturing votes. There was even danger of an open division between Sir Roy Welensky and Sir Edgar. The threat of division was particularly unfortunate for the U.F.P. at a time when there was growing criticism within political circles and the civil service of government inefficiency and methods. Sir Edgar tried to counter this criticism by reshuffling his Cabinet in September 1962 to give it more efficiency and drive.[3] Eventually the internal party dispute was patched up, the members rallied behind Whitehead, a U.F.P. poster showed a picture of a smiling Sir Roy with 'I back Sir Edgar all the way' written underneath it.

Another problem which faced the U.F.P. was its identification with the Federation at a time when the Federation's future was so uncertain. The party leaders were convinced that the British Government, by arranging the Nyasaland conference and the Northern Rhodesian elections before the election in Southern Rhodesia, had imperilled the party's chance of success. They felt that the growing fears about the Federation's survival must count against their party. The reaction of many of the European electorate would be that the U.F.P. had failed to stand up effectively against the British Government in the federal dispute, and that the party's policies had

[1] *The Rhodesia Herald*, 10 November 1962.
[2] Op. cit., 12 December 1962.
[3] Cleveland, the Minister of Education, had been ill for some time and wanted to resign, while Knight, the Minister of Law and Order, wanted to return to his legal work. The personal wishes of these ministers coincided with the Prime Minister's anxiety to introduce new and more lively blood into the Cabinet. The two new Ministers were Ellman Brown and Ewing. (See Appendix I.)

produced a rapid not a gradual change to majority rule in
Central Africa.

The R.F. in its campaign made play of the emphasis it
would give to economic expansion but this, like all issues, was
related to the central problem of race relations. The R.F. contended that the Government was following a reckless policy
which endangered Southern Rhodesia's whole economic and
social structure. Chaos and racial conflict would only follow
from the Government's irresponsibility. The new Constitution
was attacked because the franchise was far too wide and the
high standards of the past had been abandoned. The official
party policy statement read: 'The Front recognizes that inherent in the new Constitution there is the intention to ensure
the dominance by the Africans of the Europeans before the
former has acquired adequate knowledge and experience of
democratic government. The Front believes that this must be
avoided. It will therefore, *inter alia*, seek in consultation with
other groups, amendments to the Constitution to avoid the
situation arising.'[1] In the eyes of the R.F., the Constitution was
a glaring example of how Whitehead was prepared to follow
the British Government's policy of appeasement, and they foresaw that, if another U.F.P. Government were returned, the
same pattern of appeasement would continue. The Front was
fond of drawing gloomy conclusions from events in Kenya
where, they claimed, the white minority had been betrayed.
After quoting how property and land prices had fallen, how
Europeans had been forced out of the country, an R.F. pamphlet said: 'This happened in Kenya. This can be happening
here also—only you can prevent it.'

The retention of the Land Apportionment Act, with its
acceptance of racial separation, was a central pillar of R.F.
policy. Dr. Olive Robertson called it the Europeans' 'Magna
Carta'. The party contended that, to repeal the Act and to
legislate to remove all racial discrimination, was to have
'forced integration'. They rejected the argument that the
existing situation was 'forced separation'. The R.F. said that
each race should develop along its natural and traditional
lines, but for those people who wanted to live in mixed communities small areas would be set aside for them. The Africans,

[1] National Archives, Salisbury (R.F. documents).

living under their chiefs and stimulated by a policy of Community Development, would build and expand their community life in the Tribal Trust Lands. John Howman told a television audience that Africans must be given a greater chance to help in moulding the country, 'but', he added, 'I know their limitations.' He contended that tribal loyalties were still stronger than national loyalties and therefore it was only logical that Africans should play their major part in government in tribal areas rather than in central government. A policy of regional development was prepared which would permit the races, who were at such different stages of development, to advance at their own speed, and which would give Africans protection from unscrupulous exploiters and traders.

Fear is an element used in any election campaign—fear that the other party will change the school system or bring more unemployment or higher taxes. This is normal, but the degree of fear which entered the Southern Rhodesian 1962 election was exceptional. The U.F.P. used it in warning Europeans of the consequences of not facing up to realities in Africa, but the strongest fears were those expressed by the R.F. The party did not create these fears but it crystallized them within a political movement. The first of the fears was of nationalist violence. This fear rested upon the pattern of disorders and destruction which had developed in African areas and was reinforced by dramatic incidents near election time. In mid-October an African police reservist was burnt alive after petrol had been poured on him.[1] During September and October threats of destruction and rebellion were issued by the Zimbabwe Liberation Army, an underground branch of the banned nationalist party. The nationalist leaders had agreed that if Z.A.P.U. were banned they would concentrate on organizing a small, efficient band of saboteurs. The result was 'the Army' which issued its threats in the name of 'General Chedu', but was in fact organized by two members of the Z.A.P.U. national executive and one member of the Youth League. 'The Army's' most successful piece of sabotage was the burning of a large section of the British South Africa Company's forest estate in

---

[1] *Daily News*, 15 October 1962.

the Eastern District.[1] In public the Z.A.P.U. leaders protested that they knew nothing of 'the Army'.

In addition to violence there was another firm foundation for European apprehension. This was the realization that African participation in government, African competition for jobs, African rights to mix socially and to live in white areas, were no longer the far-off mirage of 'not in the foreseeable future', for Whitehead's policy had brought these possibilities into the very foreseeable future. The fear of social integration found expression in R.F. advertisements; one showing a large empty house with a 'For Sale' notice on it, and another showing multi-coloured girls' legs with a school in the background.[2]

The fear was most easily understood and expressed in terms of everyday living and property rights. In a letter to his constituents the R.F. candidate for Braeside, Lieutenant-Colonel H. D. Tanner, asked them whether they agreed with the 'integration of the two races in a common community, including the area in which you live? . . . Do you agree that the existing provisions of separate facilities and amenities for the racial groups should be sustained to enable them to preserve their customs and way of life, as opposed to integration of the races being imposed by law?'[3] The way fear was feeding European doubts, even among U.F.P. supporters, is shown in the correspondence of the local newspapers. On 6 February 1962, in *The Rhodesia Herald*, a letter signed '*Sauve qui Peut*' said: 'The Government contemplates legislation enabling Africans who, as yet, have not one iota of knowledge regarding hygiene and sanitation to live in European residential districts with the resultant devaluation of property and racial strife.' On 20 February, a man who signed himself 'I voted Yes—what Now?' wrote:

I have faithfully followed the Huggins-Welensky line for over twenty-five years. But at the next election I shall be asked to vote away the Europeans' long-standing protection against their swamping by hordes of primitive people, and agree to having them live

[1] Shamuyarira, op. cit., p. 74.
[2] The photograph was of Girl Guides' legs, and after this had been uncovered by the U.F.P. the R.F. withdrew the poster.
[3] Salisbury, National Archives (R.F. documents).

next door to me and attending school with my children. This I cannot do . . . call it prejudice if you will but however liberal-minded we are, we can never cease to shrink from close and intimate contact with the Africans.

In the same paper on 28 November 1962, E. G. Scammell wrote to say:

As a present member of the U.F.P. I wish to have information on the following:
(1) Does the Prime Minister intend if re-elected to make merit and merit alone the only qualification for advancement?
(2) Does he envisage a lowering of the franchise at an early date? On both these points I am worried lest panic measures may be taken in the face of increasing pressure from the British Government and the United Nations.

The Citizen, a right-wing weekly, expressed the same fears. Early in November, under the headline, 'Africans in White Flats', the newspaper said that U.F.P. policy meant integration in flats and in schools. The choice was 'to vote for the U.F.P. and therefore to agree to forced integration and the handing over of power to the black nationalists within two to five years' time, or to stand firm and declare stoutly and resolutely, "This far and no further". All other considerations must be swept aside as being of little or no consequence compared with the vital issue.' *The Citizen* warned that U.F.P. policy would force whites 'to become wanderers over the face of the earth with no country of our own to call motherland'.[1] In the issue before the election the newspaper stated that 'the voter has a choice to build a nation based on European and Western standards or to prepare for a mass evacuation such as is taking place at the present time in Kenya'.[2]

As the election campaign developed, so within the European society the parties established their social 'images'. The U.F.P.'s was already well known. It was the party of 'the Establishment' —the businessmen, the great mining companies, the professional classes and Civil Servants, the commercial world. Its strength was in the urban areas. The R.F. became associated with an

---

[1] *The Citizen*, 2 November 1962.   [2] Op. cit., 7 December 1962.

amalgam of farming interests and white artisans. The groupings reflected common economic and social interests. Although
the farmers and artisans made strange bedfellows, they had the
common overriding interest that their positions were challenged
by African advancement. While business and commerce had
interests in wider markets, in seeing that money flowed to all
sections of the community, and had interests in the growth of
an African artisan class to break the high labour costs of the
white 'guild system', the farmers, anxious for their land and
crop prices, the artisans, anxious for their jobs, drew together.[1]
The big query in the European society was whether the R.F.
could make substantial inroads among the white-collar
workers, the Civil Servants, and professional men of the cities.

Another strong characteristic of the R.F. was the emphasis it
placed upon war service. The party published a list of their
candidates (thirty-three of the fifty 'A' Roll candidates) who
had 'fought against tyrannies in the past to preserve freedom'.
There was a hero for every taste, from Brigadier Dunlop to
Sapper Cary.

The forces were gathering against the U.F.P. Government,
but most politicians and political commentators were confident that 'the Establishment', unopposed at the polls by the
nationalists and therefore certain to win most of the 'B' Roll
seats, would retain power. This conviction persisted right up
to the election itself. The editorial in the November edition of
The Examiner assured its readers: 'Let no one doubt that the
U.F.P. will win hands down; the Establishment always does in
Southern Rhodesia.' Mr. J. Savanhu, writing in *The Rhodesia
Herald*, a few days before the election was equally certain that
the U.F.P. would win, as was the newspaper's political corre-
spondent on the day before the election. John Reed, writing in
December in support of Z.A.P.U.'s boycott of the election, said:
'A U.F.P. victory is inevitable and abstention is the only un-
mistakable voicing of opinion open to those who see that the
constitution will prevent a transition which is inevitable coming
about constitutionally.'[2] Even the right-wing politicians,
although they had strong hopes of gaining ground against the

---

[1] I am indebted to my colleague Dr. G. Arrighi for this analysis.
[2] *The Examiner*, December 1962.

U.F.P., doubted their ability to gain a parliamentary majority.[1]

The misplaced confidence in U.F.P. invincibility told heavily against that party. Both the extremes—the nationalists and the European right wing—saw the U.F.P. as their major opponent and largely ignored each other. The U.F.P. Government therefore had to fight opposition on both sides. The Prime Minister appreciated this. He said: 'We face two oppositions. They are both bitter and they are both intransigent.'[2]

As it became apparent that European opinion was drifting to the right, the African vote became vital for U.F.P. success. Right up to the election the nationalists opposed participation. From his restriction Joshua Nkomo issued a leaflet advising Africans to ignore the elections. The Government seized most copies of the leaflet but one had been sent to *The Daily News*, a newspaper with a large African following, and so Nkomo's opposition could be read by all. Nkomo stated that, as the Constitution and election had been rejected by the African people, now Africans must 'refuse to dig [their] own graves'. He affirmed that all existing parties would soon disappear, and therefore Africans should not divide themselves by following transitory policies and false leaders. 'They are all supporting an evil document which we reject.'[3]

The nationalist leaders had already succeeded in dissuading many Africans from registering for the vote. At the election they were equally effective in dissuading those who had registered from voting. Either from fear or from persuasion the majority of those who had previously defied the nationalists by registering stayed home on election day. In the electoral districts only 24·24 per cent of the 'B' Roll voters cast their vote. Only 22·54 per cent used their cross-voting rights in the constituencies. Although the U.F.P. drew the great bulk of the 'B' Roll votes which were cast (81 per cent in the constituencies and 72 per cent in the districts), and although the U.F.P. won fourteen of the fifteen 'B' Roll district seats, while all fifteen R.F.

---

[1] Lord Alport (*The Sudden Assignment*, p. 230) said that Winston Field was so sure that the party would not win that he, Field, arranged a South American holiday immediately after the election, but Mr. Field told me that he had strong hopes of winning but did not bother to cancel a previously arranged trip until the results were known.

[2] S.R.L.A. Hansard, 1 August 1962, col. 1179.

[3] *Daily News*, 29 November 1962.

district candidates were defeated, the U.F.P. had suffered a severe blow. African failure to participate meant that in the 'A' Roll constituencies the 'B' Roll participation was too small to tip the balance for the U.F.P. Only in one constituency, Mtoko, did the 'B' Roll cross vote alter the result in favour of the U.F.P.[1]

The Africans rejected Whitehead's policy of partnership by abstention. The Europeans rejected it by voting against it. In an 'A' Roll constituency poll of 74 per cent, 56 per cent voted for the R.F. and 42 per cent for the U.F.P. When the final count of seats was made, the R.F. had won 35, all in 'A' Roll constituencies, the U.F.P. had won 29, 15 in constituencies and 14 in districts. (There was one Independent, Dr. Ahrn Palley, returned for the Highfield electoral district.)[2]

Somewhat to their surprise the R.F. formed the new Southern Rhodesian Government.

Both the R.F. and the African nationalists claimed the 1962 election as their triumph. For the R.F. it was a triumph over appeasement with the very tangible reward of forming the new Government. For the nationalists it was a triumph over deceit, the deceit of the 1961 Constitution and the deceit of partnership as preached by the U.F.P. The nationalists had no immediate tangible reward to show, but they claimed that the election had clarified the issues, that for the future there would be a direct racial contest for power, a contest which Africans would certainly win.

The nationalist claim to have triumphed in 1962 was based upon two assumptions. First, that Africans could not participate in an election under the 1961 Constitution without compromising their demand for majority rule. Therefore refusal to participate either as candidates or as voters was the logical and right course. The second assumption was that Europeans would never voluntarily agree to share political power with Africans, and therefore the U.F.P.'s policy of partnership was a façade behind which European rule would be entrenched. The

---

[1] There were seven constituencies in which a heavier 'B' Roll vote could have changed the result (Bulawayo District, Eastern Constituency, Greendale, Marandellas, Matobo, Mazoe, and Wankie). But only in Matobo was the election result very close. All the other constituencies would have required a very substantial 'B' Roll vote for the U.F.P.

[2] For an analysis of the results see Appendix II.

nationalists argued that partnership still implied a relationship which Lord Malvern had once described as that between a horse (the African) and a rider (the European). They argued that the policy was a sham, that a U.F.P. government would be prepared to let Africans drink in the hotels, swim in the pools, but never share political power.[1] Shortly after the election an unsigned article entitled 'Victory over Hypocrisy' appeared in *The Examiner*. This stated that for the nationalists the election was important not because the R.F. had been victorious, but because

the U.F.P. is vanquished. The removal of the U.F.P. and Whitehead from control has long been the *sine qua non* for a happy solution to Rhodesia's troubles. No one now, looking back to February 1959 [the banning of the African National Congress] can fail to see the remorseless step-by-step progress to disaster along which Whitehead dragged the country.

The article contended that there were no firm, no golden principles of honour guiding the U.F.P. It was just 'a hand-to-mouth affair', and 'the unwholesome total sum came to the one thing—hypocrisy'. 'What's to choose between the dogmatic paternalism of the U.F.P. and the paternal dogma of the R.F.?' asked the author. The defeat of the U.F.P. was seen as a great triumph for nationalist tactics and 'with its strength now proved African nationalism can go forward with growing confidence'.[2] Eighteen months after the election, W. D. Musaruwa was still confident that the 1962 election results had been in the best interests of Africans, that by abstaining the African voters had rightly rejected the deceitful policy of partnership. 'According to our scale of evaluation', he wrote:

Ian Smith and Whitehead are equally bad. Both want to prevent the advent of majority rule; both believe that the end justifies the means; both have a very low regard for Africans; both believe in white supremacy which they euphemistically call 'white civilization'; both use harsh means to suppress the legitimate aspirations of 95 per cent of the country's population . . . They [the Africans] will not vote for a white supremist party because it contains a white man who dislikes Africans less than other whites do.[3]

[1] Dr. Ahrn Palley, the Independent M.P., also shared this belief (personal information).

[2] *The Examiner*, February 1963.

[3] Op. cit., June 1964.

If the nationalist analysis of partnership was accurate, then the result of the 1962 election was irrelevant to the main course of Southern Rhodesian politics. If, as the nationalists argued, the U.F.P. were as committed as the R.F. to retaining white rule then the struggle between the races lay ahead, whatever the election result. The U.F.P. lost and therefore there can be no proof either way of the party's real intentions, but the nationalist analysis seems unsound. In the Legislative Assembly, in the party conferences, in the election campaign, the U.F.P. leaders had emphasized time after time their determination to eliminate racial barriers knowing that in doing so they were alienating some white support. Even if this is dismissed as the façade, even if U.F.P. leaders were in fact unenthusiastic about sharing political power—and there is no clear evidence to show this, but even assuming they *were* unenthusiastic—the reality of the situation in December 1962 was that a victorious U.F.P. would have had no choice but to share power between the party's black and white supporters. The U.F.P. was relying upon African votes to swing the constituencies in its favour. It was relying upon African Members of Parliament from the district to give it a governing majority. The party could not have ruled without the combined support of both races and therefore it would have been essential to retain African support by sharing power.

The nationalists would retort that Africans who were prepared to co-operate with the U.F.P. were those who were protecting and enhancing their own interests, who, to obtain power and status, were prepared to sacrifice the interests of the great mass of under-privileged Africans. They were therefore attacked by the nationalists as 'traitors', 'Tshombes' and 'sell-outs'. There may have been substance in the nationalist accusations, but, if there was substance, it was that Africans who supported the U.F.P. were prepared to make political distinctions on criteria other than that of race. However, the nationalists attacked African U.F.P. supporters not as 'traitors' to the poor or the needy, but as 'traitors' to their race. In this there was an assumption that a sharing of power between the races, even a sharing between the privileged, was impossible and that a struggle based upon race was inevitable. If in 1962 this assumption was not sound then the Africans who were prepared to support the U.F.P. could reply that it was they who offered the greatest hope and opportunities for Africans, for they would avoid racial conflict but obtain an increasing share in government which would lead to majority rule.

Whitehead's policy of partnership interpreted through the new constitution was an attempt to avoid a simple conflict of race. Perhaps this attempt would have failed. Perhaps a conflict of race was inherent in Rhodesian society. Perhaps racial conflicts would have developed within the party. Perhaps the African party members would have been rejected by other Africans and become isolated from them and their aspirations. Clearly, winning the election would only have been the first of a series of problems for a party that was trying to cut across racial barriers, but equally clearly the 1962 election result meant that the experiment would not even be tried. Despite the existence of the new Constitution, with its direct African representation in the legislature, the result preserved the existing racial power structure. The whites ruled, the blacks were ruled.

But the election did mark a significant change. Previously the struggle for political power had been a struggle within white society between parties representing different white interests. This ended in 1962. Even though most Africans boycotted the election they had become, through the nationalist movement, competitors for power. After 1962 the increasing realization of this within European society made divisions among Europeans relatively unimportant. The Europeans were soon massed behind the white government, conscious that the real opposition was outside the legislature and that it was black. This was the very situation which Sir Edgar had tried unsuccessfully to avoid.

The accusation which can justifiably be levelled against Sir Edgar Whitehead and his party is not that they were pursuing a hypocritical policy, but that they made a serious error of political judgment. The U.F.P. policy failed because both races distrusted it. Rightly or wrongly most Europeans decided that partnership implied a betrayal of their interests, but perhaps even more significant was the party's failure among Africans. The party still had substantial, if minority, support among Europeans and drew more than 40 per cent of the 'A' Roll vote. Had this been reinforced by a substantial vote from

Africans the U.F.P. may have won the election. Sir Edgar Whitehead later estimated that had 5,000 more 'B' Roll Africans voted and used their cross-voting powers, his party would have won. As it was only 2,396 'B' Roll votes were cast in the constituencies from a total 'B' Roll register of 10,623. Africans, from fear of intimidation, or from distrust of partnership, or because the U.F.P.'s form of partnership was irrelevant to their ambitions—or from a combination of these motives—failed to support Sir Edgar's party.

The 1962 election was a critical point of recent Southern Rhodesian political development. At the election both races in rejecting a compromise solution thereby implied that the struggle for political power which lay ahead was a racial struggle. In this sense the R.F. and the nationalists were both right in claiming the election as their triumph for they were the parties of the extremes, parties which believed that race was the great political divider. Before the election it had appeared that a party drawing support across the races had a strong chance of success, and even at the election the U.F.P. still had considerable support, at least from Europeans, but after its defeat the party rapidly grew weaker as the races moved even further apart, as they decided that compromise was impractical. The election had set Southern Rhodesia firmly on the road to U.D.I. for a European party had been returned to power committed to retaining the existing social order with its European predominance. In the negotiations for independence which lay ahead the R.F. could never abandon this stand, for it was their *raison d'être*, but because they could not abandon it they could not negotiate independence. The negative aspect of the victory was admitted even by supporters of the new government. The editorial of *The Citizen* said: 'The Rhodesian Front was returned to government through no abundance of pre-election promises—in fact they made none. They simply gave voice to the anxieties of the common people (i.e. Europeans) at the rate the last Government were going about the enforcement of their multiracial policies and the disastrous effect their speed would have on the very existence of the country and their voice found an echo in the hearts of the electorate.'[1]

---

[1] *The Citizen*, 21 December 1965.

CHAPTER VIII

The End of Federation and the Search for Independence Under Winston Field

There were many unique features about the Southern Rhodesian Legislative Assembly which met in February 1963. With its sixty-five members it was more than twice the size of any previous Assembly, but perhaps more striking was that for the first time Africans and Europeans sat together. All the Africans had been returned in electoral districts and sat with the U.F.P. opposition. The R.F. Government retained the tradition of an all-white ruling party, but it could call upon little experience of government. Its members had been outside 'the Establishment' and therefore had never practised political power. There was not a single member of the new Government with previous ministerial experience, and many R.F. Members of Parliament were new to Parliament. Winston Field himself, although he had sat in the Federal Assembly, had never been a member of the Southern Rhodesian House and therefore had the extraordinary experience of delivering a maiden speech as Prime Minister. In assembling a Cabinet Mr. Field looked for men with parliamentary and administrative experience. His two most important ministerial appointments were Mr. Ian Smith, as Minister of the Treasury and Deputy Prime Minister, and Mr. Clifford Dupont, Minister of Justice and Industrial Development.[1] Naturally the combined and individual inexperience led to uncertainty and difficulties, which, initially, the U.F.P. leaders were able to exploit, but the Ministers soon gained in experience and assurance even though there continued to be doubts about the administrative ability of some of them.

As well as the change in its composition, the new Legislative

---

[1] For the full R.F. Cabinet under Field, see Appendix I.

Assembly had a different atmosphere. Despite party divisions the old House had been a clubby, intimate place, but in the new Assembly there was a colder and increasingly bitter atmosphere. The bitterness developed around the old dispute about African rights and aspirations, which was exacerbated by the new circumstances of a right-wing ruling European party facing an opposition with a substantial number of African members. The U.F.P. African Members of Parliament were 'moderates' but they brought with them personal knowledge of the humiliation and discrimination which almost all educated and feeling Africans had suffered. Mr. J. M. Gondo, speaking about discrimination, said that 'a number of times in this House, Hon. Members of the opposite benches have said, "We are sick and tired of this sort of thing." I highly regret that they have never been black. If they were black and in the category which I am and meeting the treatment such as the kind I meet, the position would be quite different'.[1] Frequently African Members of Parliament retold personal experiences of humiliation and discrimination. In the House inevitable clashes occurred between the more extreme personalities: between Mr. P. H. J. Chanetsa, an African Member, who on occasions praised Mau Mau, called for 'one man, one vote' and admitted sharing nationalist aspirations, and Europeans like Mr. W. J. J. Cary and Colonel G. H. Hartley, bristling with pride in their own race and doubts about the ability of any other race.

The new Government was soon faced with major problems. Within a few days of the R.F. taking office, the British Government announced Nyasaland's right to secede from the Federation. This was the logical outcome of recent British policy, but it created an immediate political stir and reopened the vexed question of the Federation's future. For the British Government Mr. Butler explained that new talks would be required to settle future relations between the territories, but he reaffirmed his Government's 'constructive purpose to secure in Central Africa, conditions in which a stable and expanding economy can be maintained and people of all races can live in harmony'. Sir Roy Welensky saw it differently. He saw in Nyasaland's secession the end of his dream of a strong, rich Central African state,

[1] S.R.L.A. Hansard, 26 November 1963, col. 210.

a dream he had continued to strive towards despite the increasing evidence that the Federation would not survive. His bitterness overflowed. He told the Federal Parliament:

The history of our dealings with the present British Government now makes the Federal Government believe that there is little if any honour left among them. I say that Britain has lost the will to govern in Africa and that Britain is utterly reckless of the fate of the inhabitants of the present Federation. By contrast we in the Federation have neither lost faith in ourselves nor in our will to govern decently and fairly.[1]

Despite the Nyasaland setback, Sir Roy continued to fight for a political Federation between Northern and Southern Rhodesia.

Winston Field was not emotionally committed to the Federation. His main interest was to secure as favourable terms as possible for Southern Rhodesia. He behaved with great circumspection, refusing to be drawn into hasty decisions or statements, not taking any initiative but at the same time accepting that major changes were inevitable. Unlike Sir Roy he believed that the political links would disappear, but hoped to retain as many economic ties as possible. He told the Legislative Assembly that 'there is no doubt that Southern Rhodesia has benefited economically . . . we should like that part of the association to continue. Politically we have not benefited as we have delayed our real independence for economic reasons'. He said that there was no point in deceiving themselves about the future. Nyasaland would secede and the dominant political parties of Northern Rhodesia also wanted to break away politically. There would be great difficulties in the dissolution, but these must be faced and as many economic benefits as possible retained. He confessed that he favoured a clean break and then negotiations on an equal footing, not because of 'a desire for Southern Rhodesia to go it alone; it is facing up to hard reality and it is quite time we did this.'[2]

The British Government made clear that Nyasaland's right to secede did not automatically give Northern Rhodesia the same right. But in Northern Rhodesia Mr. Kenneth Kaunda was establishing himself as the predominant political figure and

---

[1] *The Rhodesia Herald*, 20 December 1962.
[2] S.R.L.A. Hansard, 13 February 1963, col. 35.

he had no doubts about what he wanted. He said: 'There is no question but that the Federation must be dismantled completely and then it must be left to the peoples of the territories concerned to decide if there is any chance at all of any Federal links.'[1] On another occasion he warned the British Government that if Northern Rhodesia were not given the right to secede, 'we will make it impossible for any Federal department to operate.'[2]

It was difficult to see how the British Government could deny Northern Rhodesia the right of secession but, early in 1963, there was still an element of uncertainty. Northern Rhodesia with its rich copper belt was a much greater prize to fight for than impoverished Nyasaland. Sir Roy Welensky was prepared for this fight. In a broadcast early in March he pledged himself to 'devote all his energies . . . to ensuring that the Rhodesias will remain linked together as a constitutional and political entity'.[3] Later in the month, when he left for talks in London, he was in a pugnacious mood. 'I am going into a fight', he threatened, 'and will punch at every head that rises.'[4] Sir Roy must have missed some of the heads, for at the talks the British Government decided that no territory could be kept in the Federation against its will, and so granted each one the right of secession. This was the end of the Central African Federation, for it was inevitable that Northern Rhodesia under an African Government would follow Nyasaland's lead.

The break-up of the Federation created problems of forbidding magnitude and complexity, for Central Africa had been welded into a constitutional and economic unit. Such questions arose as: How were the Federal debts to be paid and who would pay them? How would common services like air and rail communications be maintained? Who would be responsible for the mighty Kariba Dam, which had been built by funds raised by the Federal Government? What was to happen to the members of the Federal civil service? How were the Federal armed forces to be divided? These problems could not be underrated, but for Southern Rhodesia the dissolution created a separate problem, a problem which overshadowed all

[1] *The Rhodesia Herald*, 6 March 1963.   [3] *The Examiner*, April 1963.
[2] Op. cit., 11 March 1963.   [4] *The Rhodesia Herald*, 23 March 1963.

else. Would Southern Rhodesia be granted its independence and, if so, on what terms? Mr. Field said he would not attend a conference to make arrangements for the break-up of the Federation unless Southern Rhodesia were first guaranteed independence. But as the independence negotiations dragged on it became obvious that the Federal conference would be held before independence was confirmed. Field faced the dilemma of having stated publicly that he would never attend such a conference unless his conditions were satisfied, but, realizing that the interests of Southern Rhodesia would suffer if they were unrepresented, he pocketed his pride, explaining that the nation's interests must come first, and attended the conference at the Victoria Falls late in June.

The Federal conference was a triumph for Mr. Butler, both in persuading all the delegates to attend and then in persuading them to an agreed policy for the break-up.[1] Working parties were created to make the detailed arrangements for the formal dissolution, which was set for 31 December. As these final arrangements were made Sir Roy Welensky, although bitterly disappointed, showed that he was not a man to harbour grudges and offered the full support of the Federal Government.

In the final arrangements it was agreed that some important services, including the railways, Central African Airways, and the Kariba Dam, would be controlled jointly by the territories. Also an understanding was reached whereby the bulk of trade in domestic goods between the territories was free of duty. The most controversial decision concerned the division of the armed forces. At the conference the general agreement stated that when the Federal Government ceased, 'control of the forces should revert to that which obtained before 1953 when Southern Rhodesia was responsible for her own forces and the United Kingdom Government had operational control of the forces in the Northern territories'.[2] It was also agreed that in most cases units would be transferred according to their present dispositions. When the detailed negotiations were completed Southern Rhodesia had acquired one of the strongest defence forces in Africa. By 1964 she had an air force of sixty aircraft,

[1] Nyasaland was represented only by advisers, as Dr. Banda refused to attend.
[2] Report of the Central African Conference (Cmnd. 2093), para. 43.

including Hunters, Canberras, and Meteors, and an army of 3,400 men, including two infantry brigades, each with one regular and two active territorial battalions. One of the regular battalions was exclusively European while the other was officered by Europeans.[1]

There was international criticism of the transfer of forces, and in the Federal Assembly Mr. J. J. Simukonda and Mr. J. Savanhu attacked the arrangement,[2] but despite the criticism the transfer went through. It was costly for Southern Rhodesia for, as well as the recurrent costs, she had to accept the existing financial liabilities of these forces, but the Government thought it a price well worth paying. Winston Field said: 'There are timorous ones who say, "But we cannot afford a worthwhile defence force." My only reply in this day and age in Africa is: "We have got to." '[3] The Southern Rhodesian Government's direct control of these forces was an important factor in weighing the decision for unilateral action.

Although Southern Rhodesia had acquired military forces and did not suffer the predicted economic collapse, the dissolution of the Federation was not greeted with enthusiasm by Europeans, even by those who had opposed its existing structure. Field said that . . . 'it was with no sense of jubilation that we returned from the Falls Conference. We did our best for Southern Rhodesia and I think that, bearing in mind the whole unfortunate circumstances of dissolution, the result so far is satisfactory. We must look upon this as the beginning of the end of uncertainty'.[4] To most Europeans the great economic opportunity, the chance to spread 'responsible' government across Central Africa had been thrown away, not by an internal failure to settle relations between the races, or to resolve the conflicting territorial ambitions, but by the British appeasement of African extremism. They believed Sir Roy when he spoke of treachery, of deserting the path of racial 'partnership' to placate African extremists; they believed him when he spoke of weakness and the lack of moral fibre. Sir Albert Robinson, a

---

[1] J. Symonds, *Southern Rhodesia: Background to Crisis*, London, Oxford University Press, 1965, p. 55.
[2] Federal Assembly Hansard, 16 October 1963.
[3] *The Rhodesia Herald*, 10 May 1963.
[4] S.R.L.A. Hansard, 16 July 1963, col. 231.

former Federal High Commissioner in London, said the dissolution was a triumph for dedicated left-wing revolutionaries in Britain, and also laid part of the blame on the power wielded by a few demagogues on British television. Julian Greenfield, the Federal Minister of Law, said that the Federation '. . . has been destroyed by outside forces. In particular it is the British Government that had the legal power to destroy it . . . whatever the Federal Government might have done, the forces that were arrayed against the Federation would have probably proved too strong'.[1]

The end of the Federation was a severe blow for the U.F.P. The party had already suffered defeat in the territorial elections and now the Federation, to which it was so closely linked, had failed. Even the old name, the 'United Federal Party', announced the failure. The party had to be reorganized. It was divided into four sections: a Federal section which would disappear at the dissolution of the Federation, and three separate territorial parties. In Southern Rhodesia the new party was called the Rhodesia National Party (R.N.P.), with Sir Edgar Whitehead as its leader. Sir Edgar said that the R.N.P. was 'virtually the old party carrying on under a new name', although new policies would be needed for external affairs and defence.

The end of the Federation was only one of the new R.N.P.'s troubles. On paper it had considerable strength. It had twenty-nine M.P.s against the R.F.'s thirty-five. It had leaders of Cabinet experience. But the paper strength was deceiving. The party, in losing the election, had suffered a great blow to its prestige and confidence. Almost half its parliamentary strength consisted of members returned from 'B' Roll districts with minimal electoral support. In the 'A' Roll constituencies it had won only fifteen seats against the R.F.'s thirty-five. Long and loud were the post-mortems and recriminations.

The R.N.P. was pulled two ways: on one side by a European section which was convinced that the election had been lost by over-liberal policies, and, on the other, by African and some European members who were convinced that the party must continue and even expand its liberalism. From the right wing H. D. Wightwick, a U.F.P. Federal M.P., attacked the leaders

[1] *The Examiner*, August 1963.

in Southern Rhodesia, claiming that 'their immoderate and intellectual conceit had rushed their own political party into headlong political suicide.'[1] At Que Que, the old U.F.P. party branch, led by Dr. M. I. Hirsch, broke away from the R.N.P. and formed the Reform Group, which decided to follow a less liberal policy than the main party. On the other wing of the party Arnold Chaza, the chairman of the Highfield branch, resigned. He wrote to Sir Edgar:

There was a time I would never have thought of parting camp with you, and I would have gone, and I actually did go through, thick and thin with you in spite of all the intimidation which I suffered including petrol bombs and other attempts on my life and family. The white electorate of Matobo voted callously in a way to suggest that they would not stand any co-operation with the black.[2]

There were many similar examples of the drift away from the R.N.P. by both races.

Under these pressures the R.N.P. leadership did not distinguish itself. Sir Edgar was an 'Establishment' figure, he seemed out of place in opposition. Although he continued to speak with great logic and sincerity, he did not have the fire or personal magnetism to re-inspire his party. Nor, bereft of authority, did the other leaders display the confidence and poise of their days of power. In the Legislative Assembly some Members—Blair Ewing, Mrs. Watson, J. R. Nicholson, and J. M. Gondo—kept up a strong and lively opposition, but the divided voice of the party too often revealed itself, and frequently it was left to the lone Independent, the radical Dr. Ahrn Palley, to press home attacks on the Government.

The final factor which began to tell against and to divide the opposition was the independence issue. While to the European electorate, the party appeared less dedicated to achieving independence than the R.F., to many Africans it appeared all too ready to follow the Government's lead, which would result in perpetual white domination. The party of compromise was disintegrating. The followers were retreating to their racial camps.

While the opposition was enduring its tribulations, the R.F.

---

[1] *The Rhodesia Herald*, 8 April 1963.   [2] *The Daily News*, 4 June 1963.

Government under Winston Field was increasing its strength. The Prime Minister himself grew in stature as a respected honourable leader, while his fellow Ministers basked in the aura of authority. The R.F. leaders emphasized their pride in the existing structure of Southern Rhodesia and their determination to fight for its preservation. When the Federal Government made gloomy economic predictions, the Southern Rhodesian government, although admitting the difficulties, affirmed its absolute faith in the country's future. This confidence embraced the certainty that African extremism could be fought and defeated. It was a rallying-cry for Europeans. Here was a Government prepared to say that appeasement and compromise were unnecessary, that African nationalism was not irresistible. It gave Europeans a cause, a hope for the future that they could dictate the terms of a national settlement.

The growing strength of the R.F. was revealed at a by-election for the Matobo constituency held in May 1963. At the General Election six months earlier, the R.F. candidate had been returned with a majority of only thirty-four, in a poll in which 70·17 per cent of the 'A' Roll, but only 16·34 per cent of the 'B' Roll voted. The by-election demonstrated two marked and very different developments. First, many more of the 'B' Roll electorate voted: 196 at the by-election against only 59 at the General Election (54 per cent against 16 per cent). The vast majority of the 'B' Roll voters continued to support Sir Edgar Whitehead's party, and the R.N.P. attracted 194 of the 196 votes. Had as many 'B' Roll votes been cast at the General Election the U.F.P. would have won the seat. But, at the by-election, this increase in 'B' Roll votes was unable to counter the second marked development, the swing of the European electorate to the right. At the General Election the R.F. had a majority of 77 'A' Roll votes from a total poll of 1,247. At the by-election the R.F. had a majority of 463 in a poll of 1,187.

As the R.F. strength increased, greater attention became riveted on the major objective: independence. Independence for Southern Rhodesia had become an immediate problem with the dissolution of the Federation. When it became known in March 1963 that Northern Rhodesia was to follow Nyasaland to independence outside the Federation, the Southern

Rhodesian Government made immediate and formal application to Britain for independence.[1] It marked the start of protracted and often bitter negotiations. What is striking about these negotiations is how little the attitudes of the two Governments changed, whether the Southern Rhodesian Government was led by Field or Smith, and whether the Labour or the Conservative Party was in power in Britain. Neither Government was prepared to give way on some vital issues, and neither Government fully trusted the other.

At first Mr. Butler, for the British Government, tried to cloud the issue by stating that Southern Rhodesia's independence could not be decided until the final arrangements had been made about the Federation and, as we have noted, Mr. Field replied by refusing to attend the Federal Conference until independence was first guaranteed. This was shadowboxing, but the basis of the dispute soon became clear: it was the differing interpretations of the role Africans were to play in Southern Rhodesia. The dispute quickly reached a constitutional stalemate, with Britain tied by the convention of non-interference in internal affairs, and the Southern Rhodesian Government legally powerless to cut off the final bonds with Britain and so change her international status. It was a frustrating position for both sides.

In Southern Rhodesia the Government and its supporters claimed that, in fact, the constitutional changes in 1961 had implied a guarantee of independence if the Federation broke up. Colonel Hartley told the Legislative Assembly that 'the United Kingdom Government owes independence to Southern Rhodesia as a debt, an outstanding debt, which stems from the assurances which were given at the time of the Constitutional Referendum [1961] and which should be honoured.' 'Hear, hear,' interjected Mr. Ian Smith.[2] Mr. Smith repeated the point in his own speech. What, he asked, were Southern Rhodesians to do if Britain went back on past pledges and rode rough shod. 'Are we going to acquiesce and lie down and accept this, or are we going to stand up for our own rights and stand firm on our beliefs?'[3]

---

[1] Cmnd. 2073, Field-Butler, 29 March 1963.
[2] S.R.L.A. Hansard, 26 November 1963, col. 641.
[3] Op. cit., 26 November 1963, col. 191.

In April Mr. Field set out the case for Southern Rhodesia's independence in a letter to Mr. Butler.[1] It was a case which was to be repeated persistently by the Southern Rhodesian leaders over the next two and a half years. Mr. Field said that Southern Rhodesia had enjoyed virtual self-government for forty years, that had it not joined the Federation it would have achieved its independence a decade before, and that the 1961 Constitution had been agreed as a basis for independence. During its forty years of self-rule Southern Rhodesia had developed in peace and prosperity for the benefit of all its inhabitants, to become a model of stable government and economic development. Nor had it called upon Britain for large-scale economic aid. It had stood on its own feet and yet had shown outstanding loyalty to Britain, as witnessed in the two World Wars.

It was further argued that independence was essential to frustrate outside interference, either by Britain or a hostile foreign nation or power bloc. So far Britain had honoured the convention but she might wilt under increasing international pressure. In the United Nations Britain was being urged to take direct action, and at the summit conference of the Organization of African Unity at Addis Ababa in May 1963 direct action by the black African states had been threatened if Britain failed to interfere. The danger existed even in British political circles. On 13 March Mr. Harold Wilson, the Labour Party leader, said in the B.B.C. 'African Forum' programme that, if Labour were returned to power, the Southern Rhodesian Constitution would be amended 'to allow the people of these territories to control their own destinies'. These incidents heightened the already acute Southern Rhodesian suspicions. If there was one issue above all others which could rouse Southern Rhodesian Europeans to anger, it was the claim of foreigners to be able to settle the country's affairs. Interference by the United Nations, by the black African states, or by the Commonwealth was despised and rejected. Europeans agreed that a settlement should only involve the Southern Rhodesian and British Governments but, in their eyes, even the British role was limited, for they thought that Britain should not have

[1] Cmnd. 2073, Field-Butler, 20 April 1963.

the right to dictate internal policy. They argued that with independence the Africans would also be made to realize that they had to concentrate their energies on solving problems within the country, instead of constantly running to Britain or some other outside body for help. With genuine indignation the Europeans asked: 'What right has Britain to tell us how to run our own country when we have been doing it very well ourselves for forty years?'

The Southern Rhodesian leaders were probably also quite genuine in their surprise at not being granted quick independence on their own terms. There was certainly a great deal of hurt pride at the obvious doubts and reluctance of the British Government when that same Government was prepared to give independence to an impoverished country like Nyasaland after only a few months of self-government and under the control of inexperienced and, in European opinion, highly suspect leaders.

From time to time Britain suggested a Commonwealth initiative in settling the deadlock. This was always rejected. Field described the new African members of the Commonwealth as 'mainly republics with their varying degrees of one-party dictatorship; some just flirting with communism, some obviously in love with communism if not already married to it'. They wished, he said, to interfere in Southern Rhodesia to take attention away from the appalling inefficiency, nepotism, and corruption in their own states.[1] Britain saw it in a very different light and earnestly sought a solution which would satisfy the Commonwealth. In December 1963 Duncan Sandys suggested informal discussion with Commonwealth leaders not 'to sit in judgment but to advise'. He suggested this because he thought an independent Southern Rhodesia would not like to be left out of the Commonwealth and because the risk of a break-up of the Commonwealth over the Southern Rhodesian problem was 'a risk which we would be most willing to undertake'.[2] Field rejected this 'unprecedented' proposal, because it would be a breach of the agreement that the decision lay solely between Britain and Southern Rhodesia, and because the attitude of the Commonwealth countries would 'be doctrinaire

[1] S.R.L.A. Hansard, 26 February 1964, col. 45.
[2] Cmnd. 2807, Sandys-Field, December 1963.

or governed by national interests' and not those of Southern Rhodesia.[1]

The R.F. Government further claimed that independence would provide the opportunity for its policy of gradual evolution to take root for the benefit of all races. Each race would develop in its own way and at its own pace, in a society based upon merit. The country would not be forced into hasty and ill-prepared political developments which could only result in disorder and misery. Mr. Smith often stated how well off Africans were in Southern Rhodesia. He told the Legislative Assembly that one lesson of the Federation had been to show the advantages Africans enjoyed in Southern Rhodesia. They had better schools and hospitals than the other territories and, he claimed, they were better off politically because they had access to a common roll. He thought Southern Rhodesia was the only remaining place in Africa in which the ideals of 'partnership' could be achieved.[2]

The arguments put forward to substantiate the desirability of gradual evolutionary progress were developed by some Europeans to present Southern Rhodesia as a fortress of high moral and Christian standards, of justice and order and good government, in a world which was torn by corruption and chaos. To preserve their 'standards' these Europeans were prepared, if necessary, to oppose all comers. Lieutenant-Colonel Macleod declared that: 'As Rhodesians we are ready to take up the challenge and prove to the world that we have the faith, the courage and the will to go forward against undoubted opposition and create here the real bastion for Christian civilization in Southern Africa.'[3] Mr. Lance Smith, after warning against 'the dark forces of evil such as our unfortunate cousins in Kenya have been subjected to', affirmed the R.F.'s determination to continue to pursue policies 'which have raised this country from a primitive forest area where most of the Hon. Members for the electoral districts would have been running around in skins'.[4] Another R.F. member, Mr. J. A. Newington, told the House:

Presumably they [the Opposition] believe that this descent into degeneration is inevitable. It's not inevitable unless we make it so,

---

[1] S.R.L.A. Hansard, 13 December 1963.   [3] Op. cit., 26 February 1964, col. 11.
[2] Op. cit., 26 November 1963.   [4] Op. cit., 19 June 1963, col. 53.

that good should be replaced by bad, that honour should be replaced by dishonour or justice by injustice and sadly enough that is what is happening elsewhere in Africa where honour goes and where independence and democracy come in. . . . Everything that has been said today has been said elsewhere in Africa and because the forces of courage and honesty have not been strong enough these countries have gone under.

There could, he continued, be no retreat from 'certain standards of honesty and justice and what we believe to be right'.[1]

These ideas were embraced by ill-defined phrases like 'the Rhodesian way of life' and 'keeping up standards'. They pictured a life in which Europeans had a reasonably affluent life, in which the sunshine and space of Southern Rhodesia could be enjoyed in a relaxed, friendly way with people of similar tastes and ideas. In this picture Africans were subordinate but not ill-treated, they benefited enormously from the presence of the white man and his skills, and were themselves gradually acquiring the same skills and possessions. It was a society of degree, order, and place. Ulysses' judgement in Shakespeare's *Troilus and Cressida* was accepted:

> Take but degree away, untune that string,
> And hark what discord follows.

Some of the Europeans who so passionately defended 'the Rhodesian way of life' were of well-established Southern Rhodesian families or had spent the greater part of their lives in the country, but the majority were immigrants. In 1961 only 35 per cent of the European population had been born in Southern Rhodesia.[2] Many had come in the post-war years, mainly from Britain and South Africa, but they had quickly been absorbed into the European society and accepted its standards as their own. The sociologist who said that it took a

---

[1] S.R.L.A. Hansard, 19 June 1963, col. 129.

[2] 1961 Census (Central Statistical Office), p. 38. Of the European population in 1961 26·2% had been born in South Africa and 26·1% in the United Kingdom. The Census report states: 'Both censuses (1956 and 1961) show that more than three-fifths of all Europeans enumerated in Rhodesia were born outside the Federation. At the same time, because of the ageing of the population and a decline in immigration, nearly 50% cent of Europeans born outside the Federation had been in the country more than ten years at Census date 1961, as compared with only 31% in 1956.'

white immigrant half an hour to become a Rhodesian was exaggerating, but his exaggeration had more than a grain of truth.[1]

The British Government accepted many of the Southern Rhodesian claims. The record of forty years' self-government was not disputed, nor the loyalty Southern Rhodesians had shown to Britain in the wars. Mr. Butler in his correspondence with Mr. Field agreed that the settlement of Southern Rhodesia's future could only be made between Britain and Southern Rhodesia and that the convention of non-interference would be respected and that the constitutional changes leading to independence would be made in Salisbury and not in Westminster.[2] Indeed, the principle that Southern Rhodesia should proceed to independence was readily accepted but dispute centred around the terms on which this was to be granted. The Southern Rhodesian Government insisted that independence should be granted on the basis of the 1961 Constitution without any substantial alterations. The British Government insisted that changes must be made to ensure the end of racial discrimination and a greater African share in government. Mr. Sandys told Winston Field that the Southern Rhodesian Government's claim that Britain was treating the country less favourably than any other was quite inaccurate. 'The present difficulty', wrote Sandys, 'arises from your desire to secure independence on the basis of a franchise which is incomparably more restricted than that of any other British territory to which independence has hitherto been granted.'[3]

So convinced were the Southern Rhodesian Ministers of the strength and justice of their case that they could not believe that the British Government's doubts were based on any justifiable principles. They concluded that the British Government was, for her commercial interests, trying to appease the Afro-Asian bloc and the Commonwealth, and also trying to avoid unpopular decisions which might tell against the Government in internal British politics. The picture which emerged in the eyes of Southern Rhodesian Europeans was one of honest, high-principled Southern Rhodesian politicians negotiating with a

[1] *The Observer*, 21 November 1965, Colour Supplement, p. 32.
[2] Butler-Field, 2 May 1963 and 16 May 1963 (Cmnd. 2073).
[3] Cmnd. 2807, Sandys-Field, 7 December 1963.

group of unprincipled, deceitful, selfish British leaders, prepared to abandon anybody or anything in their desire to retain power and wealth. In particular, the British Government—any British Government, Conservative or Labour—was prepared to abandon Southern Rhodesia to chaos and economic ruin for its own selfish ends. In Colonel Hartley's opinion:

The interests of the British Government in our affairs are totally selfish. The United Kingdom Government has only one object and that is to appease the national ambitions of nationalists throughout the continent of Africa. She seeks to present a façade which is designed solely to enhance her image in world affairs and the interests of Southern Rhodesia in relation to that are of no account.

'Quite correct', interjected Mr. Ian Smith. Yet, continued the Colonel, they hoped to retain the allegiance of the Europeans while arranging their suicide, and 'at the same time prate of principles'.[1] In November, after eight months of unsuccessful negotiations, Winston Field said: 'I think the United Kingdom Government regards only what is important to win the general election and please new members of the Commonwealth. . . . I do not believe the British Government is at this time concerned with the justice of our case.'[2]

The British Government was open to the pressures of which the Southern Rhodesian politicians were so critical. But this did not imply that one side was principled and the other unprincipled in its behaviour. Much of the misunderstanding stemmed from the different angles from which the two sides saw the problem. The Southern Rhodesians saw it in the context of their daily lives and the intimate affairs of their own Government. The British saw it in the context of international relations and world problems. Britain, as an international power, had interests in preserving her standing in the United Nations and in the Commonwealth. She did not believe, as did some R.F. Ministers and supporters, that the vast majority of nations, new or old, could be dismissed as Communist, corrupt, despotic, and unprincipled. Successful international relations depended upon a degree of tolerance, and therefore Britain was prepared to listen to the voices of other nations, even if on

[1] S.R.L.A. Hansard, 26 November 1963, col. 640.
[2] Op. cit., 26 November 1963, cols. 685 and 689.

occasion she thought that those voices lacked moderation or good sense.

Southern Rhodesia was a particularly vulnerable point for Britain. In the United Nations she was facing increasing pressure to replace the white minority Government by one elected on a popular franchise. In 1962 a special subcommittee of the United Nations' Committee on colonialism was created to investigate the situation in Southern Rhodesia. The subcommittee concluded that the 1961 Constitution did not provide satisfactory African representation and recommended that another constitutional conference should be called. Britain ignored this, claiming that the government of Southern Rhodesia was an internal affair outside the United Nations' competence. On 31 October 1962, the General Assembly, by eighty-one votes to two votes, with nineteen abstentions, requested Britain to take immediate steps to give the people of Southern Rhodesia 'the full and unconditional exercise of their basic political rights, in particular the right to vote'.[1] The dispute dragged on, with Britain becoming more and more isolated. A serious setback to Britain's stand was the resignation in October 1962 of her representative, Sir Hugh Foot, because he could no longer support British policy on Southern Rhodesia. The visit to the United Nations of Southern Rhodesians, including Sir Edgar Whitehead, did little to counter this blow.

In May 1963 a second report of the Committee on Colonialism was published, in which Britain's claim that the United Nations had no power to intervene was rejected. Britain was accused of ignoring all principles of justice and democracy, by denying $3\frac{1}{2}$ million Africans their legitimate rights for the sake of a constitutional convention. A crisis was reached on 9 September 1963, when the Security Council discussed the transfer of the Federal air force to Southern Rhodesia. In the Council Britain was asked not to grant 'any power or attributes of sovereignty . . . [nor] to transfer . . . the armed forces and aircraft as envisaged by the Central African Conference 1963.'[2] Britain was forced, for the first time since Suez, to use her power of veto to defeat the resolution.

[1] U.N. Security Council S/5403, 28 August 1963 (Ghana's case on Southern Rhodesia).
[2] U.N. S/5425, 11 September 1963.

There was similar pressure on Britain in the Commonwealth. Even the older, 'white' Commonwealth countries had little sympathy for the Southern Rhodesian Government's claims, and all Commonwealth countries saw the danger of a break-up over Southern Rhodesia. After the 1964 Commonwealth Prime Ministers' Conference, Lester Pearson said: 'If we can solve the Rhodesia problem, the Commonwealth will grow greater still in world importance. If we cannot, then the future of the Commonwealth is dim indeed.'

Obviously this was tremendous international pressure on Britain. The Southern Rhodesian Europeans might regard her as the appeaser of the Afro-Asian bloc, but the Afro-Asian countries saw her as the defender of a white, racist Government. During the early 1960s, Britain bore the brunt of an international assault on the white minority Government of Southern Rhodesia.

The British attitude to Southern Rhodesia was dictated not only by international pressures. During and since the war there has been a revolution in British thinking, involving a re-assessment of British society itself, where a more equal distribution of wealth and status has been accepted, and a re-assessment of Britain's international role. Partly from necessity, partly from conviction, it has been recognized that the Empire would disappear and that its place would be taken by independent, democratic states. In achieving this there have been mistakes and disappointments, but also great achievements, and the conviction has grown firm in Britain that the people, all the people, of a new state should have a say in their government. To accept that this should not apply to Southern Rhodesia would be to go against the grain of British opinion. There has been opposition to this thinking among right-wing Conservatives but the predominant British opinion has been reflected in the policies of both the major political parties.

While the Southern Rhodesian Government did not trust the British, equally the British Government did not trust the R.F. The British believed that, for all their protests that there would be gradual development to majority rule, the R.F. had no intention of keeping to their word. This conviction had been reinforced by the European rejection of the U.F.P. policy of moderation, and by statements of R.F. leaders that they did not foresee an African Government in their lifetime.[1] Because the British Government did not trust the R.F., it would not grant independence on verbal promises but wanted to see entrenched constitutional arrangements leading to majority rule.

The distrust and doubts on both sides came out in the detailed negotiations. The early negotiations between Field and Butler were vague and general, but in discussions before the Victoria Falls Federal Conference the British terms became clearer. The British wanted an end to racial discrimination, which would involve amendments to the Declaration of Rights and the repeal of the Land Apportionment Act. They wanted the qualifications for both the 'A' and 'B' Rolls lowered, and an increase in the number of members returned by the 'B' Roll districts to provide a 'blocking one-third' in the Legislative Assembly.[2] The changes to the Constitution, which the Southern Rhodesian Government under Field was prepared to consider, were slower in emerging. The furthest they went was in private proposals which Winston Field put to Duncan Sandys in February 1964, and which he, Field, was not certain would be supported by his colleagues. These proposals were that amendments should be made to the Declaration of Rights to make it more effective; that the Land Apportionment Act should gradually disappear, although schools would not be integrated; and that discrimination in public places should be abolished, although individuals, like hotel-keepers, would have the right to restrict entrance. On the franchise some lowering of 'A' Roll property qualifications would be accepted, and for the 'B' Roll there would be a considerable extension, or 'simplification' as Field called it, of the franchise. But the number of 'B' Roll seats would not be increased to provide a 'blocking one-third', and cross-voting between the Rolls would be abolished, as would the separate referenda of each race as a means of changing the Constitution's entrenched clauses.

Although the British Government had doubts about the

[1] For example, Winston Field answering a questioner at a Matobo by-election meeting said he did not believe there would be an African Government in his lifetime, although by natural evolution it would presumably come some time (*Rhodesia Herald*, 22 May 1963).

[2] S.R.L.A. Hansard, 17 July 1963 (Field's speech). (A two-thirds majority of the Legislative Assembly was required for changes to the 1961 Constitution, other than the entrenched clauses).

qualifications Field attached to the repeal of the Land Apportionment Act, his proposals went a long way towards satisfying
the British terms for abolishing racial discrimination. However, Field's proposals were refused because the changes in the
franchise were unsatisfactory. Sandys noted that the amendment to the 'A' Roll qualification would put only a few of the
more prosperous farmers on the Roll, while the 'B' Roll proposals did not provide any extra seats and would deprive that
Roll of its cross-voting powers.[1]

The power to be given to the 'B' Roll was one of the critical
issues on which neither side would compromise. The question
arose: 'Why, if the main terms of the Constitution and future
majority rule were accepted, should the R.F. Government
oppose the safeguard for Africans of the "blocking one-third"?'
They refused this because they were not prepared to make any
substantial concessions on the balance of powers contained in
the constitution. An increase in 'B' Roll seats would have
brought forward the potential date of African majority rule.
The R.F. attitude to the Constitution was confused, almost
schizophrenic. The R.F. Government based their claims for independence on the Constitution because they hoped its terms
would be acceptable to the British. Yet the Constitution implied a gradual development to African majority rule, while
the R.F.'s objective was to retain European control for an indefinite period. At one time or another all the R.F. leaders had
criticized the Constitution and even in the 1962 election had
campaigned for a revision of some of its clauses. They could
never quite rid themselves of their distaste for its liberalism.
They looked on the 'B' Roll as a bastard franchise conceived
by appeasement out of extremist agitation. In working the
Constitution at all, they felt they had gone further than could
reasonably be expected, but the British Government kept
pressing for greater concessions. It was more than flesh and
blood, at least R. F. flesh and blood, could stand. Ian Smith
asked: 'Do we accept that we are prepared to lower our standards? It is no use talking about widening the Roll. It is a
polite way of saying exactly the same thing.'[2]

By early 1964 it was obvious that the chances of a quick

---

[1] Cmnd. 2807, Sandys-Field, 22 February 1964.
[2] S.R.L.A. Hansard, 26 November 1963, col. 191.

negotiated independence were very slight. The Governor, in his speech at the opening of the Legislative Assembly session on 25 February 1964, said: 'It is now plain that the British Government are not prepared to be brought to any conclusion except on the most extravagant terms.' The Prime Minister followed this by saying that to accept the British terms 'would lead to the passing of Government authority from responsible hands to those not yet trained or responsible in government, and so to a lowering of standards in all walks of life—standards of justice, daily discipline, freedom, the lowering of standards in the professions, apart from a death blow to our economy'.[1]

The search for independence which became the focus of the Government's activities, also became the central issue of internal politics. The Government called for a united front. However, although the R.N.P. opposition was anxious to achieve independence, it was suspicious of R.F. aims and methods and therefore refused to give the Government unqualified support. At first it appeared that the difference between the two parties would be slight. When the dissolution of the Federation was announced, Sir Edgar Whitehead stated that he did not see how Britain could refuse independence, for 'when we drafted our new Constitution, we had full independence very much in mind', but he added that Britain would require some amendments to the Constitution.[2] Sir Roy Welensky, emotionally upset at his failure, was even more emphatic. He called on Southern Rhodesians to close their ranks and claim immediate independence. He declared: 'I think no one here, such as the European, the moderate, anyone who believes in our standards of civilization, culture and integrity must have the slightest illusion that this kind of thing is going to be protected and supported by the present Government in Great Britain.'[3]

These early statements could not hide for long the divergence of opinion which existed between the parties. The R.N.P. were almost as suspicious of R.F. motives as were the British. Blair Ewing said that the R.F. was 'a complete anachronism', prepared to accept that African rule was possible elsewhere, but

[1] S.R.L.A. Hansard, 26 February 1964, col. 44.
[2] *The Rhodesia Herald*, 3 April 1963.
[3] Op. cit., April 1963.

not in Southern Rhodesia. The R.F. would not accept 'that the day when one section of the community can impose its will on the rest has gone for ever from this land'.[1] Sir Edgar White-head criticized the Government for fostering 'the fallacy that interests of the European section of the community and the African section of the community politically must always be different, that there is no real hope of working together; either you have a white Government or an African nationalist Government.'[2] This difference of opinion meant that while both parties wanted independence there was a contrast of moods, of approaches. The R.N.P., being more sympathetic to African aspirations, claimed that they would have been able to negotiate independence with little difficulty. They accepted that, while the 1961 Constitution should be the basis for the negotiations, changes in the franchise and pattern of representation could be made without abandoning its spirit. Indeed Sir Edgar claimed that the Constitution had been designed to absorb such changes. The party was strongly opposed to a U.D.I.

The increasing demand for independence rallied Europeans behind the R.F. Government, which accused the opposition of appeasement and insincerity. But while the R.F. was gaining increased support in its demands for independence, the issue was creating strains within the party. As the unsuccessful negotiations dragged on, frustration and dissatisfaction arose. The frustration revealed itself in demands for more positive results in the negotiations, and in criticism from the right wing of the party that promises made at the election, such as the end of interracial swimming, had not been fulfilled. During 1963 Winston Field was able to absorb this criticism and remain in undisputed control. This was confirmed at the Party Congress of September 1963, the first since the election victory.

At the Congress the party was in a strange position. It was very new; it had had little time to establish a definable shape or image; and the relations between the leaders and Congress delegates was still uncertain. The party had been formed on a wave of reaction to internal events, yet it had become the governing party involved in complex international issues. As the Congress assembled, there was an air of uncertainty, with rumours that the delegates would dictate terms to the

[1] S.R.L.A. Hansard, 12 March 1963.   [2] Op. cit., 26 November 1963, col. 197.

leaders, and that there existed policy clashes among the leaders. The Congress was lively and outspoken. It appeared that, although the leaders were trusted, the branch delegates wanted a voice in forming policy. The Chairman, Mr. F. Alexander, denied that the party's tail was wagging the head, but warned against the head taking complete control. It was, he thought, the Government's duty to implement policies decided by the party. Direct criticism of the leadership was confined to the failure to keep the country fully informed of the Government's actions and policies but the predominant tone of the Congress was to exert right-wing pressure on the Government, to prevent it straying towards moderation. Independence was strongly urged, but the Congress affirmed that there must be no concessions on the 1961 Constitution, and there were hints of unilateral action if all else failed.

The Congress revealed another strong R.F. characteristic: an intense dislike of criticism and opposition. The party supporters hold their views so strongly that there is frequently an air of aggrieved disbelief that R.F. policies should be challenged. At the 1963 Congress strong attacks were made against the Argus Press,[1] and the radio and television services, for alleged anti-Government reporting. Despite opposition from Mr. Field the Congress passed a resolution 'deploring inaccuracies, mis-statements and misrepresentation of news'. This was followed by the Greenwood branch proposing that the Government should withdraw its grant to the University College, a centre of opposition to the R.F., and put the money 'to better use'. Ian Smith successfully opposed the move saying: 'If there is something wrong with the university—and I must concede on many occasions I have raised my eyebrows at what seems to go on there—I would suggest the correct procedure is to put it right and not try to push it down.'

The delegates to the Congress had been critical and lively, but they also revealed great personal devotion to their leaders and were prepared to follow the main outline of their leaders' policies. Winston Field appeared to emerge with enhanced prestige. He re-emphasized his determination to gain independence without major concessions. He attacked party

[1] The Argus Press controls the two largest dailies, *The Rhodesia Herald*, and *The Bulawayo Chronicle*, which have generally supported the U.F.P./R.N.P. policies.

members who spoke of abandoning allegiance to the Queen and leaving the Commonwealth, and carried the Congress with him when he declared that the aim was to achieve independence within the Commonwealth with the Queen as head of the state. For the leaders the lesson of the Congress was not that they were directly challenged, at that time, but that to retain the full support and confidence of the party it was essential to keep to the right, to avoid compromise.[1]

In September the leadership was still secure but the weeks, the months passed without independence. By February 1964 Field said that 'remaining a member of the Commonwealth must go by the board if this impedes our progress to independence', but he hoped to retain a special relationship with Britain. He admitted that he was 'bitterly disappointed' at the failure to achieve independence, but he intended to 'pursue any course within the framework of the Southern Rhodesian Constitution'.[2] This was interpreted to mean that he had decided against U.D.I. There was further confirmation when on 27 March the Prime Minister was reported as saying that he did not see how Britain could legally refuse Southern Rhodesia's claim, but added: 'I do not visualize any immediate unilateral action by ourselves unless the British Government gives us cause to take such action.'[3]

Winston Field's failure to gain independence was his undoing. On 13 April 1964, he was forced to resign the Premiership after a Cabinet revolt. Only John Howman, the Minister of Internal Affairs and Local Government, stood by the Prime Minister and chose to resign with him. The leadership change was brought about by an internal party manœuvre and therefore is difficult to assess as it was surrounded by intrigue and rumours. The pressure for change seems to have started in the party branches and to have spread upwards where it found an echoing voice in the parliamentary party and in the Cabinet. The Prime Minister himself was unaware of the revolt until a late stage. The first rumours of Field's resignation were reported in the Press on 11 April. During the week-end of 11 and 12

---

[1] Reports of the Congress are contained in *The Rhodesia Herald*, 20 and 21 September 1963, and the *Sunday Mail*, 22 September 1963.

[2] S.R.L.A. Hansard, 26 February 1964, col. 45.

[3] *The Rhodesia Herald*, 27 March 1964.

April, party meetings were held throughout the country. At one of these in Bulawayo Mr. George Rudland, the Minister of Trade, Industry and Development, made an extraordinary statement for a Cabinet minister. At the time of the meeting Winston Field was still Prime Minister, yet Rudland told his Bulawayo audience that at a secret meeting members of the Cabinet, with one exception, had decided that the Prime Minister must go. Rudland said that he admired the Prime Minister as a person but he, Field, was a 'middle-of-the-road man leaning to the left'. Rudland denied that the independence issue was the cause of the revolt, and instead cited Field's lack of consultation with his colleagues, his failure to implement election promises, and his failure to inform the country of government plans.[1]

There was speculation at the time that Field might fight back and have enough personal support to succeed, but partly from increasing ill-health, partly from lack of ambition and perhaps doubt about the size of his support, he did not do so. Instead he issued a statement which said: 'Serious disagreements have arisen between my party in the House and myself, in relation to policy, and I have been requested to retire in order to make way for someone else.' The 'someone else' was Mr. Ian Smith. Mr. Smith was the natural successor. He had been nominated as Mr. Field's deputy; he was hard-working and ambitious; he was liked personally; he had considerable parliamentary experience; and although he was not regarded as a party extremist his determination to achieve independence and his toughness as a negotiator were well established.

Mr. Smith is a dedicated man, sincere in his dedication, but fixed, narrow, and simple in his beliefs and ideals. He has a strong sense of mission, a conviction that his course is the only right course for Rhodesia. Such attributes have served him well as the leader of the Europeans as they have moved into their 'white laager'; they have singled him out as the chosen leader, but the same attributes have made him suspicious and mistrustful of opposition, they have blinded him to problems within his own society, and as a negotiator have made him intransigent and inflexible. Mr. Smith has been so deeply committed to the white-dominated Rhodesia he knows and loves that he has

[1] *The Rhodesia Herald*, 13 April 1964.

failed to see, or failed to recognize, the tension which this society breeds. He has dismissed those who represent these tensions as trouble-makers out for personal gain. In the events which lay ahead, Mr. Smith was sometimes uncertain in his tactics, often vacillating, ambiguous, even devious in what he said, and the way he negotiated, but in the end he always came down on the side of his more intransigent followers, the men who believed that there could be no deviation, no compromise from the path which the R.F. was following. Therefore from conviction or inclination, or from the desire to hold on to office, Mr. Smith chose to identify himself with the intransigent group. 'Thus far and no further' became a favourite and characteristic phrase. As the political leader of the white Rhodesians, Mr. Smith has concentrated on two main tasks. First, to gain independence from Britain without making concessions. Second, to unite and consolidate white Rhodesians behind him. In both these tasks Mr. Smith has revealed considerable flair and skill and judged within these narrow limits he has been an outstandingly successful politician. The characteristics of inflexibility and narrowness of vision which are major weaknesses within a non-racial or international context are strengths within the confined world of white Rhodesian politics. When Mr. Smith decided that whatever the means, whatever the cost, the existing Rhodesian society must be preserved, he echoed the feelings of the majority of white Rhodesians.

On taking office the new Prime Minister denied that there had been any policy split or that the party would move further to the right. He said that the break had been over leadership, not direction. He reaffirmed Rudland's claim that the independence issue had not been involved. This is very difficult to accept. Undoubtedly there was some discontent with Field's leadership. Within the party he had been criticized for his moderation on racial issues, for practising if not advocating multiracialism, and critized as a poor party man in his failure to appoint party followers to such posts as High Commissioner in London and the Chairmanship of the Lowveld Development Corporation. Within the Government there had been criticism of his remoteness, of his failure to consult colleagues and publicize government policy, while in the Cabinet there had been a clash between the Prime Minister and John Gaunt, the Minister of Mines, whom Field thought was incompetent.[1] But all the criticisms would have been inconsequential if Field had achieved or looked likely to achieve the major goal of independence. Mr. Smith, at his first Press conference as Prime Minister, said: 'I think it has been said on numerous occasions that we have no intention of weakening on the question of independence.' He said that he hoped it could be achieved by negotiation, 'but we have made it quite clear that we can visualize circumstances which might drive us to do something else'. This was the heart of the matter. Winston Field had decided against unilateral action; Ian Smith had not.

There were some disturbing aspects of the fall of Winston Field. He was overthrown by party not national pressure, and the whole incident was kept tightly within the party. Mr. F. A. Alexander, the Party Chairman, stated: 'As is well known to all Rhodesia it has been found necessary to make a change in the leadership of the Rhodesian Front Government.'[2] But it was not just the Rhodesian Front Government, it was the Southern Rhodesian Government. Mr. Smith said that he could see no point in holding an election on the issue.

The new Prime Minister, himself, was soon reminded of his own vulnerability. Mrs. D. C. Lilford, the wife of a powerful background figure in the R.F., wrote to the *Sunday Mail* a month after Mr. Smith had taken office. She said:

We in Southern Rhodesia have assumed the obligation of maintaining government of the people best able to assure just rights, freedom from fears and the privilege of serving and working for such a community in their own ways of life. If at any time this government finds its leader wearying of the tug of war he, too, will have to make way for a fresher and a more resolute man.[3]

The danger of this scarcely veiled threat was that an R.F. Prime Minister might consider that his first duty was to the party and not to the country.

[1] Palley, op. cit., p. 460.
[2] *The Rhodesia Herald*, 14 April 1964.
[3] *The Sunday Mail*, 17 May 1964.

CHAPTER IX

The Rhodesian Front Government and the African Nationalists

The African nationalists interpreted the 1962 election as a clear victory. The unbeatables, 'the Establishment', had been overthrown and with them the bogus but confusing appeal of 'partnership'. For the future, as the nationalists interpreted it, the issue was simple, it was a straight fight between the white extremists and the cause of African majority rule. The nationalists did not doubt their own invincibility. Events elsewhere had demonstrated that once the African people recognized where their interests lay the white Governments crumbled before them.

When the R.F. came to power, Z.A.P.U. had been banned and its leaders restricted. The new Government lifted the restriction orders, released the A.N.C. detainees held since 1959, and announced that in future it would use the courts to deal with any breaches of law and order. If the Government expected a conciliatory response from the nationalists, it was disappointed. Joshua Nkomo confirmed that the struggle would continue unabated but, because of the disruption and expense caused by their banning, no new party would be formed. He quoted the example of Algeria, where a nationalist movement had fought a successful campaign without a party organization. Z.A.P.U. would therefore continue to exist but without party machinery.

Nkomo said that he would not negotiate with the new Prime Minister unless it was at a conference presided over by the British Government. Southern Rhodesia, he declared, belonged to Africans, but Europeans would be welcome provided they did not want to be masters. 'Settler minority rule, which has now gone uninterrupted for more than seventy years—all the time in flagrant defiance of my people's wishes and in open war against their aspirations—must be forced to a halt.'[1]

Despite these strong words the nationalist movement lacked life and purpose in the early months of 1963. It was the Government which dictated the pace. A permanent ban was placed on Sunday political meetings, the main day for nationalist meetings; the nationalist leaders were regularly brought before the courts for alleged breaches of the Law and Order (Maintenance) Act. In February Mr. Nkomo, himself, was arrested at Rusape, together with George Nyandoro, only recently released from detention, Robert Chikerema and Boniface Nyagumbo. Mr. Nkomo was charged with leading an illegal procession from the railway station to the African township and for assaulting a policeman by poking him in the ribs with a stick. Nkomo was convicted on some of the charges but later appealed successfully.

In April there was a further setback to nationalist activities when Mr. Nkomo led his executive to Tanganyika to form a government in exile. He did this partly to gain greater freedom of activity: to have easier and closer contact with other nationalist leaders and to avoid the constant harrying and pressure of the Government: and partly because he miscalculated the independence negotiations. He decided that independence would be achieved quickly, either by negotiation or by a unilateral declaration, and therefore thought it wise to remove himself and his executive before the full strength of the Government, no longer restrained by Britain, was brought against him. Later, Mr. Nkomo's opponents within the nationalist movement were to accuse him of a further reason for the move to Tanganyika. They accused him of personal cowardice. In the absence of the leaders nationalist activity was at a low ebb, but in mid-June a fresh wave of activity started when Mr. Nkomo returned to rally the forces of 'our people to final victory'.[2] He left the executive behind in Dar es Salaam. Mr. Nkomo called for the lifting of the ban on Z.A.P.U., and dismissed a suggestion from Patrick Matimba, President of the small Zimbabwe National Party, that the two parties should unite, 'because', said Mr. Nkomo, 'they represent nobody except themselves.' On the surface at least he was full of

---

[1] *The Rhodesia Herald*, 9 January 1963.   [2] *Daily News*, 17 June 1963.

confidence and on 24 June declared: 'I know majority rule is just around the corner',[1] but he gave no evidence to support this belief.

Early in July Mr. Nkomo's surface confidence became transparent when rumours spread of plans for the formation of a new nationalist party which would exclude him from leadership. On 1 July leaflets were pinned to the houses of political leaders in Highfield calling for a new party. It was rumoured that the exiled Z.A.P.U. executive was meeting to decide whether it should take the initiative. Nkomo came out strongly against these moves. A pro-Nkomo pamphlet, which was circulated in Bulawayo, stated: 'Imperialists are using several stooges formerly their agents to disseminate an anti-nationalism to lead the new party to the people's detriment.'[2]

The rumours of opposition to Mr. Nkomo's continued leadership were well founded. Within the exiled executive there was deep discontent, which some of the members decided to translate into action. Mr. Nkomo received factual proof of this when he intercepted letters which Edson Zuobgo was carrying from the discontented members to nationalists in Southern Rhodesia.[3] The storm broke when Mr. Nkomo made a dramatic announcement to a mass rally in Salisbury. He named four of the exiled executive—Robert Mugabe, Leopold Takawira, Moton Malianga, and the Rev. Ndabaningi Sithole —as 'rebels' who had instigated the new party move. Mr. Nkomo's announcement was greeted by a roar of disapproval against the rebels, and there were shouts of 'sell-outs' and 'Tshombes' as he named other rebels within Southern Rhodesia, including Enos Nkala, Nathan Shamuyarira, and Stanley Parirewa. On the following day Nkomo sent a telegram to Dar es Salaam, dismissing the four rebels. When the telegram was received the executive broke up, with the four rebels on one side and the other three members who were still in Dar es Salaam—J. Z. Moyo, Joseph Msika, and Clement Muchache— remaining loyal to Mr. Nkomo.[4]

Joshua Nkomo's action marked the beginning of a deep and bitter split in the nationalist movement. It was a struggle for

---

[1] *Daily News*, 24 June 1963.
[2] Op. cit., 3 July 1963.
[3] Shamuyayira, op. cit., p. 181.
[4] Loc. cit.

leadership, a division based upon personalities not upon objectives. It had some similarities with the later revolt against Winston Field, for it was a 'Cabinet' revolt based upon frustration at failure to achieve the party's main objective, which, in the case of the nationalists, was majority rule. However, there were also clear contrasts in the two situations. Mr. Nkomo fought back and, although he lost some support and a substantial section of the executive, he remained the outstanding figure in the nationalist movement. He never lost his ability to draw the crowds and therefore countered the rebellion by summoning up massive support. Added to this he energetically reorganized his supporters so that they retained control of the majority of local nationalist groups. The rebels had hoped to overthrow Nkomo without prior publicity by deposing him at an executive meeting or at a party congress when, by good management, they might have been able to remove him without too much fuss, but, after Nkomo's statement, they had no choice but to fight in the open. They had to discredit Nkomo in his followers' eyes. Violent verbal, and later physical, attacks became common, committing both sides to attitudes which they later found impossible to relinquish.

Immediately the rebel executives heard of their denunciation, they sent a telegram to their supporters in Southern Rhodesia saying: 'Fear not Nkomo who is enemy of the people. Nkomo must go.'[1] A meeting of the rebel executive decided to dismiss Nkomo and accused him of fostering tribalism. A further statement spoke of 'Nkomo's political treachery, cowardice, tribalism and nepotism'. The elements loyal to Nkomo replied by speaking of 'Quislings, saboteurs and Tshombes'. The bitterness rapidly spread through the ranks. On 15 July, supporters of both sides assembled at Salisbury Airport to await the return of Sithole from Tanganyika. Sithole did not arrive but emotions and antagonisms were so high that a pitched battle broke out between the rival groups in front of the airport terminal building. This incident was the first of a series of fights and clashes between the rival groups. One aspect of nationalist violence had always been the attempt to eliminate opposition and defection within the African ranks. This aspect reached a new pitch as the rival groups fought to impose their will upon each other.

[1] *Daily News*, 10 July 1963.

The battle of words continued to rival the battle of fists, sticks, and petrol bombs. One pro-Sithole group accused Nkomo of 'watered leadership, his unmatched cowardice, his purposeless manœuvres and his connivings with settlers and imperialists'.[1] His 'sell-out' at the 1961 constitutional talks was constantly brought up against him. Nkomo was accused of spending his time and party funds in fruitless world trips. For Nkomo, James Robert Chikerema, one of his closest followers, replied that there was no division among the people: 'It is only a handful of power-hungry and so-called intellectuals who want to divide the people.' He warned African students at the university college that their degrees would not be recognized if they supported the rebels.[2]

The Reverend Ndabaningi Sithole emerged as the leader of the rebel group. He is a man of clear conviction, simple tastes, and great determination; less earthy and less easygoing than Joshua Nkomo. Sithole returned to Southern Rhodesia on 28 July, but was immediately arrested by the police and charged with offences under the Law and Order (Maintenance) Act. Leopold Takawira, the 'Lion of Chilimanzi' and one of Sithole's lieutenants, had met a similar fate the previous week. Sithole obtained bail and then launched his campaign against Nkomo but already he, Sithole, had lost valuable time which Nkomo had used to rally his own followers. Initially Sithole said he had no intention of forming a new party. Further, he claimed that he had no personal quarrel with Nkomo, but the very nature of the attack upon Nkomo made personal friction inevitable. Sithole said that Nkomo's leadership lacked decision and boldness because he was a coward who feared to go to gaol. He claimed that whenever danger was near Nkomo fled, that during his restriction at Kezi, Nkomo had tried to arrange for a private aircraft to fly himself and the executive out, and that when there was a threat of U.D.I. Nkomo, after declaring 'We shall be bundled up', had decided to lead the executive into exile. Sithole also accused Nkomo of being 'a law unto himself', of taking decisions without consulting his executive, and of making 'arbitrary, unconstitutional and undemocratic' dismissals from the executive.[3] Finally, Nkomo

[1] Op. cit., 18 July 1963 (statement by fourteen Harare residents).
[2] Op. cit., 29 July 1963.   [3] Op. cit., 22 July 1963.

was said to have misled the executive about leading a government into exile. It was claimed that no arrangements had been made, that the Tanganyika Government had known nothing of Nkomo's plans and finally President Nyerere, backed by the opinion of other African leaders who had met the Southern Rhodesian nationalists at Addis Ababa, told Nkomo to return home.[1] According to Sithole and his supporters, Nkomo had failed as an internal leader and was discounted and despised internationally.

On 9 August the rebels announced the formation of a new party, the Zimbabwe African National Union (Z.A.N.U.). Sithole became the President and his executive included Leopold Takawira, Herbert Chitepo, Robert Mugabe, and Enos Nkala. The policy statement of the new party revealed no great diversions from previous nationalist aims, although it had stronger socialist overtones.[2] The announcement of the new party was made the day before Nkomo held a large conference at Cold Comfort Farm, just outside Salisbury. There Nkomo announced that the leadership of the movement would be

[1] Shamuyarira, op. cit., pp. 177–9.
[2] The Z.A.N.U. policy statement said that the party was non-racial, believed in the African character of Zimbabwe, and stood for democratic rule. Its aims, *inter alia*, were:

(1) To establish a nationalist, democratic, socialist and Pan-African Republic within the fraternity of African states and the British Commonwealth;
(2) To introduce universal adult suffrage;
(3) To uphold the rule of law and the separation of powers.
(4) To restrict European immigration to technicians and investors, but to welcome Africans, other than the whites of South Africa or Portuguese territories.
(5) To repeal all colour discrimination and repressive laws.
(6) To entrench a Bill of Rights with retrospective effect from September 12th, 1890.
(7) To place all land under national control, with the government as the people's trustee—'owned but unoccupied land' to be communal.
(8) To grant an amnesty to all political prisoners.
(9) To give African courts the right to enforce African customary laws.
(10) To create a Ministry of Economics for long-range planning and 'vigorously encourage foreign investment and nationalize major industries that form the basis of the main economy.' (It was not explained how these apparently irreconcilable aims could be achieved.)
(11) To integrate education and make it compulsory to secondary Form II.
(12) To maintain a strong national army for defence and the liberation of Africa from colonialism, settlerism and imperialism.
(13) To provide a free health service and to give unemployment relief.

settled by popular choice, but Z.A.N.U. boycotted the conference, claiming that Nkomo had packed it. Therefore the
conference became a great pro-Nkomo rally, at which it was
decided that Z.A.P.U. would continue to exist, that no new
party would be formed, but that a People's Caretaker Council
(P.C.C.) would be appointed to provide guidance for the
movement. Other conference decisions were that less reliance
would be placed on outside support, that a fresh call would be
made to Britain to transfer power to the majority, and that the
Government's policy of Community Development, which was
declared *apartheid* in disguise, would be opposed. Z.A.N.U.
was condemned.

With the formation of Z.A.N.U. and the appointment of the
P.C.C. the nationalist split was complete and formalized. All
subsequent attempts to bring the two together have failed.
There was no easy rule of thumb by which the nationalist
followers divided between the two parties. At first it was
suspected that there might be a tribal division, with the
Shona supporting Z.A.N.U. and the Ndebele supporting
Z.A.P.U./P.C.C., but this division did not materialize. What
did emerge most clearly was that the Z.A.N.U. leaders had
badly miscalculated the amount of personal support Mr.
Nkomo could summon. Despite the energy of the Z.A.N.U.
campaign, despite support for Sithole from some foreign
nationalist movements, despite initial wide publicity for
Z.A.N.U. in the *Daily News*,[1] Mr. Nkomo retained his hold on
the great mass of nationalist supporters. Z.A.N.U. attracted a
substantial section of the old nationalist leadership and the
support of many 'intellectuals', but not all the old guard deserted Mr. Nkomo. Among his supporters he could boast
James Chikerema, George Nyandoro, Jason Moyo and George
Silundika. As it became apparent that Z.A.N.U. had failed to
recruit majority support, those Africans who had hesitated or
even given doubtful support to Z.A.N.U. drifted back to support Mr. Nkomo. Z.A.P.U. clearly became the party of the
majority, but the split had greatly weakened the nationalist
movement. The few men with experience or ability as leaders

---

[1] The *Daily News* later changed its policy and generally supported Z.A.P.U. and
Nkomo. See Shamuyayira, op. cit., p. 141. Shamuyarira edited the newspaper for
three years, resigning in September 1962.

were divided and they, instead of concentrating their efforts on achieving their main goal of majority rule, spent their energies in fighting each other.

Relations between the R.F. Government and the nationalists were of undisguised hostility. They—the R.F. and the nationalists—represented in its clearest form the conflict of race within Southern Rhodesian politics. The R.F., whose case rested on the belief that Europeans should and must continue to rule, were prepared to use all the powers and authority of the Government to resist those who challenged this basic belief. At first the Government was more severe on the P.C.C. than on Z.A.N.U., for according to government officials Z.A.N.U. initially tried to use peaceful methods but, to defend itself against P.C.C. attacks and to establish a suitably militant image, Z.A.N.U. also began to practise violence. Z.A.N.U. supporters were even accused of the murder of the father of a European family which was attacked in the Eastern Province.[1]

The Government fought and, at least temporarily, defeated the nationalists by means of fierce security legislation. The effectiveness of the R.F. Government's security measures is indisputable. Here the Government moved with a sure step. It was decisive, it had clear objectives in mind and eventually secured a very large degree of order. However, the very effectiveness of the Government's measures raises two major questions. First, whether the means have not defeated the very ends of justice, freedom, and Christian virtue, which it was said they were designed to defend. Second, whether repressive security measures can offer more than a temporary solution to the problems of frustration and discontent which lie at the base of the nationalist movement.[2]

In its election campaign the R.F. had stressed the need for strong security measures, and after assuming office the new Government fulfilled its pledge. It inherited from the U.F.P. Government formidable security legislation, but quickly it added to this. In February 1963 the Government introduced the 'hanging' Bill. This was an amendment to the Law and

[1] Report of Secretary for Law and Order (1964).
[2] The R.F. Government's attempts to provide outlets for Africans will be discussed in the next chapter.

Order (Maintenance) Act which, *inter alia*, laid down a mandatory death sentence for crimes involving the use of fire, explosives, or petrol bombs against a residential building, whether or not the building was occupied at the time of the attack. Death was also mandatory for a similar attack on occupied vehicles or aircraft whether or not the accused knew that people were inside. The penalty for possession of offensive weapons was increased from ten years' to twenty years' imprisonment. The 'hanging' Bill caused a great outcry inside and outside Southern Rhodesia. There were demonstrations outside the Legislative Assembly, Church leaders made a strong protest, and the R.N.P. opposition contested the Bill, clause by clause, but the Government refused to be diverted and the Bill was pushed through.

Further legislation (The Preservation of Constitutional Government Act) aimed at countering attempts to organize a *coup d'état* from outside the country, and an amendment to the Unlawful Organization Act, by which ex-officers of a banned party could be prevented from activity in other organizations) added to the Government's armoury. Also, although the restrictees and detainees were released by the new Government, the pressure against the nationalist leaders was sustained by frequent action through the courts, and by restriction of their political activity. From time to time European opponents of the government were declared prohibited immigrants and deported. In January 1963 Dr. Terence Ranger, a history lecturer at the university college, who had been a nationalist supporter and associated with attempts to break discriminatory practices, was told to leave the country. (The U.F.P. Government had made the decision to declare Ranger a prohibited immigrant before the R.F. came into power.)

Ranger was followed in September 1963 by Mr. Jack Halpern, a South African journalist, and in July 1964 by two American missionaries, Bishop Ralph Dodge and the Reverend Robert Hughes. Each of these deportations raised criticism. For example, when Dr. Ranger was deported the Association of University Teachers issued a statement saying: 'No charge of illegal or subversive activity has been brought against Dr. Ranger in a court of law. Nor have any reasons been given for his deportation.' The Anglican Bishop of Mashonaland attacked laws by which persons could be declared prohibited immigrants without 'accusation, trial or cause given'.[1] The Government ignored the criticisms.

Mr. Clifford Dupont explained the extension of government powers in terms of an international struggle in which Southern Rhodesia was in the front line. He claimed that the original laws had been designed for normal conditions, but now the country faced international revolutionary and subversive powers. He spoke of a force of evil 'creeping gradually towards us down the whole length of Africa. Yesterday it was the Federation, today it is Southern Rhodesia.'[2] On another occasion he told the Legislative Assembly:

Southern Rhodesia today is in the front line; but we are fighting not only our own battle for existence but theirs [i.e. that of America and Britain]. Is it too much to ask even for their sympathy and understanding in this struggle? I do not think I am being melodramatic in stating that small as we are at the present moment in the battle for Africa we are the keystone, and I have no hesitation in saying that if we go the way of Central and East Africa then it is only a question of time before Western civilization also has to go.[3]

The source of the evil, in his view, was Communism, which used the nationalist movement as a tool for its ambitions. Mr. Dupont said it was ironic that democracy, which was considered one of the foundations of Western civilization, could be used by the communists to defeat its own ends. They, the Communists and nationalists, cried for political equality, they claimed all men are equal: 'and in our case that [means] the lowering of the franchise—and so undermine the established order to replace it with their own brand of dictatorship'. Mr. Dupont urged Southern Rhodesian Europeans to fight not only to preserve themselves but Western democracy and Christian standards.

The R.N.P. opposition was ill fitted to oppose the increasing powers of the Government, for the R.F. was only building upon a structure which the U.F.P. had created. The main line of opposition criticism was that the U.F.P. Government had combined the security measures with an attempt to deal with

---

[1] *The Examiner*, February 1963.
[2] *The Rhodesia Herald*, 18 March 1963.
[3] S.R.L.A. Hansard, 13 March 1963, col. 832.

the root cause; the frustration and discrimination which fostered nationalist support; but that this had been abandoned by the R.F. Government. Sir Edgar Whitehead frequently mentioned the problem of unemployment, which led many dissatisfied young men into the nationalist camp. Some opposition members were more cutting than Sir Edgar. Mr. G. R. J. Hackwill asked: 'If our system here is so marvellous, if there is nothing wrong with our own internal system in Southern Rhodesia, why do Southern Rhodesians give this apparently heavy support to the African nationalist movement?'[1] He protested that the Government offered nothing to attract Africans away from nationalism. Early in 1964 Mr. C. Hlabangana told the Government that the additional security measures were a confession of failure. 'You are struggling against Africa; who are you to measure yourself against the strength of Africa? You are struggling against the whole world.'[2] The protests were made, but the R.N.P. opposition was hesitant and timid for, while it opposed the general trend of government policy, it shared the Government's determination to maintain order, if necessary by repressive legislation.

For most of 1963 there was relative calm in Southern Rhodesia, the nationalists were dispirited and disorganized, and the Government strong. However, late in 1963 and increasingly in 1964, disturbances started again. They followed the pattern of the past. Their foundations lay in the frustration and discrimination of a divided society, but particular incidents and grievances set off the chain of events, events which were now complicated by the struggle between the nationalist parties. An example of the way in which a particular grievance became absorbed into the wider struggle was provided by the urban schools. These schools had always been overcrowded, and there had been bottlenecks at various stages, which meant that many children could not complete their education. Until 1965 there was only one African Secondary school in Bulawayo which had places for about 320 children and offered education only to Form III. In 1964 the Director of Housing and Public Amenities wrote: 'The scandal that there should be only one secondary

---

[1] S.R.L.A. Hansard, 17 March 1964, cols. 897–8.
[2] Op. cit., 17 March 1964, col. 923.

school for a population of 160,000 Africans has been commented on more than once in my reports.'[1] Yet the government urban schools had been popular, partly because no fees were charged; it was common for children from rural areas to stay with relatives in town to attend the government school. Naturally this exacerbated the problem of overcrowding. In 1964 the Government decided that, because of rapidly rising education costs, school fees would be charged. For African Primary education the scales ranged between 19s. and 29s. per term. For the poorer African workers this was a substantial sum and naturally there was a strong reaction which was allied to the general dissatisfaction of inadequate school facilities.

As the discontent grew, it was used and stimulated by the nationalists, so that the urban schools, and particularly the Salisbury schools, became the centre of a struggle between the Government and the nationalist movement. The Secretary for Education called 1964 '*gore remtanbudziko*' ('the year of the troubles'). Schools were boycotted, some were burnt down, teachers were assaulted, and their cars burnt. At one stage African school enrolment in Salisbury schools fell from 20,000 to a few hundred. Gangs of young nationalist supporters roamed the townships threatening and attacking those who tried to break the boycott. When two African women social workers tried to negotiate a settlement they were badly beaten. The Government responded by trying to give protection to the schools and teachers and then, at one stage, by closing all Salisbury African schools.

The schools were, however, only one section of the disorders of late 1963 and 1964. Government property was attacked in both urban and rural areas. Fighting and intimidation became rife between the rival nationalist parties, but as in the past the violence was, in the main, contained within the African population.

The Government responded energetically to the disorders. In November 1963, Joshua Nkomo was banned from all meetings for three months and the P.C.C. was prevented from holding meetings for the same period. In February 1964 the Government

---

[1] Director's Report, 1963–4. In 1963 there were 328 children attending the school. By 1965 new government and missionary Secondary schools had been opened, and 917 children in Bulawayo were receiving Secondary education.

abandoned its attempts to work through the courts and resorted to restrictions without trial. One hundred and forty-four men, described by the Director of African Administration in Salisbury, as 'terrorists and hooligans', were rounded up and restricted under the Law and Order (Maintenance) Act, which gave the Minister power to restrict people for ninety days. There were no charges laid, no court case, and there was no right of defence except an appeal to the Minister. The restricted men were sent to a camp (called a 'concentration camp' by the Government's opponents) at Wha Wha. The following month the Government extended its powers again with further amendments to the Law and Order (Maintenance) Act. The Minister's powers of restriction without trial were increased from ninety days to one year, greater powers were introduced to control crowds and processions, the police received increased powers of confiscating, and prison sentences of between five and twenty years were specified for subversive training outside Southern Rhodesia.

As the Government increased its powers so it indulged in a degree of self-deception, for, while it was prepared to use severe legislation to retain order, it was also anxious to demonstrate that Southern Rhodesia was a model for all African states. On 13 March 1964, Mr. Dupont admitted to the Legislative Assembly that: 'conditions in the African townships today are such that life for the majority of the inhabitants who, by nature, everybody will admit are law-abiding, has become almost unbearable'. Yet a minute or two later he said: 'In comparison with many other parts of the world, Europe, Asia, South America and even in the United States of America themselves, I venture to suggest that the situation here today is comparatively a haven of peace.'[1]

The struggle between the R.F. Government and the nationalists continued over the period of the change of Premiership and, if anything, the Government's efforts were intensified after Mr. Smith's appointment. On 16 April 1964, only a few days after Mr. Smith had become Prime Minister, Joshua Nkomo, Joseph Msika, of the P.C.C. executive, and Mr. and Mrs. Josaiah Chinamano of the Highfield Community School, were restricted for one year to a remote area at Gonakudzingwa.

[1] S.R.L.A. Hansard, 13 March 1964, cols. 825 and 826.

They were followed by a steady stream of nationalist leaders until all the leading figures of Z.A.P.U. and Z.A.N.U. were in detention or restriction. Mr. Dupont, explaining Nkomo's restriction, said that in spite of persistent warnings 'there has been a build-up of tension in the larger African townships and in the rural areas and an increase in the number of politically-inspired incidents'. The restriction of Nkomo set off further outbreaks of violence. On 17 April, in the Salisbury townships of Mufakose and Highfields, gangs were out stoning houses, overturning cars, and setting up road blocks. In Bulawayo there were stoning and rioting, which the police broke up with gunfire, killing one man. In both urban and rural areas the number of incidents increased. Mrewa was a particularly bad rural area. In that district between April and June there were, among other cases, 97 cases of arson, 55 of malicious injury to property, and 1,030 cases of intimidation and threatening violence. Five hundred and twenty-two people were brought before the courts, of whom 485 were convicted.[1]

It is impossible to know how much of this violence was organized or inspired by the nationalist leaders, and how much was a direct reaction to the Government's curtailment of nationalist activity. The Government claimed that in Nkomo's case gangs of thugs followed him around causing fighting and disorder. At the time he was restricted he was on a country-wide tour, which had taken him to Fort Victoria where his arrival was said to have signalled the outbreaking of lawlessness, including stoning, breaking into houses, and the stabbing of an African schoolmaster. However, before their restriction the nationalist leaders themselves were showing increasing concern at the pattern of events, in particular the inter-party fighting, and early in the year both the P.C.C. and Z.A.N.U. issued statements condemning violence. Even if the nationalist leaders did condone some of the violence, it took forms and directions which they disliked. It took on a life of its own no longer directed to any specific objectives or with any real purpose other than trying to suppress opposition within the African community or paying off personal scores. It was a struggle of African against African. No one was safe: traders, schoolteachers, politicians were all attacked. Far from being

[1] S.R.L.A. Hansard (Lardner-Burke), 5 August 1964.

'havens of peace', the townships, in particular, became centres of fear and terror. The Director of African Administration in Salisbury wrote: 'This is the worst year on record for violence and breakdown of law and order. However, the violence and intimidation is not continuous but rather spasmodic.'[1] Gangs of youths moved around at night demanding allegiance and funds for their particular cause. A parliamentary committee which was strongly anti-nationalist reported that, if the demands of the youth gangs were not met, 'bands of ruthless thugs known as the "Zhanda" descended to wreak reprisals'. The report continued:

Such was life in Harari and Highfield, and to a lesser extent in the smaller townships around Salisbury. The inhabitants were subjected to mob law; compelled to follow the dictates of mob rule; beaten and molested if they failed to comply; compelled to contribute to the funds that sustained the gangs; and to join in acts of violence; their sons forced to social outrage; their daughters defiled.[2]

Many Africans became disillusioned with the sterility of the violence and the fear in which they and their families spent their lives. The African newspaper, *The Daily News*, carried an increasing number of protest letters. On 6 August Michael Makaya wrote: 'Terror in the African townships is no longer strange but an accepted order of the day.' On 10 August Tadius Mutongwizo wrote:

Men are stoned and set alight, mostly for no other reason than political differences that seem more petty and unreal as the weeks go on. Life has become hell in Rhodesia for the thousands of decent law-abiding citizens who live in the townships. It is true that the whole country and the African people especially are going through a time of intense frustration. It is true that poverty, cold, and hunger lead to bitterness and that bitterness leads to wickedness and crime. It is true that restricting leaders to camps in the back of beyond gives the people who worship these leaders a feeling of hopelessness. All this can be said. But nothing excuses the violence and hatred that has grown up between Africans in recent months.

On 20 August, H. Mkhuhlane wrote: 'Life in the townships has now become a Hell to us. Fear is ruling our lives because

[1] Director's Report, 1963–4.
[2] Report of Select Committee on Political Boycott, 3 February 1966, L.A.S.C., 8–65.

one does not know who is the next man to be attacked.' A similar protest at the futility of it all was made by A. C. Majongwe in the Legislative Assembly.[1]

On 26 August the Government banned the two main African parties, declared a state of emergency in Highfields, and banned *The Daily News*. Announcing the action Mr. D. W. Lardner-Burke, who had replaced Mr. Dupont as Minister of Justice and Law and Order,[2] said: 'Both the People's Caretaker Council and the Zimbabwe African National Union made strenuous attempts to promote violence in order to create the impression of an explosive situation in this country prior to and during the recent [Commonwealth] Prime Ministers' Conference.' He said that 'alleged grievances such as increased dipping fees, school fees and rents have been used as instruments to promote violence', but 'the Government is determined to take all steps to maintain law and order. We are not going to allow rank subversion to take place under our very noses when a remedy is available'. He confirmed that the Government would respect any party which kept within the law but stated that the nationalist parties had refused to do so. The nationalists did not represent the majority of the African people in the country, and they 'have no means of advancing their cause except by violence and the threat of violence'. He admitted that there were probably 70,000 to 80,000 people living in Highfields, which had been designed to accommodate 45,000 and that 'the unemployment and overcrowding are fully exploited by nationalist elements'. The Government counter to this had been to throw a cordon 'around the township by the police and the army and thugs and hooligans are being rounded up and will after screening by the police, be moved to detention centres'.[3]

The R.N.P. opposition did not challenge the banning of the nationalist parties and the declaration of emergency in Highfields, but there were some dissenting voices in the House. Mr. J. M. Gondo said that the 'Government was merely treating the problem from the top and not seeking to find out what the

---

[1] S.R.L.A. Hansard, 5 August 1964, cols. 375–6.
[2] Mr. Dupont retained his position as Deputy Prime Minister and became Minister of External Affairs.
[3] S.R.L.A. Hansard, 26 August 1964, cols. 1258–62.

real causes are and then deal with the problem from its root cause'.[1] Ahrn Palley asked how the Minister intended to deal with the 30,000 excess people who lived in Highfield. The Minister could put some in detention camps but not all of them. 'The remainder of this enormous number of people will', said Palley, 'be more or less directed and deposited into the Tribal Trust areas on the basis that what is out of sight is out of mind. And the Government has been criminally neglectful in avoiding the necessary attention to the Tribal Trust areas to make these places capable and fit to deal with and hold the large number of African people who are resident there.'[2]

The banning of the newspaper, *The Daily News*, met much stronger opposition from the R.N.P. The Government's action was defended by Lardner-Burke, who said that the country was fighting a psychological war against external and internal subversion but 'the Government is fully aware of its responsibilities to the electorate and must therefore insist that the freedom and the privileges normally accorded to the Press are inseparable from responsibility'. He accused *The Daily News* of being a nationalist propaganda weapon, with an editorial policy 'designed deliberately to promote dissatisfaction and hostility towards the Europeans in the minds of a largely unsophisticated reading public'. He said that the paper had played upon sensationalism, created a Nkomo personality cult, and had made false accusations against the Government that 'have followed the standard pattern and can only be considered as part of well-tried tactics for loosening the bonds of society and creating a state of revolution'.[3] For the R.N.P., J. R. Nicholson, after dealing with *The Daily News*' editorial policy, which he said had opposed violence, had spoken out against U.D.I. and had supported majority rule, concluded that the ban had been imposed not for a breach of law but because of the paper's 'advocacy of support for moving towards African majority rule'. P. H. J. Chanetsa declared that 'this is a deliberate move by Government to suppress African opinion in the event of the forthcoming declaration of independence'.

---

[1] Op. cit., 26 August 1964, col. 1314.
[2] Op. cit., 26 August 1964, col. 1329.
[3] Op. cit., 26 August 1964, cols. 1278–85.

By the end of 1964 the R.F. Government had largely suppressed the nationalist movement. The parties were banned, political meetings were severely curtailed, the leaders were in detention or restriction without trial for periods up to five years. No new outstanding leaders emerged, partly because the Government was quick to restrict any potential leaders, and also because schoolteachers were prohibited from taking part in any political activities and teaching was the main outlet for educated Africans. Relative peace and calm returned to the African townships, and overt signs of nationalism largely disappeared. The government security forces were strong and well organized.

During most of 1965 nationalist activity was confined to the party organizations in exile with Lusaka in Zambia as the main centre. There both Z.A.P.U. and Z.A.N.U. had offices, from which poured out a stream of news, propaganda, and ideas, much of which was wild and violent in its nature. During the final negotiations before U.D.I., and in the weeks immediately following, there were some signs of African opposition to the Government's actions. This revealed itself in crop-slashing, damage to property and, more openly, in the great crowd singing nationalist songs which greeted Mr. Harold Wilson at Salisbury airport. However, these actions appear to have been individual and spontaneous, and not centrally organized. Direct action by the nationalist parties has centred on smuggling saboteurs—young Africans trained in Ghana or China or Russia—into the country. Many of these young men have been arrested, but in April and May 1966 at least one Z.A.N.U.-backed band was at large. The police clashed with this band near Sinoia, killing seven of the saboteurs, but some escaped and were later held responsible for the murder of a European married couple on a farm near Hartley.

The tragedy of the nationalist movement in Southern Rhodesia is not that it has lacked a justifiable cause, not that it has lacked popular appeal or numerical strength, but that it has been badly led. The leaders have misjudged the political circumstances; by refusing to work for reform within the Constitution they were open to extreme pressure from the constitutional government and had not the strength to combat this pressure. Too easily they have accepted violence as a legitimate means of action, violence which has usually been directed against fellow-Africans; and finally they have quarrelled bitterly among themselves. The degree of intransigence and inflexibility shown by the nationalist leaders may be the stuff from which martyrs are made, but martyrs do not make good politicians.

Even in the long weeks of restriction the leaders have refused to abandon publicly their intransigence and internecine strife. Z.A.N.U. leaders have made conciliatory gestures to the Z.A.P.U./P.C.C. leaders, but the terms have been unacceptable.[1] Also it is said that privately Joshua Nkomo and Ndabaningingi Sithole are willing to consider a compromise constitutional solution, but are afraid to state this publicly because the rival party would brand whoever compromised as a stooge of the Government. There was, however, no indication of willingness to compromise when Lady Judith Listowel visited Joshua Nkomo in restriction in mid-1965. He told her: 'Power must be handed over to us, who represent the majority of the people. As Smith and his men will not do this, we expect the British Government to send troops to compel them to do by us what is right and proper.' Mr. Nkomo rejected any suggestion that the nationalists had been mistaken in not trying to work within the 1961 Constitution. Judith Listowel concluded: 'Apparently nothing short of becoming Prime Minister of Rhodesia immediately would do, even if it meant armed conflict, even if armed conflict were to escalate to war', and she reported that in a three-hour conversation, 'he had not made a single constructive statement, he was unwilling to compromise on any point'.[2] Harold Wilson met the same intransigence and refusal to compromise either between themselves or with the Government when he met the Z.A.P.U. and Z.A.N.U. leaders in October 1965.

The suppression of Nationalist violence and disorder is an achievement in which the R.F. Government takes great pride. Obviously there is some justification for this, as any government must aim at preserving order. But in Rhodesia there has been a heavy price to pay. The price has been a substantial loss

---

[1] Shamuyarira, op. cit., p. 190.
[2] 'Rhodesia; Both Ends against the Middle', *The Listener*, 15 July 1965.

of individual freedom. There has been an easy, a frightening logic behind the growth of government and police powers. Both under the U.F.P. and the R.F., the government leaders have been convinced that their policies have been based upon indisputable standards of justice and honesty. They have followed policies which they have claimed would in the long term give equal opportunities to all individuals, regardless of race, in a society based upon merit. But they have seen these policies challenged by opponents who, backed by a large section of the population, have refused to believe or accept these claims. Their nationalist opponents have fought to change the structure of power, to replace white minority control by black majority government, as the only way of satisfying African aspirations, economic and social as well as political. In meeting this challenge the Government has taken unto itself fiercer and fiercer powers. The Government spokesmen have argued that exceptional circumstances have called for exceptional powers, that they have acted for the good of all, for the preservation of the society.

Against these arguments must be balanced the erosion of individual rights. Restriction and detention without trial, bans on public meetings, mandatory sentences, censorship of all publications including the Press, police searches, and seizure of private property, have all become features of Rhodesian life. This has come about partly from the hardening of European attitudes following nationalist violence and partly from sheer necessity if Europeans are to retain their minority control. Defences of the Government's actions have usually been clothed in general terms, in talk of saving the country from chaos, of countering external subversion, of the need for order to ensure economic development. There is perhaps substance in these points, but they obscure the main issue that there has developed a power struggle in Rhodesia between a black and a white nationalism. Because the African nationalists have refused to work within the Constitution, the struggle has taken place outside the Legislative Assembly. The African movement has used such weapons as civil disobedience, boycotts, international pressure, violence, and destruction. The white movement has replied by using the powers of the Government which it controls.

A defence of the powers already exercised by the Government and a plea for an extension of these powers was contained in the report of a Select Committee on political boycotts.[1] The committee, which investigated boycotts in 1963 and 1964 of firms and shops which were said to have refused to support the African nationalists, did not confine itself to boycotts but ranged over the wider field of the powers which a government could justifiably use to retain order. The committee, assuming that the nationalist supporters who caused trouble were only a small section of the African population, dealt with the problem of the peace of the majority being disturbed by a minority. It concluded that: 'If the only methods by which this [the achievement of order] can be done are methods which would not be found in a normal peaceful society the Select Committee should not be unduly disturbed.' The committee accepted that, if its recommendations were implemented, 'it is inevitable that some innocent citizens will be inconvenienced and unjustly treated', but the objective was to control the militant minority without losing all individual rights. The report continued: 'Any steps which the Select Committee may recommend will inevitably in some degree strengthen the arbitrary power of the Government. If the Select Committee finds it necessary to make some such recommendation it should not feel any sense of shame in doing so.'

After such an introduction it was hardly surprising that the committee recommended severe action and legislation. Among the recommendations the committee said that in cases of intimidation when the normal laws were insufficient, 'the persons responsible should be unhesitatingly removed from that locality at the discretion of the Minister of Law and Order— such persons should be held *incommunicado* from the outside world, thus preventing them from continuing their nefarious activities'; and 'as a corollary regard for the rights of the individual must not be allowed to outweigh the suffering that the

---

[1] L.A.S.C. 8–65. The committee originally contained R.F. and R.N.P. members, but after the R.N.P. defeat the committee's work was continued by the three R.F. members—J. A. Newington (Chairman), Colonel G. H. Hartley, and J. H. Howman (who became Minister of Information). In thirteen of the last sixteen meetings only Newington and Hartley attended. The committee's report was published after U.D.I.

vast majority must endure if there is delay in taking appropriate action'. The committee thought that in the case of 'irreconcilable fanatics', after two periods of restriction, they should lose property and tenancy rights and when released not be allowed to return to the township from which they were originally removed. The committee then made revolutionary suggestions for amendments to the rules of procedure and evidence in cases of intimidation, boycotts, and encouraging violence. The recommendations were based upon their conclusion that the existing rules of evidence and procedure were aiding 'the guilty', and therefore 'consideration should be given to placing the full burden of proof of innocence on the defence, on the grounds that such offences endanger the security of the state'. They also suggested that in cases of violence it should be permissible to conceal the identity of witnesses to save them from intimidation, 'and that consideration be given to the admission of hearsay evidence in cases of this nature'.

The Government is not committed in any way to accepting the recommendations of the committee, but the report is important in that it reflects the thinking of a group of R.F. Members of Parliament including a Minister, and is a defence of the Government's extensive powers.

Similar thinking is found in many Government reports and statements. For example, in his 1965 report the Secretary for Law and Order, appealing for powers of preventive detention,[1] wrote:

When a country is fighting for its existence against subversive forces which take every advantage of the law to defend themselves, but at the same time employ unlawful means to attain their political ends, it means that a situation is being created in which democracy is being used to defeat itself and the administration of justice is in fact being abused.

Perhaps the ablest case for the Government's repressive and restrictive powers was made in the debate on the Select Committee's report by Mr. Howman, who said that the duty of the Government is:

to maintain the conditions under which and in which the law may exist and hold sway. The critics of this Government seem to believe

[1] For the distinction between 'restriction' and 'detention', see Chapter III, p. 55, n. 1.

that the rule of law itself preserves and maintains those conditions, but, as we have shown in this report [the Select Committee on Boycotts], the lawless few can destroy the whole fabric of government and with it the very basis upon which the rule of law is founded. I think all of us who have held responsibility in the last year or three know the extraordinarily fine balance between liberty on the one hand and order on the other. We all know that order without liberty can lead to slavery, but we equally know that liberty without order becomes licence and anarchy.[1]

Against this the African nationalists would argue that Mr. Howman's 'rule of law' is a rule of laws made by white men to preserve white control.

As the powers of the executive have increased, so those of the judiciary have been restricted. The courts have retained high standards of objectivity, but have been circumscribed by the laws they administer.

When Richard Mapolisa, who had been a party to an unsuccessful arson attempt (in which no one was hurt and in which Mapolisa had not thrown the bomb), was convicted under the mandatory hanging law, the Judge said: 'The legislature has seen fit to take away from the court any discretion in a case such as at present. I am therefore obliged to pass the death sentence.'[2] Other examples of the judiciary upholding its standards, but the executive having its way, have concerned restriction and detention orders. In 1964 the nationalist leaders were restricted to two areas, Wha Wha and Gonakudzingwa. The areas surrounding the restriction centres were declared protected areas under the Protected Places and Areas Act, by which entry was controlled and restricted. The nationalists contested the terms of their restriction and Mr. Justice Young in the High Court found that neither Wha Wha (five acres) nor Gonakudzingwa (110 acres) were 'areas' within the meaning of the Law and Order (Maintenance) Act, for within the terms of the Act a restrictee was entitled to all such freedoms as the residents of the area and in particular 'economic liberty as a worker'. The restriction areas did not, in the judge's opinion, allow this exercise of personal freedom. The Government

---

[1] S.R.L.A. Hansard, 25 February 1966, col. 1043.
[2] *The Examiner*, October 1963.

appealed against the judgment, but the Appellate Division of the High Court, sitting under Sir Hugh Beadle, not only upheld the original ruling but further found that it was illegal to restrict a person in a protected area, as this legislation had been intended to guard strategic and vital areas, not to confine individuals. The appellate court found that two separate Acts were being wrongly used to achieve a result which neither of the Acts alone had been designed to achieve. After the appellate court's decision had been given on 13 August 1964, the restrictees were released, but immediately the great majority of them were re-arrested under new restriction orders. This time they were sent to an extended, 400-square-mile version of the Gonakudzingwa restriction area in which, explained Mr. Lardner-Burke, 'some Africans have their homes . . . and there is a trading store. The restrictees will, if they so desire, be allocated land on which to build their homes and cultivate crops'.[1] It was most unlikely that any restrictee would choose to build his home at Gonakudzingwa, for it is a hot, desolate, inhospitable place in the far south-east of Rhodesia, against the Mozambique border.

In November 1964 the Appellate Division of the High Court ruled that the detention without trial of Mr. Nkomo and sixteen other nationalists was unlawful. It was held that the Preventive Detention (Temporary Provisions) Act under which they were held was inconsistent with the Constitution's Declaration of Rights.[2] Mr. Nkomo and his fellows were therefore released from prison but returned to restriction. However, in 1965 states of emergency were declared within the restriction areas and under the terms of the emergency regulations individuals can be detained without trial. A few days before U.D.I. a country-wide state of emergency was declared, and under this cover the main nationalist leaders were detained in prison.

The R.F. Government has said that the steps it has taken are 'for the preservation of justice, civilization and Christianity',[3] but the Europeans of Rhodesia enjoy no monopoly nor even a

---

[1] S.R.L.A. Hansard, 13 August 1964, col. 712.
[2] Palley, op. cit., pp. 446–7. For the distinction between 'restriction' and 'detention', see Chapter III, p. 55, n. 1.
[3] Mr. Smith's independence broadcast, 11 November 1965.

disproportionate share of Christian virtue or superior moral standards. They do, however, have a Government which they ardently support and which is committed to defending their economic and social order. In a nation which is deeply divided into two racial camps the R.F. are committed to defending the existing white predominance. Opposed to the Government is an African nationalist movement which aims to replace minority European control by African majority rule. The R.F. Government, like other governments which have faced large, popular, internal revolutionary movements; like Ghana under Nkrumah, South Africa under Malan and Verwoerd, or Hungary under Matayas Rakosi; has defended itself by restrictive and repressive laws, by asserting that the rights of 'the State' are superior to those of the individual, by proclaiming that power must be concentrated in a few 'safe' hands. The judgement which all Rhodesians have to make is not whether the R.F. is defending a superior moral order, but whether a particular form of government, a particular economic and social order which the R.F. represents, should be preserved.

CHAPTER X

The Rhodesian Front and the Administration of Africans

Communication and contact between the central Government and Africans was a problem which the R.F. Government inherited from its U.F.P. predecessor. It was however an even greater problem for the R.F. because, as a virtually exclusive white party committed to defending Europeans' rights, it had no contact with Africans via party channels.

The R.F. relations with Africans were coloured by the overall commitment of the party to retain the existing social structure. A halt was called to the changes initiated in the U.F.P. 'partnership' policy. In mid-1963 the Director of African Administration in Salisbury wrote: 'There are already signs that a slowing-down process will replace the policies of non-racialism espoused by the previous Government and the re-establishment and preservation of "separate" facilities for the two races appears to be evident'.[1] The signs of change were revealed over a wide area. African schools for the children of servants and employees in white areas were closed down, and the children were forced to abandon their education or seek it in the African townships, often miles away. The civil service remained non-racial, but the Government placed 'emphasis on the essential factor that there will be no lowering in standards of qualification or of conduct'.[2] In practice, this meant that emphasis on years of service and experience was retained so that at best Africans could not expect to fill top administrative posts for many years, while in some branches, such as district administration, the experiment of introducing Africans was abandoned. When Sir Edgar Whitehead asked the Legislative

[1] Director's Report, 1 July 1962–30 June 1963.
[2] Governor's speech, S.R.L.A. Hansard, 12 February 1963.

Assembly to eradicate racial discrimination against African Members of Parliament, 'with particular reference to his place of abode and his entry into any premises licensed to serve the general public',[1] Mr. D. R. Lardner-Burke said it was the 'thin end of the wedge' and Mr. Smith rejected it on behalf of the Government.

The clearest indication of change came in relation to land, where the new Government implemented its election promises to retain the existing racial land division. In March 1963 Lord Graham announced that the Government would not recommend any further transfer of European land to the 'unreserved' category (i.e. purchasable by people of any race). The new Government said that it was prepared to provide small, separate, urban areas in which people who chose to live in a mixed community could stay, but otherwise the Land Apportionment Act was to stand.[2] The Government argued that racial discrimination in land-holding was already embodied in the Constitution, by the entrenchment of the African Tribal Trust Lands, and therefore it was illogical to ask for the repeal of the Land Apportionment Act on discriminatory grounds. For the opposition, Whitehead replied that the division recognized in the Constitution was between those who lived in a communal society in the Tribal Trust Lands, and the remainder who lived in an individualistic economy. 'The remainder', so Sir Edgar argued, included people of all races and therefore all races should have freedom to live, and to purchase land and property wherever they wanted.

A heated dispute over land took place in March 1964 when Whitehead introduced a motion to repeal the Land Apportionment Act. Sir Edgar's action followed an adverse report on the Act by the Constitutional Council, the watchdog of discriminatory legislation. In its report the Council said that the Act was inconsistent with the Declaration of Rights, for it 'is the embodiment of racial discrimination and . . . in express terms and with penal sanctions enforces it'.[3] In a bitter debate the R.F. back-bencher Colonel Hartley said:

[1] S.R.L.A. Hansard, 20 February 1963.

[2] In practice only one residential area, Westwood, which is adjacent to an African township has been designated for multiracial living, and now no Europeans live there (Palley, op. cit., p. 638).

[3] The R.F. Government's attitude to the Constitutional Council's report on the

My own feelings in regard to the report of the Council is that it is howling indictment of African failures and inability to stand on their own feet. It is a pathetic pandering to complexes and emotionalism which lends support to those who suffer from the innate fixation that to force their way into the society of people who prefer to keep themselves to themselves will give them a status which they cannot achieve in any other way.[1]

Mr. Chigogo of the R.N.P. countered by saying that he could understand why his fellow-Africans followed the nationalists. It was because of discrimination and frustration which 'has gone so far and is so deep that these people have found only one thing—that this land is their God-given inheritance and therefore they must take it back . . . and I do believe that is the right course—is to take their own God-given property back'.[2] He told those who thought of themselves as Europeans and not Africans to 'go back to Europe'. Cabinet Ministers confirmed the Government's opposition to any change in their land policy. Lord Graham said: 'The coloured man all over the world seems to be chasing a chimera of his own imagination. The magnitude of the mental dragon is accentuated by the common use, unfortunately, of the word "prejudice" of one group for another when, generally speaking, it is in reality no more than preference of each group for its own kind.'[3] In an earlier debate Mr. Howman had declared that the Land Apportionment Act 'remains so long as it is necessary in so far as the Europeans are concerned; so long as violent nationalism aims at elimination of the European, so long as that kind of thinking dominates the African thinking, so long will this legislation be necessary'.[4]

The decision to retain the Land Apportionment Act implied that, although the races would continue to work together, they would live in separate areas and therefore could develop and be governed in distinct ways. This was accepted by William

---

Land Apportionment Act was characteristic of its general attitude to the Council. It would note Council reports but it was not prepared to take any action which threatened the existing social order. The watchdog was lively but had no teeth.

[1] S.R.L.A. Hansard, 4 March 1964, col. 341.
[2] Op. cit., 4 March 1964, col. 347.
[3] Op. cit., 10 March 1964, cols. 566–7.
[4] Op. cit., 2 October 1963, col. 2058.

Harper, who became Minister of Internal Affairs after Howman's resignation. Mr. Harper, whether in opposition or in government, had consistently maintained that the races must be allowed to develop separately according to an evolutionary process. He affirmed that 'so long as there is a Land Apportionment Act there will be a tendency that Africans will run their part of the country and the Europeans substantially run their part'.[1]

The R.F. Government has placed great emphasis on 'community development'. This policy had been introduced by the U.F.P. Government, but the R.F. reorganized it and laid much greater emphasis on it. The R.F. Government affirmed that community development was not confined to one race or to any particular areas but decided that initially concentration would be centred on the African rural areas.

'Community Development' is not a precise or easily defined policy. In Southern Rhodesia there has been considerable confusion even among Ministers about whether it included local government or whether local government was quite separate. The policy cannot therefore be measured in absolute or precise terms. The organization of a local community to satisfy what, in the policy jargon, is called 'its felt needs', is a gradual process which need not find expression in any formal organization. But the R.F. Government has placed such great importance on the policy that an examination of its implications will be attempted.

The very enthusiasm with which community development has been pursued has had its dangers. Some R.F. supporters have seen it as a cure for all ills, a magic formula by which Africans can develop without challenging the existing social structure. In 1963 Professor J. F. V. Phillips, who had been the Government's adviser on community development, warned of this danger. He explained that to succeed community development had to be largely spontaneous, but because too much had been expected of it there had been too much planning and a temptation to impose rather than help or advise. Community development, he wrote, 'could be nullified by direct administrative means and party policies and slogans', and advised that the Government should talk about it less and avoid the 'mystique'

[1] Op. cit., 6 October 1964, col. 1291.

approach. Community development, he said, could not solve all problems and the greatest danger was a growing loss of faith and confidence among Africans.[1] Similar comments came from the Director of Housing and Amenities in Bulawayo, who wrote in his 1963 Report that the policy had been practised in the past with some success but that now 'unfortunately it has become something of a political philosophy instead of simply a sensible administrative attitude and so has become suspect in the very circles [in which] it should have been welcomed'.[2]

Community development became an issue early in the R.F. Government's life when John Howman was Minister of Internal Affairs and Local Government.[3] In Mr. Howman's words, community development meant . . . 'that the people of each local community are given responsibility for their own development in specific areas, a responsibility which can only be discharged through communal organization formally or informally for democratic planning and action'. There are different cultures, but 'it is not for Government to determine what emergent cultures will be. Only the people can decide this'. The Minister explained that 'community development is political development and I do not mean party political development . . . One of the advantages of the policy, the creation of local viable communities, the conferment of responsibility, is that with the development you get the local government development and that community and local government development are the two sides of the self-same coin'. It is 'an inculcation within the people of an understanding of what is local government at local levels and responsibility at that level . . . a philosophy of politics, of people of varying cultures, kinds, creeds, and colours living together in the national boundaries, having respect for one another and living together in harmony and community of purpose.'[4]

The early ministerial statements revealed a developed theory

---

[1] *The Examiner*, October 1963.

[2] Director's Report, 1962–3.

[3] Roughly, the Ministry of Internal Affairs is responsible for the administration of rural African areas, while local government looks after both the African and European areas of the towns. Local government in European rural areas is not highly developed. It consists of bodies providing individual services, such as road boards and conservation boards.

[4] S.R.L.A. Hansard, 22 August 1963, cols. 1878–9 and col. 1880.

of community development, but there was, from the beginning, the major difficulty of understanding what this theory implied in practice. Howman was questioned closely on this in a long Committee of Supply debate in August 1963 and under pressure he admitted that the practical implications of the policy were as yet ill-defined and little understood. He said that outside the Tribal Trust lands 'we lack an awful lot of information and an awful lot of study and quite frankly I am not now in a position to express clearly, exactly how we see the pattern going'.[1] Later he further explained that, even in the Tribal Trust Lands, the Councils established by the U.F.P. Government were 'unfortunately not anchored to the communities to which they should have been . . . which was the tragedy of that administration', and said of relations between chiefs and councils: 'I am not entirely certain in my own mind what is the best attitude to adopt.'[2] He called it 'a fascinating problem'.

The imprecision of the Government's plans was criticized both by the R.N.P. opposition and by the independent Dr. Ahrn Palley, who said: 'The Government may have certain philosophies for community development but they have in fact no plans at all.' There was evidence to support Palley's comment in both the African rural and urban areas. The annual report of the Secretary for Internal Affairs called 1963 'a most frustrating year'. He complained of lack of co-operation from other departments because a view had emerged 'that community development was some strange obsession of the Ministry of Internal Affairs which it must tolerantly be permitted to get on with provided other ministers were not concerned or unduly molested, that was the dominant element in the frustration of the year'.

Early indecision was understandable but the indecision continued. In October 1964 Mr. Harper, who had succeeded Howman, said: 'I think, looking back over the last twenty months or so, in the matter of community development that community development in itself has, in fact, benefited from what I call a lull.'[3] He explained that two important pieces of legislation—a new Local Councils' Bill and a Tribal Trust

---

[1] Op. cit., 22 August 1963, col. 1947.
[2] Op. cit., 22 August 1963, col. 1937.
[3] Op. cit., 6 October 1964, col. 1252.

Land Bill—had been under consideration for some time and were then being drafted. Neither Bill had appeared when U.D.I. was declared. In his report for 1964 the Secretary for Internal Affairs wrote: 'Despite some progress having been made there is still an urgent need for clear-cut decisions by Government on many matters involving the implementation of its policy of community development and local government.' When in 1965 the Prime Minister issued a White Paper on community development it was still felt necessary to explain what community development was about and to urge ministries to co-operate. The White Paper stated: 'Each ministry must now address itself to the tasks of defining its role in relation to community development, of planning the necessary changes in its organization, of ensuring co-ordination of its efforts with those of all other ministries and arranging that its officers are fully instructed in the new approach.'[1] A Cabinet co-ordinating committee was to be established (an earlier co-ordinating committee had been set up in Field's time but had become defunct), which would ensure that the policy was given high priority by all Government departments. At a local level it was affirmed that:

The district commissioner, as the representative of Government in his district, is responsible, as a whole, for all ministries in so far as they impinge on the local communities. All ministries share in the process of community development—for it includes better productivity, economic growth, better health of man and beast, better education, conservation of the soil as well as conservation of the community in its capacity for collective action and control—but the district commissioner is the guardian of the process of community development and is charged with the task of fostering and supporting local government.

In African rural areas officials have been busy 'identifying' and 'defining' communities, the district commissioners have been busy encouraging and co-ordinating the policy, and community advisers have been appointed. These advisers:

have no specific policy to get across, no programme to promote, but are simply there to find out what the people *want*, within the law,

---

[1] *Local Government and Community Development*, C.S.R. 44–1965, Salisbury, Government Printer.

and help them to achieve their aspirations within the 'local good' by local organization, by their own programme planning, their own order of priorities, and with the maximum reliance on their own resources, supplemented by assistance from outside the community.[1]

In the tribal lands a major task of the government officials has been to try to improve the standard and output of African agriculture, but progress in moving away from a largely subsistence economy has been slow. The R.F. Government has accepted that the already moribund African Land Husbandry Act had to be abandoned. In his 1964 report the Secretary for Internal Affairs wrote: 'Further implementation of the African Land Husbandry Act, in so far as allocation of land is concerned, has been suspended.' The crucial power of land allocation was returned to the chiefs, thereby confirming the tribal structure of land-holding.

Local government, if not an integral part of community development, is closely related to it and its development provides one measure of the Government's aims and achievements. Like the U.F.P. before them, the R.F. have relied upon local councils and chiefs, but the emphasis has changed sharply, for the chiefs have clearly become the main foundation of the Government's policy. However, local councils have not been neglected and their powers and functions have been increased. In 1964 it was decided to transfer responsibility for Primary education to local councils and, despite tardiness in implementing the decision, it could be of great significance in increasing interest and vitality in the councils. There are other responsibilities, such as cattle-dipping, road maintenance, forest work, medical dispensaries, and provision of water supplies, which have been transferred to some, but by no means all, councils.

Within the councils Africans have been encouraged to accept more responsibility. At the end of 1963 only nine councils had African chairmen, but a year later there were twenty-five.[2]

---

[1] White Paper C.S.R. 44, 1965, para. 31.

[2] In councils with an African chairman, the District Commissioner retained the office of President of the Council with the right to attend and speak at all meetings in an advisory capacity. The personality of the D.C. largely dictates whether he does advise or whether he tries to dictate.

Against these increases of power and responsibility have to be balanced the old problems of paternalism, the complete ineffectiveness of some councils, and clashes of interest between the needs and desires of rural Africans and the policies of the central Government. For example, early in 1964 women in the Tanda tribal area refused to dip their cattle as a protest against the lack of government services (schools, roads etc.). Three hundred women were arrested and fined an average of £10 each. Some refused to pay and instead served twenty-two days in prison.[1] I attended a meeting of the Mondoro Council at which there was a dispute over the Council's request to take over road works. As the central Government refused to give the Council the degree of control it wanted, the Council decided that it would refuse responsibility for any road works.

The most striking of the old problems also remains: the lack of finance. In 1964 the total revenue collected by all councils was only £164,387, to which was added £15,679 in Government grants. The Secretary for Internal Affairs complained that . . . 'the need for some clearcut decisions on the financial support to be given to local government is now most urgent. Councils cannot be expected to assume additional responsibilities without knowing how they can finance them.'[2] The Government has taken steps to improve the situation. A review of community development published in 1966 stated that:

In the current financial year, the Government will pay to councils approximately twice as much in salary, block, percentage and *ad hoc* grants as in 1965. Apart from the normal rate system, councils are allowed to take over powers of taxation on dogs, bicycles and receive a proportion of the amounts paid in all motor vehicle licences in respect of vehicles in the council area. Subject to certain provisions [the collection of a set percentage of tax], persons living in council areas may be exempted from personal tax, enabling the council to take advantage of the money which is thus freed for the improvement of the area.[3]

Clearly these steps will help many councils, but the problem of devising efficient means of collecting council rates remains,

[1] *The Examiner*, May 1964.
[2] Report of Secretary for Internal Affairs (1964), p. 28.
[3] Community Development Review, Salisbury, Government Printer, Vol. 1, No. 1, January–March 1966.

16

as does the even more basic problem that the councils represent wretchedly poor communities whose ability to finance services is severely restricted.

One thing above all others stands out in the R.F.'s policy of African administration. This is the increase in the powers, prestige, and rewards of the chiefs. In 1963 Mr. Howman, as Minister of Internal Affairs, declared that: 'Our whole purpose is to try to restore the power and authority of the chiefs [as] the head of the community in matters religious or spiritual and judicial and in the allocation of land.'[1] But while Mr. Howman's statement implied enhanced importance for the chief's traditional role, it became increasingly clear that the Government intended to extend chiefs' powers even further than their traditional claims. Their administrative and advisory functions were extended, and firm suggestions were made to have direct representation of chiefs in the Legislative Assembly. In July 1965 Mr. Harper said that the Government had been unable to extend the chiefs' powers as far as they had wanted because of the restrictions in the Constitution, but that the chiefs' authority over the allocation and use of land had been restored, and the Government had extended their powers 'in the administrative field where chiefs have been encouraged to exercise their influence and power in a much wider field than ever before, and they have been provided with special chiefs' messengers to assist them'. Also, said Mr. Harper, chiefs had been appointed to important councils and boards, such as the Constitutional Council, and the Chiefs' Council had been used as a government advisory body.[2]

In recognizing the chiefs as the leaders of the African people, in recognizing them as the main representative organ of African opinion and a channel for the implementation of government policy, the R.F. Government has been severely criticized both inside and outside Southern Rhodesia. The controversy reached a crisis with the Domboshawa *indaba* of October 1964 when the chiefs were called together to represent African opinion on independence.

In explaining why the *indaba* was called, the Government claimed that, as most Africans still live in a communal, tribal

[1] S.R.L.A. Hansard, 29 August 1963, cols. 185–6.
[2] Op. Cit., 23 July 1965, col. 1341.

community, it would be 'unrealistic to approach the communal African in the same manner as . . . the individualistic European'.[1] It was said that, as the chiefs have time-honoured methods of sounding opinion, they can speak out not only for themselves but all Africans. The chiefs shared this belief. At the *indaba*, one chief said :

> According to our custom it is not permissible for such an important matter [independence] to be discussed by youngsters [lesser men] . . . we are the rightful people who should discuss the important matters in connection with this land . . . Many people say that it is not proper that we, the tribal leaders, should become involved in politics, but we always had the power to govern. These people who have so much to say are the youngsters.[2]

Another chief said : 'I would say that we represent both the Africans who are on the voters' roll as well as those who are not, because they come under our jurisdiction. Even the ones on the voters' roll come under us because when they are sick, hungry, or in trouble and want land, who do they come to? We the chiefs.'[3] Later, after suggesting that the British Government might invite chiefs and African politicians to negotiate together, he said : 'If they expect us to sit at the same conference table as these upstart children of ours, we will dismiss these children because it is not our custom to discuss matters of importance with minors.'[4]

Undoubtedly the chiefs play an important role in the tribal life of Southern Rhodesia. They have important traditional powers, they are a focus of tribal loyalty, and they have religious functions. But, even accepting this, there are still grave doubts as to whether the chiefs can be regarded as a representative voice on such issues as independence, or can be an effective and efficient executive of government policy. The first doubt regards the nature of the chiefs' office. It is an hereditary office based upon a traditional structure, but African society, while retaining aspects of the past, has undergone enormous changes during the twentieth century. Can men who base their authority on a social structure, which largely ignores these changes,

---

[1] *The Domboshawa Indaba*, Salisbury, Government Printer, 1965, p. 34.
[2] Op. cit., p. 19.
[3] Op. cit., p. 27.
[4] Op. cit., p. 29.

claim to reflect African opinion on contemporary, as opposed to traditional, problems? A group of anthropologists and sociologists from the University College of Rhodesia and Nyasaland thought not. With specific reference to the independence issue they commented:

In Southern Rhodesia Africans are no longer organized solely on the basis of a tribal system. Therefore African opinion on the national issue of independence cannot be tested within the framework of this system. Approximately half of the adult men in the population live and work outside the tribal areas at any one time.[1]

Before government policy became so orientated to support of the chiefs the same doubts had been expressed by an officer in the Department of Native Affairs. He said:

We have been, and still are, so busy transforming African society on the land that it is absurd to think we can insulate and preserve the one feature of chieftainship while everything else moves on. It is equally absurd to claim that chiefs are still leaders of their people, as if that were true for all chiefs and that other leaders were non-existent. The danger of political leaders would not be there if the leadership of chiefs was so firm, so deep, so certain as some claim.

He added: 'There is no moral justification for government to hide behind, or utilize, a chief's power to back its policy, and experience suggests to conserve and preserve the unifying and somewhat unique function of a chief, he should be left out of the development or important sphere of administration.'[2]

Another doubt which had arisen in U.F.P. days was how the chiefs could reconcile their increasing administrative role, their 'civil service' functions, with their claim to represent Africans and not government opinion. Dr. Ahrn Palley stressed this problem. He said that chiefs might become 'an absolute shuttlecock of politics; they are dependent on Government for their salaries, they are dependent on Government for their allowances, and it would be a brave chief who would run counter to Government political policies and express them independently'.[3] The Government's reply to this was that chiefs were appointed by a traditional system and the rewards they

[1] *The Rhodesia Herald*, 22 September 1964.
[2] Second Report, Commission of Inquiry into the Organisation and Development of Southern Rhodesian Public Service (Patterson Report), Salisbury, Government Printer, C.S.R. 35, 1962.
[3] S.R.L.A. Hansard, 27 August 1963, col. 184.

received from the Government were not salaries but subsidies and allowances paid for their government functions. These rewards were only an addition to the tribute and presents given by their own people. The critics, according to the Government:

. . . conveniently overlook the profound and complicated processes whereby each tribe by infinite discussion, application of principles of tribal law and custom, spiritual appeals and ceremonial rites eventually chooses its own hereditary chief for the Governor's approval. They can ignore the tribal process of consultation and representation which make a chief's decision an expression of his people's view.[1]

However, despite the Government's protests, it is indisputable that the Government has considerable influence and power over the chiefs. Indeed, whether a chief is recognized as such depends upon the Government. In the African Affairs Act it states: 'The chief in charge of a tribe shall be appointed by the Governor and shall hold office during his pleasure and contingent upon good behaviour and general fitness.' In cases of succession disputes it is usual for the tribe to seek the advice of the District Commissioner. Dr. Kingsley Garbett, discussing the role of spirit mediums in chiefs' succession disputes among the Korekore, a northern Shona people, wrote:

Nowadays the medium's nomination, though it is still earnestly sought after, does not necessarily bring a succession dispute to its conclusion because the District Commissioner makes the final appointment and all royals know this. The Commissioner, too, considers public opinion when making his final choice.[2]

Hereditary right has been an important, but not the sole, criterion used by the Government for the appointment of chiefs. In the last ten years, twelve disputed cases of succession among the Shona have been settled by a form of election. Three of the seven Ndebele chiefs who sit on the Chiefs' Council are not customary heirs to chieftainship. Among these is Chief Simon Sigola, the successor to a chieftainship which his father was given because of good service as a government messenger.[3]

[1] *Domboshawa Indaba*, p.42.
[2] 'Religious Aspects of Political Succession among the Valley Korekore' in E. Stokes and R. Brown (Eds.), *The Zambezian Past*, Manchester University Press, 1966.
[3] Palley, op. cit., p. 467.

The Government's power to dismiss chiefs is rarely used and normally is restricted to occasions when a chief has committed a criminal offence. But the power is there. In 1951 there was a complete reorganization of chiefs, in which eighty-nine chiefs were told that they would no longer be recognized as such. Between 1958 and 1961 five chiefs were dismissed, including Chief Mangwende, whose dismissal caused great controversy. The Government may also discipline chiefs short of dismissal, and it is the Government's decision whether a chief draws a personal allowance in addition to his subsidy. The payments which chiefs receive from the Government have risen sharply. In July 1965 it was announced that 128 chiefs with 500 followers or more would receive a subsidy of £420 per annum and the twenty-nine chiefs with less than 500 would receive £240 per annum. In addition, fifty-four chiefs were receiving personal allowances ranging from £6 to £240 per annum.[1] By Rhodesian African standards, the chiefs' rewards from the Government place them in a high income bracket.

The powers which a chief exercises are derived partly from tribal tradition, but these are confirmed and added to by the Government. A chief allocates land not only because it is a traditional right but because the Government says he may do so. Chiefs' powers are balanced between those they claim as traditional rulers and those they derive from the Government. As the government-granted powers have increased, so the chiefs' reliance upon traditional powers has become relatively less important and so their position within their own society has changed. As they are drawn more into political decisions, so they become identified with particular political ideas and identified with government policies. Therefore they have become increasingly controversial figures. The dilemma which this can represent for the individual chief was shown in the case of Chief Shumba, who in 1963 was the President of the Chiefs' Council. Chief Shumba signed a petition which opposed independence without increases in African political rights. Within the Chiefs' Council he met opposition and in May 1963 was forced to resign as President.

Another problem of placing such reliance upon chiefs is the unevenness of their individual abilities. They are not chosen

[1] S.R.L.A. Hansard, 21 July 1965, cols. 1217-8.

for their efficiency or skill or knowledge and therefore while some happen to be men of ability, distinction and strong personality many are not. In 1953 the Chief Native Commissioner commented: 'A description of chiefs, particularly in Mashonaland, takes on the nature of a catalogue of the vices and virtues of an old men's home. So many are beer-ridden, old, blind, opposed to all new ideas, senile, swayed by an entourage of hangers-on, lethargic and chronic invalids that they are of little use administratively.' In 1963 he raised the same problem, although in less colourful language. He wrote that so many Shona chiefs:

are very old and unable to carry out the onerous duties of chieftainship in this modern age. Not only does this system invariably mean that a chief can only expect a few more years of life, but it also precludes any possibility of training his successor in the role of chief because the likely choice, besides being too old to train, might well die before the chief.

These personal inadequacies must throw considerable doubt on the ability of many chiefs to understand the complex political and constitutional problems which have faced Rhodesia, and doubt on their claim to represent African opinion and feeling on these issues. Probably the most satisfactory judgment of the chiefs' position was that made by the Chief Native Commissioner in 1961, which has already been quoted. He said:

in the political field chiefs should be able to express their views, and Government should attach as much importance to their views as it does to any other responsible and organized representative group such as a Chamber of Mines or Commerce, but in no way a substitute for or to exclude normal political expression and other representative organs of African thinking.

Yet by 1965 the R.F. Government was claiming that the chiefs and the chiefs alone could represent African opinion, that they were the sole voice of African aspirations. Obviously such a claim was based upon political convenience, not upon a reasoned assessment.

It is easy to understand why the R.F. Government has placed such emphasis upon the chiefs. Both the R.F. and the chiefs have a vested interest in preserving the existing social order. They are both conservative, even reactionary, forces. The retention of a tribal structure is naturally attractive to the chiefs for the power, prestige, and rewards it affords them, but it is equally attractive to the R.F. because it distinguishes the African and European communities and therefore preserves the old divisions. The Africans who most threaten the existing order are those who have left the tribal structure, who claim individual rights, who want to share the rewards and privileges of the Europeans. These claims have been encouraged by nationalist activity, but they are undermined by strengthening the tribal structure. In their search for African support, the R.F. have discovered that the one powerful group in African society whose interests coincide with their own are the chiefs and therefore the powers and rights of chiefs have been emphasized to the exclusion of all else.

As the chiefs' powers have increased, their relations with African politicians and elected representatives in the Legislative Assembly and the councils have become more strained. The chiefs have become closely identified with a Government which many Africans distrust, and therefore suspicion of the chiefs has grown. The Government has overvalued the chiefs, but the African politicians have underrated their position in African society and, for the nationalists in particular, the chiefs have become little better than 'government stooges'.

In African rural areas, the R.F. Government can claim that a clear policy is emerging, but no such claim can be made for the urban areas. The large urban African population (Salisbury, c. 230,000; Bulawayo, c. 170,000) presents enormous problems, but they are problems which no government can afford to ignore. The urban areas, with their social disruptions and frustrations, have been the breeding-ground of African nationalism, and if the Government wishes to counter nationalism by policies other than unmitigated suppression it must solve these problems.

African urban problems were not created by the R.F. Government, nor did they first appear during that Government's lifetime, nor are the problems unique to Southern Rhodesia. They are the common problems of a country with a rapidly expanding population and a rapidly changing economic order. In Rhodesia many of the Africans who have come to the towns had little choice—the land was overworked, there was no alternative employment in the tribal areas, and so in their search for employment or adventure or a quick fortune they have moved to the towns. There they have found an economic and social order very different from the tribal areas, and they have mixed with people of different tribes and even different races. Often their hopes of quick money or employment in any form have been dashed. It is a situation ripe for frustration, discontent, and disillusionment. The problems have been so great that some Europeans and Africans have sighed for the past when there was no African urban population. The urban African has been seen as a man who has lost his standards and identity. At a meeting at which Ian Smith was claiming substantial African support he said: 'I don't mean all these city slickers. I mean the real African in the rural areas.'[1] This attitude is completely unrealistic, for the urbanization of a large section of the African population is inevitable with the rapidly changing economy. The problems are very real, but they cannot be ignored.

The R.F. Government's policy of community development has offered little for urban Africans. There is even doubt whether there has been any policy at all, except to keep the races in their separate residential areas. The Director of Housing and Amenities in Bulawayo reported in 1965 that: 'Little has been heard of the Government's community development policy, which in a number of places was said to be moving into the active stage'; and in another section of his Report he complained that no decision had been made about policy in the African townships. 'We hope', he wrote, 'a clear and decisive statement will not be long delayed, as it is difficult to make far-reaching plans for the future without a policy'; also, the lack of policy was having a depressing effect upon the staff.[2] In his 1963 Report he had written: 'Perhaps things are better in the rural areas, but in the urban areas "Community Development" has so far stultified development rather than promoted it.'[3]

Even among R.F. members there has been criticism. In

[1] *Daily News*, 21 July 1964.
[2] Director's Report for 1964–5.
[3] Director's Report for 1962–3, para. 10.

October 1964 P. Palmer Owen, an M.P., referring to both African and European local government, stated:

When the Government took office one of the first statements made in this House, and this was in the Speech from the Throne, was that we, as a Government, would blanket the country under a system of local government. We have been in Government for close on two years and as matters stand now we have done nothing whatsoever to blanket the country with local government.[1]

Urban Africans are divided between those who live in the European areas, as servants, and those who live in the African townships. In some European suburbs the number of African servants and their relatives outnumber the Europeans. For example, in 1963 there were 7,700 Europeans and 8,356 people of other races in Highlands, and in Mabelreign 8,100 Europeans and 8,500 people of other races, yet Highlands and Mabelreign are 'European suburbs' of Salisbury. For the African living in the European areas there are few if any social amenities and during 1965 the R.F. Government started to close the few African schools which had been established.

In the African townships, which are divided between those administered by municipalities and those directly administered by the central Government,[2] there have been enormous problems. (Again it must be stressed that they were not created by the R.F. Government.) These problems are revealed in the reports of the officials responsible for administration of Africans in the two main cities: the Director of African Administration in Salisbury and the Director of Housing and Amenities in Bulawayo.[3]

There has been serious unemployment. In 1964 the Director in Salisbury reported: 'It is a well-known fact that hundreds of Africans stalk the premises of large industrial concerns waiting patiently to be taken on or given any menial task only to be turned away.' In Bulawayo a survey in May 1964 revealed 3,121 adults and 328 juveniles unemployed on the streets, but the Director thought this was a low estimate as many

[1] S.R.L.A. Hansard, 20 October 1964, col. 36.
[2] At the end of 1964, 33 of 64 townships were administered by the central Government.
[3] Reliance for conditions in the towns has been placed on the annual reports of these two officials.

unemployed would have been indoors because the survey was taken on a cold day. In 1962–3 in Bulawayo 2,087 youths registered for employment but only 1,374 were placed. The position for females was much worse as 14,473 registered but only 106 vacancies were notified to the exchange (some of these women would find employment by personal contact without the help of the labour exchange).

The position of Primary school-leavers was particularly tragic. In 1963 the Director at Bulawayo reported: 'Even more worrying is the number of children and youths from Bulawayo and other areas as far away as Umtali who are crowding into the Youth Employment Service in search of work. The future of these youngsters is bleak.' In the following year he wrote: 'There has been no improvement in the employment prospects for the school leaver and it is depressing to see the enormous crowd which gathers outside our Employment Exchange after a strike in some factory, hundreds turning up on the prospect of a job.' He denied the oft-repeated assertion that Africans simply refused to undertake particular jobs, especially in agriculture. The Director asserted that those who were capable would take any job.

There has been overcrowding and lack of accommodation. The situation has been especially bad for married couples. In July 1963 there were 16,679 African families accommodated in Salisbury, but there were 9,553 on the waiting list. When a government 'aided self-help' township was planned at Kambuzuma, with 1,425 units, there were 5,000 applications. In 1964 the Director in Salisbury wrote: 'I cannot stress too strongly the need for additional housing . . . There are literally hundreds of Africans who are still recorded on the waiting list and who have priorities for married housing which date as far back as 1949, and they are still waiting.' In Bulawayo the situation was equally serious. In 1963 it was estimated that there were 7,000 families waiting for accommodation. The Director estimated that at least 9,000 unauthorized Africans were living in the townships. In a particularly bad area, Makokoba, 'a room originally designed for four single tenants, might house seven or eight men and a scattering of women and children'.

There has been poverty. In 1963 a survey was made of the 'Old Bricks' area of Harare Township, Salisbury. This area was theoretically designed for 1,920 single men, but a census in the previous year had revealed that it was housing 2,610 men, 683 women, and 749 children. There were 548 families 'illegally' living in the area and, of these, four-fifths were living under the 'poverty datum line'. This 'line' had been defined in the previous year by David G. Bettison as £15 per month for a married family with two children, but Bettison had stressed that it 'must be viewed as a measurement far removed from what a given family in practice requires to sustain itself in a minimum state of health and decency'. Bettison had discovered the average married man with two children in Salisbury was earning only £8 10s. od. per month. The Director in Bulawayo mentioned the problem of the older Africans. In 1964 he reported that:

Many Africans are now reaching the stage when their physical strength is declining so that they are no longer able to hold down their jobs as unskilled labourers. In the past they used to return 'home' to their land in the Reserves. But now so many have no such land and have become urbanised. They have nothing but their declining physique to offer an employer, they are practically unemployable.

These social and economic problems have naturally created deep discontent and frustration. Writing of the unemployed in 1964, the Director at Bulawayo said: 'A situation of despair and frustration has emerged and the complexities which surround these unfortunates are grave and real.' In the same year the retiring Mayor of Salisbury, Frank Clements, commented that punitive measures to retain order were insufficient in themselves, for 'while there are thousands of young men with no opportunity for either education or work idling in townships, their sense of frustration and purposelessness can only too easily be exploited . . . Evil-doers should be punished but the great mass of young men who feel themselves to be abandoned by society should be given the opportunity to do some useful work for their own people in their own community', he suggested that revolutionary thinking was required to create employment for them. 'If', he continued, 'young people here or anywhere in the world, were treated as outcasts they would behave like gangsters.'[1]

[1] *Daily News*, 22 April 1964.

There has been no easy channel through which urban Africans can express themselves or voice their needs, for the community development policy has not yet provided a direct means of African participation in urban government. In 1963 Clair Ewing raised the problem of the mixed communities of European householders and African servants in European residential areas. Mr. Howman replied that the servants must be considered as migratory labour and therefore not part of the community. 'I think', said Howman, 'it is abundantly clear that the only persons who can be taken into account in the delimitation of a community are persons who have a stake in that community, and that migrants and persons who come there for a temporary purpose cannot be regarded as forming an integral part of that community.'[1] Ewing made the obvious point that some servants spent all their lives in European areas and had a very clear stake in it. Howman replied that he was uncertain about servants but still accepted the principle that 'the exercise of the franchise under local government legislation must be related . . . to responsibility and a stake in the community.'[2] Africans have continued to be regarded as outside this community and therefore to have no voice in it.

In the townships administered by municipalities Africans have not enjoyed direct representation in the municipal councils. Although the townships are administered by the municipalities, they lie outside the official municipal boundaries, and therefore the council electorate has been drawn exclusively from the European areas. However, in the municipal townships Africans have since the 1946 Native (Urban Areas) Accommodation and Registration Act been offered a limited and unsatisfactory voice via Advisory Boards. These Boards have no powers but can offer advice to the municipal authorities. In 1963 the Director in Salisbury reported: 'The Advisory Board system as has previously been stated is an out-moded mechanism. The fact that the body is "advisory" carries with it no responsibility and any actions taken by the governing body, viz. the Council itself, if unpopular or contentious, are never the concern of the Board.' He warned that, unless a more enlightened and dynamic system were introduced,

[1] S.R.L.A. Hansard, 22 August 1963, col. 1898.
[2] Op. cit., 27 August 1963, col. 13.

Africans would refuse to participate. His warning was well founded, for by 1965 the only functioning Advisory Board was in Harare Township, Salisbury. All the others had collapsed and attempts to revive them had met blank refusals from the African populations. In the townships directly administered by the central Government the situation is even bleaker, for in these there is no African participation even in an advisory capacity.

The U.F.P. Government had been considering a reorganization of urban administration, based upon a new Local Government Act which they introduced in 1961. Under the Act African and European local government in urban areas could have developed along similar lines and African townships could have had representation in the Councils, but this was abandoned when the R.F. came into power. For example, in Bulawayo the Council had asked a panel led by Mr. A. D. H. Lloyd to make recommendations for a reorganization. After his investigations Mr. Lloyd had suggested that the municipal area should be extended to embrace the African townships and that the whole area should be divided into wards from which councillors would be chosen. Had Mr. Lloyd's suggestions been accepted there would probably have been eight Africans in a total Council of twenty-six. However, Mr. Lloyd's report was not received until after the change of government. The Director reported: 'By February, when the panel's report was ready, the atmosphere was so cooled that no action was taken until 3 July, when Council decided to leave the matter over for six months, pending clarification of the Government's policy on community development and the devolution of certain responsibilities to Local Authorities.' The Director in Salisbury made a similar comment in 1963. He wrote:

The whole structure of future local government is very much in the melting pot . . . It will, therefore, be readily appreciated that the provisions of certain services are closely linked with the pattern of local government and more directly with the activities of this administration and in the absence of declared policies the whole tempo of this administration's future has been considerably slowed down and even stultified.

In 1964 the Minister of Local Government announced that he intended to introduce an experimental, nominated Board in the centrally administered township of Highfields, which if successful would lead to greater African participation in urban local government, but these promises had not been fulfilled when U.D.I. was declared.[1] It is probably not overstating the case to say that as yet no attempt has been made by the R.F. Government to give any practical application to the community development policy for the African urban dweller.

In this survey of the townships, there has been concentration on their problems and the deficiencies of their administration. This is not intended to belittle the efforts of the officials who have been responsible for administration of the African townships, for many of them have given devoted service and have spoken out for African rights. Nor is it intended to imply that both the central Government and the municipalities have not put substantial funds into the townships to improve housing and social amenities. For example in his 1964 report, the Secretary of Local Government stated that, during the year, new accommodation had been provided for 3,993 families (2,017 married housing units by local authorities and the remainder by the central Government). But he admitted: 'Unfortunately there is no sign on the horizon of the massive sums of money which would be required to provide a major break through in our housing problems.'

It is clear that the funds which local and central authorities have been able or willing to spend on the townships have been inadequate to overcome problems like overcrowding. It is also clear that, because of the country's economic and wage structure, most Africans have not the individual financial capacity to overcome the problem themselves. And finally there is the glaring weakness that urban Africans have no say in the way they are governed or administered. If Mr. Smith wants to find one of the major causes for nationalist support he has no need to look outside his borders for the 'Communist menace' or for 'British appeasement'. He should, to use his own phrase, 'clean up his own backyard' in the African townships.

There has been considerable speculation that the R.F.'s community development policy will lead to a form of separate

[1] Palley, op. cit., p. 650.

development and Bantustans. This has been denied consistently by the R.F. Government, but the suspicion has been very strong and has been shared by such diverse people as nationalists, R.N.P. politicians, and the Director of Housing and Amenities in Bulawayo. In 1963 Blair Ewing of the R.N.P. declared that 'this policy does seem, as its end result, a policy of separate development, of *apartheid* and Bantustans, call it what you will'.[1] To support his case he quoted an R.F. pamphlet on community development which stated it was a 'process whereby each community, whether European, African, or Asian, defines its needs, makes its plans and carries out these plans with its own resources and secures outside assistance when this is needed'. He also mentioned a newspaper article in which Lord Graham had spoken of the law of God that each shall preserve his own kind, and quoted Mr. Howman himself as saying: 'The social integration of people differing in race and culture does not conduce to harmony; indeed lessons have been drawn from all social studies which show that in such circumstances racial friction and intolerance are inevitable.'[2]

Similar misgivings were expressed by the Director in Bulawayo who wrote in his 1962–3 report that community development may 'be landed with the task of justifying the unequal development of African and European areas by reference to the "community's" capacity for self-help, and there is a real danger that it might be called upon to justify the provision of separate facilities for the races and to maintain the *status quo*.'

It is, of course, impossible to predict the future with any accuracy but, if the R.F. retain power, it seems probable that some form of separate development will be perpetuated. South African influence is likely to be strong, but in practice the two countries would differ because of the great differences in their white-black population ratios. However, there are general principles that will probably be shared in common. These are that the races will continue to live in separate areas; that within their own rural areas Africans will be given increasing responsibility, but that within European areas and the towns, Africans will have little or no say in how they are governed

---

[1] S.R.L.A. Hansard, 23 August 1963, col. 1890.
[2] Op. cit., 23 August 1963, col. 1946.

and administered; and that the central Government will remain in European hands.

The evidence for this suggested line of development does not rest upon an existing, developed theory of race relations, but upon the R.F. response to specific problems. The recent implementation of laws which forbid African servants to have their families with them, including their children, while working in European areas; the warning to private schools in European areas that they may be breaking the law by accepting African pupils; the closing of African schools in European areas; the opposition to African participation in municipal government; the growth of chiefs' powers, and the emphasis on developing tribal life: all these specific responses indicate the line of development. In addition to these, R.F. Ministers and Members of Parliament have indicated their support for aspects of separate development. John Gaunt, when Minister of Local Government, in 'thinking aloud' to a Local Government Association in 1964, said that the answer for African townships might be in separate autonomy. Two of the suggestions of the Parliamentary Select Committee, which investigated political boycotts, were that tribal courts presided over by representatives of the chiefs should be established in townships, and that the townships should be planned to group together members of the same tribe.[1] Even clearer was a statement made by Mr. Mark Partridge, who was appointed Minister of Local Government after U.D.I. He said: 'I would like to see a Constitution which recognizes racial differences and does not try to pretend they aren't there, and in recognizing them, give each main race its own homeland within the country. This would mean that the Europeans and Africans would have definable territory where their rights would be paramount.' He suggested that there should be separate African and European Parliaments.[2] Mr. Smith himself, when questioned whether R.F. policy was 'to give each main race its own homeland within the country, that is, a definable territory where its own rights would be paramount', replied that the Land Apportionment Act 'provides each of Rhodesia's main races with definable territories'. This

---

[1] L.A.S.C. 8–65, paras. 246 and 253.

[2] *The Rhodesia Herald*, 9 February 1965, quoting an article in *Shield*.

17

had been the position since 1930, 'and it remains government policy to continue with its application'.[1]

The R.F. Government claims that it is defending and developing a society in which rewards and distinctions are based upon merit, not upon race. This is difficult to believe. Even accepting that the Europeans have an inheritance of high educational and economic achievements, by what standards of merit—in a population in which there are seventeen or eighteen Africans for every European—are there no African Cabinet Ministers, no African senior Civil Servants, no African magistrates or judges, no African officers in the army or the police? By what standards of merit are the races forced to live in separate racial areas? By what standard of merit are Africans denied entry to many hotels and clubs? The inescapable conclusion is that Southern Rhodesia is a racially divided society in which political and economic power is a white monopoly, and R.F. policy is that this structure should not be substantially changed in the foreseeable future.

R.F. policy implies that within tribal areas and tribal affairs Africans will achieve an increasing say in their own government, but outside that restricted field there are no indications that Africans will be given increased responsibilities or power. Because of this many Africans see the R.F. Government as at best paternalistic—and they do not want paternalism—and at worst outright racialist. They see that it has leaders like Smith, Howman, and Wrathall who are at pains not to offend Africans personally, but they also see that there are followers, some of whom regard Africans as an inferior species, others who say that without the European presence Africans would 'return to the trees'. In the Legislative Assembly they have heard Colonel Hartley tell the African Members of Parliament: 'You are learning a little, you are beginning to rise as the result of the efforts of devoted people, but against your own opposition. For the present level to which Hon. Members, such as the Hon. Member for Ndanga [Mr. Gondo] have now risen, he can thank the dedicated efforts of missionaries and administrative officials.'[2]

[1] S.R.L.A. Hansard, 18 February 1966, col. 715.
[2] Op. cit., 23 August 1963, col. 1901.

The dangers and fears which the R.F. say lie in a rapid change to African majority rule are dismissed by many Africans as pointless and irrelevant when measured against the society which the R.F. seeks to preserve. The R.F. speak of the danger of a one-party state ruled by a black dictator and riddled by nepotism, injustice, and corruption. But, ask many Africans, what is the threat of a black one-party state when the country has always been ruled by exclusively white parties? What is the threat of a black dictator when Africans have always been dictated to by whites? What threat does injustice hold when many Africans are convinced that the land and economic benefits of the society are already unjustly distributed, and that there is one law for the blacks and another for the whites? What threat does nepotism hold when all the top positions are already filled by Europeans, or corruption when the major economic benefits are already channelled to an exclusive racial *élite*? Many Africans conclude that if the worst fears of the R.F. were realized they would lose little, but make the enormous gain of racial equality.

CHAPTER XI

The Closing of the Ranks

The fall of Winston Field did not become a national issue. It was absorbed within the R.F. ranks. At first there was speculation that Field might, with the backing of a few supporters, follow an independent line and thereby jeopardize the R.F. majority, but this did not happen. Mr. Ian Smith, the new Prime Minister, quickly consolidated his position.

The upheaval in the R.F. provided little consolation for the opposition R.N.P. It was apparent not only that there would be no break in the governing party, but that the change of leadership had moved the R.F. further right, away from the moderate policy favoured by the R.N.P. In the reorganized Cabinet the two important ministries responsible for the administration of Africans, both previously held by Howman, were divided between William Harper (Internal Affairs) and John Gaunt (Local Government).[1] Both Harper and Gaunt were well known for their right-wing attitudes, for their doubts about the ability of Africans to participate in central government.

A few days after he took office, the new Prime Minister said he did not expect to see an African nationalist government in his lifetime and, as many people found it difficult to imagine any other form of African government, this was translated as a determination to retain white rule.[2] But Mr. Smith had not publicly denied the right of Africans to participate in government. In September 1963 he had said:

[1] The full Cabinet was: Dupont (Justice and Law and Order), Wrathall (Treasury and Posts), Harper (Internal Affairs and Public Services), Gaunt (Local Government), Lord Graham (Agriculture and National Resources), McLean (Labour, Social Welfare and Health), Rudland (Trade, Industry and Development, Transport and Power), Reedman (Roads, Immigration and Tourism), A. P. Smith (Education), and van Heerden (Mines, Lands and Water Development). For details, see Appendix 1.

[2] *The Rhodesia Herald*, 10 January 1964.

We must remain flexible politically. We must maintain a position where there is hope for all. To put a wall in front of African political advancement will lead to frustration which will provoke desperation of a different kind. Equally to abandon the standard of civilization we have built up will lead Europeans to despair and provoke desperation of a different kind.[1]

On another occasion he said that his policy was to bring the two races together amicably but when asked how quickly Africans would qualify for the vote he replied: 'I believe that it is an evolutionary process and so of course it cannot be very quick.'[2] Mr. Smith's attitude was that African majority rule was a remote future possibility—so remote, some contended, that the possibility did not in fact exist.

Under Winston Field the search for independence had been the predominant issue of Southern Rhodesian politics. Under Ian Smith it became an obsession. The climax was reached in the days immediately before U.D.I. when the Cabinet sat in almost continuous session, talking, debating, disputing, drafting messages to or awaiting messages from London. But, even in the early days of Mr. Smith's premiership, the question of independence overshadowed all else.

Mr. Smith's determination to achieve independence was well known before he became Prime Minister. After his trip to London in November 1963 he had said that there was little chance of negotiating independence and that other methods would have to be considered. In January 1964 an interview was published in which Smith, after affirming that 'our resolution, in fact cannot be harder than it was when we first demanded it [independence]', was asked: 'What would be the main repercussions, apart from belt-tightening, if we declared independence?' Mr. Smith replied:

I don't think there will be any belt-tightening, when we are independent—the days of belt-tightening will be over. That's for sure. As far as the City of London is concerned it might be a three-day wonder. For that reason I think a Friday afternoon would be a good time. By Monday morning the excitement (if any) would be over.[3]

---

[1] Op. cit., 7 September 1963.
[2] Op. cit., 11 May 1964.
[3] *Newsfront*, 10 January 1964.

The militant attitude of the new Prime Minister was reflected in the correspondence with London. There was a new insistent, even threatening, tone. In his first letter to Sir Alec Douglas-Home Mr. Smith confirmed that the Southern Rhodesian Government would continue to press its claims for independence and would negotiate for as long as there was a 'possibility of fruitful results'. 'It's well known to you', the letter continued, 'that Southern Rhodesia's claims to complete independence are based on grounds which we believe to be irrefutable', and then he claimed that Britain had 'assumed obligation' to grant Southern Rhodesia independence on the basis of the 1961 Constitution if the Federation broke up. 'Should your Government deny the obligation', wrote Mr. Smith, 'I ask you to state, for the information and consideration of the Southern Rhodesian Government, the reasons for such denial and other grounds for your Government's refusal to grant independence.'[1]

Within Southern Rhodesia a new emotional climate quickly built up. Mr. Smith is not a fluent public speaker, but his unsophisticated technique suits the simple earnestness of his ideas. He conveys an impression of sincerity, of pride in country, a determination to fight for his ideals, and, what is perhaps even more important, he has reflected and captured the mood of Rhodesian Europeans. The new Prime Minister, by broadcasts and by public speeches throughout the country, invoked a crusading spirit among his followers. Broadcasting on St. George's Day, he declared that Southern Rhodesians must take the mantle of the saint and destroy the 'evil dragon which plagues us . . . The evil of unreasonable and unenlightened opinion which is levelled against our country must be destroyed by all of us standing together.'[2] In a speech at Banket he said that Southern Rhodesia 'would effectively hold her position in the next two or three years and then those who had criticized Rhodesia would see the light themselves and say "We were right after all" '.[3] He attacked the opposition R.N.P. for not giving uncompromising support on the independence issue. In Salisbury in May, when he spoke of increasing African

[1] Cmnd. 2807, Smith-Home, 6 May 1964.
[2] *The Rhodesia Herald*, 24 April 1964.
[3] Op. cit., 13 May 1964.

representation, he said: 'If we were foolish enough to do that we would be guilty of the greatest folly.' The speech was drowned with applause.[1] At Sinoia he declared: '. . . we must hold our ground and also try to regain some of the ground we were misled into giving away'. Then he stated that there had been a time when Southern Rhodesian and British moral standards had been the same, but that British standards had now fallen.[2]

At the liveliest of these early meetings, in Salisbury in July, the Prime Minister referred to the 1961 Constitution as 'this fantastically cumbersome and unworkable Constitution which is absolutely riddled with discrimination and racialism'.[3] Paradoxically he again attacked the R.N.P. for not giving full support to achieving independence on the basis of the Constitution. 'Surely', he said, 'these people should be asked to give an account of their behaviour; why they have now changed their ground'. When he declared that 'the most unfortunate aspect of this whole [independence] question is the attitude of some of our own Southern Rhodesians', R.F. supporters cried out, 'Traitors', 'Renegades', Quislings', and 'Send them to Wha Wha [a restriction camp]!'

Independence itself was an emotional issue, but even greater emotionalism was centred on the method by which to achieve it and, in particular, whether unilateral action should be taken. With Mr. Smith's appointment as Prime Minister the prospects of unilateral action became very much greater. Ministers dropped broad hints that it was a possibility. In Bulawayo in June the Prime Minister himself said: 'If anyone really believes that there is much hope of negotiating independence on the lines we want it then I think he is indulging in wishful thinking'. The statement was met with cries of 'Freedom now!'[4]

At Gwelo in the same month Mr. Smith said that independence was near, that Southern Rhodesia was not prepared to drift indefinitely, but he did not think that there was much chance of negotiating it with Britain.[5] John Gaunt, the new Minister of local Government, was reported to have made even

[1] *The Rhodesia Herald*, 21 May 1964.
[2] Op. cit., 23 May 1964.
[3] *Daily News*, 21 July 1964.
[4] *The Rhodesia Herald*, 6 June 1964.
[5] Op. cit., 16 June 1964.

blunter statements. In an interview with the *Washington Post* he was reported to have said that Southern Rhodesia would seize independence. 'There will', he said, 'be some shouting, screaming, and foaming at the mouth for a few days. Then there'll be a new outbreak of trouble in British Guinea, British Honduras or Cyprus and we'll be forgotten.' He thought that changes in the Constitution would be made, as 'it would be pretty silly to take all these risks and then in about ten years get an African majority government, wouldn't it?'[1]

The ministerial statements were so outspoken that speculation became centred on when, not if, independence would be seized. Various dates were suggested—Malawi's Independence Day, Rhodes' and Founders' Day, or perhaps to coincide with the British General Election. Each of the dates passed uneventfully. One of the reasons for this was the Government's uncertainty about European support for U.D.I. While the R.F. meetings revealed fervid support from the faithful, there was a suspicion that the illegal act might drive many of the less faithful directly against the Government. There were ominous signs. Early in July Sir Robert Tredgold said that a unilateral declaration would be treason and that it would be the duty of every soldier, policeman, or civilian to do everything in his power to defeat an action stemming from the declaration. It was known that senior army officers had deep doubts about their loyalty in the event of unilateral action.

The R.N.P. were sincerely and strongly opposed to a unilateral act and saw also that it was an issue on which they might revive their political fortunes. They thought that by concentrating on that issue, by expressing the doubts felt by Europeans and Africans alike, they could overcome the internal tensions, which had been undermining the party. They could for a time forget their internal disputes on such subjects as the Land Apportionment Act and the pace of African advancement, and fight the R.F. on an issue which would re-unite the party and gain additional European support. At a party congress in June 1964 a resolution was passed assuring the Governor of loyalty to the 1961 Constitution and pledging full support to him 'in any steps he may have to take to prevent unconstitutional action by the Government in power'. Mrs. Rosin, an ex-

[1] The interview was reported in the *Daily News*, 17 June 1964.

Federal M.P., declared that in the struggle against U.D.I. 'we are all prepared to go to Wha Wha if necessary'.[1] The congress revealed another important party move. It was decided that the party should seek a broader but unspecified base for support and, although Whitehead was re-elected leader, he told the party that he would be prepared to stand down if a more acceptable leader appeared. This was a public acknowledgement of current back-scene pressures to persuade Sir Roy Welensky to return to politics and lead the opposition party on a more moderate programme, which would regain some of the European support lost by Sir Edgar.

Early in August Sir Roy addressed the R.N.P. caucus and, despite the doubts of some of the African members, support was given for the formation of a new party under his leadership. On 6 August Sir Roy announced that a new party might be formed, and declared bluntly: 'The object is to get into power. I would lead a broadly based party which would have a much wider appeal and a party which is not so irrevocably committed to different things—a party which has room for manœuvre.' He was sympathetic with the R.F. Government's predicament but declared that a party of reconciliation was needed. On U.D.I. he was adamant. It was ruled out unless Britain broke the convention or there was other outside interference.[2] On 13 August the new party, the Rhodesia Party (R.P.), was announced. It absorbed the R.N.P. and had Sir Roy as leader with Sir Edgar as his deputy. Sir Edgar was to lead the party in the Legislative Assembly until Sir Roy obtained a seat.

The R.P. was quickly given the opportunity to test its strength. Two by-elections were set for 1 October. Both were in affluent, northern Salisbury suburbs and both had returned leading members of the R.N.P. and ex-U.F.P. Ministers. A. R. W. Stumbles, the Member for Avondale, had been appointed Speaker of the Legislative Assembly, and B. V. Ewing, who was Member for Arundel, had resigned for business reasons. If the new R.P. wanted to show its strength, it had not only to retain these seats but to retain them handsomely. The R.P. decided that Welensky would stand for Arundel, and Sidney Sawyer, an ex-Junior Minister of the

[1] *The Rhodesia Herald*, 22 June 1964.   [2] Op. cit., 6 August 1964.

Federal Government, would fight the Avondale by-election.

The new party based its hopes upon opposition to U.D.I., upon a more moderate approach to African advancement, and upon Sir Roy's personal popularity among Europeans. In its policy statement the R.P. retained many of the old U.F.P./R.N.P. policies, but they were moderated. The Land Apportionment Act would be repealed, but slowly, by phases, and there would be 'suitable legislation for the maintenance of standards'. On the franchise it was emphasized that control must remain in responsible hands. The 'A' Roll would not be changed, but the 'B' Roll would be extended by granting the franchise to some older Africans.[1]

However, the great policy issue was U.D.I. Sidney Sawyer said: 'In accepting the invitation to contest Avondale I believe that the by-election will be the first step towards the emergence of a new political movement which can organize opposition to a unilateral declaration of independence.' In the Legislative Assembly Whitehead continued the attack. In a 'no confidence' motion he said: 'We undoubtedly believe that independence is something that is desirable and should be gained but not that it is of such overwhelming importance that it warrants unconstitutional acts.'[2] He warned again of the dire consequences such an act would bring on Southern Rhodesia. When the new party's advertisements appeared in the newspapers, one of them stated: 'Reason not Rebellion', and urged that independence should be sought:

(a) Within the Commonwealth and Sterling Area: we want prosperity for our country, (b) based on Government remaining in responsible hands: we firmly reject any hand-over to Black Nationalist dictatorship; (c) achieved within the Constitution and the law: Southern Rhodesia must not become an international outlaw.[3]

The Government did not underrate the danger posed by the R.P. Mr. Smith, referring to Sir Roy, had disparagingly said: 'If anyone stands in our way we will deal with him. If it hap-

---

[1] R.P. policy statement reported in *Daily News*, 12 August 1964.
[2] S.R.L.A. Hansard, 29 July 1964, cols. 94–5.
[3] *The Rhodesia Herald*, 11 September 1964.

pens to be a rogue elephant coming out of the bush he will be dealt with accordingly.'[1] This was the public attitude but the Government's concern was real. Clifford Dupont, the Deputy Prime Minister, resigned his safe seat at Charter to fight the by-election against Sir Roy.

The R.F. had always found it difficult to understand or accept opposition. This became increasingly so as the independence issue began to dominate Southern Rhodesian politics. Independence was the vital question and therefore the clash of the political parties was inevitably centred around it, but it was an issue which had raised so much emotion, so much fervour, that the R.F. followers found it increasingly difficult to accept that their views were not the only views which loyal Southern Rhodesians could hold. In the Legislative Assembly Colonel Hartley, speaking about what he thought was the opposition's deceit over the 1961 Constitution, said: 'I say to Hon. Members opposite, are you prepared to make yourself a party to the betrayal which the country has suffered? . . . if treason there has been then it has been treason against the electorate of Southern Rhodesia.'[2]

The Prime Minister himself often confessed his inability to understand why the parliamentary opposition did not give unstinted support to the Government in the way it was seeking independence. Then, on 25 June, he made a broadcast which was full of menace. He said that Southern Rhodesia was involved in a cold war which was being fought by propaganda devices. He stated that it was difficult to deal with the danger because:

it is all mixed up with the incessant outpourings of arguments and challenges, words and more words from the legitimate opposition. . . . It is often difficult to distinguish between the enemy of the state and the Government's legitimate political opponents. Indeed, the real enemy will always do his best to infiltrate and to use as a screen all the lawful, well-meaning, loyal opposition groups. These, on the other hand, in their own eagerness to get into power are not always very particular about their friends and allies. . . . It is most necessary therefore that we draw a clear distinction between a legitimate, loyal opposition and an opposition which is merely the

[1] *The Rhodesia Herald*, 11 August 1964.   [2] S.R.L.A. Hansard, 29 July 1964.

external enemy in disguise. The disguise is sometimes so thin as to be almost invisible.[1]

It was not a far step from this broadcast to identify the Government of the day as 'the State' and therefore to translate all opposition as treason.

The R.F.'s distrust of opposition became very apparent during the by-election campaigns. The R.N.P. were persistently accused of harming the chances of a negotiated settlement, of putting their own political interests before those of the country as a whole. The R.F.'s impatience grew even clearer after Mr. Smith's visit to London in September.

Mr. Smith had been invited to talks with the British Government on the independence issue. The British Government had wanted these talks to improve the increasingly strained relations between the two Governments, but Mr. Smith had been reluctant to agree, especially after the refusal of the Commonwealth Prime Ministers to invite him to their conference in July, when Southern Rhodesia had been discussed. In September, however, Mr. Smith changed his mind and went to London. The September talks were important both in establishing the attitudes of the two governments towards independence and in the influence the talks had upon internal Southern Rhodesian politics. They were held as the by-election campaigns were in full swing.

At the London talks Mr. Smith reaffirmed his contention that '. . . the people of Southern Rhodesia regarded themselves as having made in effect an implied contract with the United Kingdom in 1961, whereby they would be entitled to receive the independence without more ado in return for accepting the 1961 Constitution'.[2] Sir Alec Douglas-Home had already categorically denied that there had been any such agreement, explicit or implicit,[3] and he reaffirmed this at the September meeting. Mr. Smith made this same claim as late

---

[1] *The Rhodesia Herald*, 26 June 1964. (It was suggested that this broadcast had been written by Mr. Ivor Benson, who had recently been employed in the government information services as 'Adviser to the Government'. The appointment, which carried a monthly salary of £375, caused heated arguments between the Government and the opposition. But, whoever wrote the broadcast, it was the Prime Minister who made it.)

[2] Cmnd. 2807, record of meeting at 10 Downing Street, 7 July 1964.

[3] Op. cit., Home-Smith, 20 May 1964.

as 29 October 1965, when he was negotiating with Mr. Wilson, but he must have realized from the beginning that it was untenable. In 1961 he had personally resigned from the U.F.P. over the question of the Constitution. He had done so not only because he disliked the new franchise, but also because the Constitution left too many powers with Britain. When, in 1964, the question of an independence agreement arose, Sir Edgar Whitehead reaffirmed Sir Alec's denial.

The September talks re-emphasized the different attitudes of the two Governments to African political rights. The British Government wanted constitutional arrangements made for a steady advance to majority rule. The Southern Rhodesian Government could not accept this and made proposals which would in fact have slowed down the pace of African advancement as envisaged in the Constitution. However, one major new point did emerge from the talks. This was Mr. Smith's acceptance that the British Government had the right to be satisfied that a majority of all Southern Rhodesians supported his claim for independence on the 1961 Constitution. Obviously the great difficulty for Mr. Smith would be to demonstrate that he had majority African opinion behind him, but he said: 'I should be a fool if I tried to go ahead without African support.' The British Government accepted that, if Mr. Smith's claim could be substantiated, it 'might change the situation radically', but there was a deep division over how Mr. Smith could prove his point.

Mr. Smith contended that African opinion could be discovered through the chiefs. 'The system', he said, 'did not require the views of individual Africans to be ascertained; the expression of a tribe's views was a matter for its chief and its members were content to leave the decision to him. Indeed any suggestion that they themselves should be committed individually would be misunderstood as a challenge to the authority of the chiefs.'[1] Mr. Smith claimed that 3 million of the $3\frac{1}{2}$ million[2] African population would be directly represented by the chiefs, and that the chiefs' views had support from 70 per cent of the African population. The British Government would

---

[1] Cmnd. 2807, record of meeting on 7 September 1964, p. 23.
[2] There were in fact about 4 million Africans in Rhodesia, but these were the figures used by Mr. Smith.

not accept this. Sir Alec insisted that a chiefs' *indaba* by itself was unsatisfactory, that it would have to be replaced or supplemented by a referendum of the African population. Mr. Smith disliked the suggestion because, he said, the vast majority of Africans could not possibly understand the complex issues involved. Also, Mr. Smith said that 'if he conceded the principle of "one man one vote" for the purpose of ascertaining the views of the African population on the issue of independence, he would have no grounds for denying it to them for ordinary electoral purposes', and this he thought would be 'folly because of the lessons to be drawn from elsewhere in Africa'.[1]

At the last point in the September discussions, when there was precise discussions about the chiefs' *indaba*, the British record of the meeting states that Sir Alec said that Britain must be satisfied that independence on the 1961 Constitution was the genuine desire of the majority. 'It would', the record states, 'be very dangerous if Mr. Smith returned to Southern Rhodesia with any misunderstanding of the United Kingdom position on this matter. He remained of the view that the proposed *indaba* would not suffice by itself; it must be either replaced or at least supplemented by a referendum or something equivalent to a referendum.' The record continued:

The Prime Minister [Home] said that a referendum or some equivalent procedure would be necessary; but, since it was apparently difficult for Mr. Smith to accept this explicitly at the present moment, it would be preferable to avoid any attempt to define in the communiqué the means by which African opinion would be ascertained.

Mr. Smith said that while in principle he agreed with the Prime Minister's view about the desirability of a referendum if it were practicable to arrange one, he had still to persuade his supporters in Southern Rhodesia to endorse his own, more limited, proposal [the chiefs' *indaba*]; and he had also to induce the tribal chiefs themselves to co-operate in putting it into effect. He would consider further the various suggestions which had been made about the means by which African opinion might be ascertained and would submit detailed proposals *after* the United Kingdom General Election.[2]

The London talks finished inconclusively. A final communiqué was issued in which the British Government reserved

[1] Op. cit., p. 28.   [2] Cmnd. 2807, pp. 28–30 (my italics).

its position whatever sounding of African opinion the Southern
Rhodesian Government made, while Mr. Smith 'accepted that
independence must be based on general consent and stated that
he was convinced that the majority of the population supported
his request for independence on the basis of the present constitution and franchise.'

Clearly the division between the two Governments was very
wide, and the chances of a negotiated settlement were still
remote. But this was not apparent in Rhodesia. There, optimistic reports from Mr. Smith were given wide publicity. He
said that he hoped that independence could be achieved by
negotiation before the end of the year, and that U.D.I. had
been 'thrown out of the window for the time being. I do not
think we will have to face up to a unilateral declaration of independence in Southern Rhodesia at the moment . . . If I
can prove to the British Government that I have the support
of the majority they will grant me independence on this constitution and this franchise.' It was, he thought, a victory for
'moderate responsible opinion' and all that was required for
complete success was a demonstration that the whole country
was behind the Government.[1]

The apparent success of the London talks and the temporary
rejection of U.D.I. changed the local political scene dramati-
cally. The major plank of the R.P.'s campaign had been removed at one blow. The R.P. claimed that it was their pressure
which had changed the situation and expressed doubts about the
firmness of the Government's change, but this held little conviction. They had to agree that independence by consent and
negotiation was their objective as well as the Government's and
they offered to help in discovering how African opinion could
be tested. Indeed, momentarily the R.P. seemed to move to the
right of the Government. As the details of the London discussions were unknown, it was thought that the R.F. might be
planning an African referendum. Sir Roy said that his party
would give its full support to any referendum designed to
achieve independence on the present Constitution, but he
warned against any departure from the principle of a qualitative franchise. He said : 'The Prime Minister's decision to seek
majority consent for independence moves sharply away from

[1] *The Rhodesia Herald*, 12 September 1964.

the qualitative franchise which is the tradition upon which Rhodesian Government has been built. The will of the voters has now been made subject to the will of the voteless in this matter.'[1] It seemed a carping criticism. A new R.F. poster proclaimed: 'This is no time for hair-splitting and quibbling, let alone artificial divisions based on political opportunism. The country *must* come first.' After forty years' wait the moment of decision had come—'United behind this man [Smith], secure your future.'

The contention that opposition to the Government was against national interests was emphasized more than ever. Speaking at Arundel Mr. Lardner-Burke said that Sir Roy should retire from the by-election because the one point he had been fighting for had been achieved. The Prime Minister appealed to Sir Roy 'not to continue to meddle in the independence issue', as he had 'come to the conclusion that we would have a far greater chance of success if Sir Roy refrained from further interference'.[2]

The emotionalism of the R.F. by-election campaign was seen at its worst in the behaviour of a thug element among the party's supporters and in the bitter personal attacks made upon political opponents. The thug element had displayed its talents at a meeting held by the Prime Minister before he flew to London. At that meeting a small group of staff and students from the University College had heckled and questioned Mr. Smith. The reactions of some R.F. supporters had been to throw lighted cigarettes into the hair of the girl students, and to manhandle and punch the men. At the end of the meeting the university group had to be rescued by the police. At some of Welensky's public meetings vicious personal attacks were made on him. The ex-champion of the European electorate was called 'a bloody Jew', 'a Communist', 'traitor', and 'coward'. Mr. Smith deprecated the behaviour but added that 'a deliberate attempt to create an incident at his meeting [the pre-London meeting] had promoted the incidents at Sir Roy's meetings'. The Prime Minister thought that 'politicians should be able to take the rough with the smooth' and treat criticism light-heartedly.[3]

[1] *The Rhodesia Herald*, 15 September 1964.   [3] Op. cit., 23 September 1964.
[2] Op. cit., 23 September 1964.

Naturally Sir Roy was attacked by the R.F. for his past policy failures and particularly his failure to preserve the Federation, but even here criticism was turned into personal attacks. One of these was made by Mr. Smith himself. A statement was issued from the Prime Minister's office stating that in London Mr. Smith had been told that he (Mr. Smith) had been 'the most forthright and tenacious protagonist of the Rhodesian cause with whom they [the British Government] had had to deal. He [Mr. Smith] had no wish to be unkind, but they had also informed him that from past experience they had found Sir Roy Welensky during his days of negotiation to be one of the weakest.'[1] Mr. Smith also said that Sir Edgar Whitehead had been most helpful in support for sounding African opinion, but Sir Roy had not. The R.P. immediately denied that there was any difference between the leaders.

The R.P. also raised one personal issue. They accused the Government of using a government official, Mr. Ivor Benson, a far right-wing political theorist, to address an R.F. meeting. The R.P. published a letter sent by the R.F. to Jews in the Arundel constituency inviting them to attend a meeting at which Mr. Benson was to speak. The R.F. meeting was intended to reassure Jews after the attacks made upon Sir Roy as a Jew.

The by-elections were a major triumph for the R.F. Government. Both seats were won by large majorities. In Arundel Mr. Dupont received 1,079 votes against Sir Roy's 633 in a 75·9 per cent poll. At Avondale Mr. J. W. Pithey, the R.F. candidate, had an even larger victory. He received 1,042 votes against Mr. Sawyer's 416. The results were greeted with great enthusiasm by R.F. supporters. When the defeated Sir Roy tried to address the crowd he was shouted down and told to go home.

The R.P. never recovered from this defeat. It left them bereft of ideas and of spirit. The new appeal to the electorate backed by the party's most powerful figure had failed disastrously. For the by-election at Charter, caused by Mr. Dupont's resignation, the R.P. even failed to raise a candidate.

October, which had started with the by-elections, was a

[1] *The Rhodesia Herald*, 23 September 1964.

month of intense activity in Rhodesia. On 7 October, a state of
emergency was declared in Harare African township, Salisbury,
because, stated the Government, the banned nationalist parties
had continued their activities there. On 14 October, Mr.
Smith informed the British Government that he had called a
meeting of chiefs and headmen for 20–21 October, 'to obtain
the views of the tribal people, most of whom are not on the
voters' roll'. The Government had arranged a referendum of
all voters for 5 November, but did not propose any method
other than the *indaba* of sounding the opinion of Africans who
were not on the voters' roll. Suggestions which were made for
other means of sounding African opinion were dismissed by Mr.
Smith as impractical or as undermining the authority of the
chiefs. Mr. Smith said that he had been forced to call the *indaba*
quickly, and before a promised parliamentary debate, because
chiefs and headmen were being intimidated and one headman
had actually been murdered.

The timing of the *indaba* had one other possible advantage
for Mr. Smith. His message was sent the day before a British
General Election. As the major parties were caught up in their
domestic political battle and, as there was a fair chance of a
change in government, it was a reasonable expectation that Mr.
Smith might have the opportunity of forwarding his plans
without strong British reaction or interference. If this was the
intention, it failed. The British Conservative Government replied immediately expressing surprise at the speed and content
of Mr. Smith's proposal. 'You will remember', the message
said:

that during the course of your meeting with the Prime Minister and
the Commonwealth Secretary they made it clear in their view a procedure on the lines you now suggest would not provide conclusive
evidence of the wishes of the people. [The British refused to send
observers to the *indaba*] . . . since this might be interpreted as implying
a commitment on the part of the British Government to accepting
your consultations as representing the opinion of the people as a
whole.[1]

The British rejection of the *indaba* was followed by a similar
rejection by the R.P. Sir Edgar Whitehead said that the joint

---

[1] *The Domboshawa Indaba*, Salisbury, Government Printer, p. 10.

parliamentary committee had reached agreement on some points, including the sounding of opinion in the Tribal Trust Lands through tribal machinery. 'But we find', he said, 'that we cannot accept that the chiefs' opinion will necessarily be that of the majority of the inhabitants.' He specifically mentioned the large number of adult Africans who did not qualify for a vote and who lived and worked outside the tribal areas.

The new British Labour Government, on taking office, immediately confirmed that, like its Conservative predecessor, it could not accept the *indaba* as an accurate reflection of majority African opinion. Mr. Bottomley wrote of a state of affairs which 'gives cause for serious concern'. He suggested that he should visit Southern Rhodesia, but said that he would want to meet a cross-section of people including the nationalist leaders. Mr. Smith replied to this by saying: 'I am shocked that a man [Bottomley] in his high position and office should want to see these people when he knows of their evil and criminal conduct and of the subversion and violent behaviour of their followers.'[1] And so the Bottomley visit did not take place.

With the strength of support behind him which the by-elections had revealed, Mr. Smith reacted sharply to the British attitude. The conciliatory talk of U.D.I. being thrown out of the window was forgotten. On 22 October he told cheering supporters at Macheke that the '. . . British Government had swung a low blow but we will only derive greater strength. Today we are far more determined than we were yesterday . . . Whether or not the British Government send observers, whatever that Government might say, whatever anyone else might say, we have set our course. This means independence for Southern Rhodesia—that I can assure you.'[2] Of even greater significance was the announcement on 24 October that Major-General J. Anderson, General Officer Commanding Rhodesia, had been retired on grounds of age. General Anderson was fifty-one and stated that he had expected to serve several more years. In a public statement the General said that, while he disclaimed any political affiliations, he had made clear his opposition to U.D.I. He said that, when questioned by the

[1] Cmnd. 2807, Smith-Wilson, 10 November 1964.
[2] *The Rhodesia Herald*, 23 October 1964.

Prime Minister, 'I admitted that I am naturally anti a government which has hinted at any unconstitutional action.'[1]

Meanwhile at Domboshawa the chiefs and headmen had been discussing independence. On 26 October the chiefs gave their findings at a public meeting. The likely outcome of the *indaba* had been known to the Southern Rhodesian Government even before Mr. Smith had left for London. Early in September there had been meetings of chiefs throughout the country at which independence was discussed. The Domboshawa White Paper reported that at the first of these meetings in the Matabeleland Provinces the chiefs 'clearly indicated to the Prime Minister of Rhodesia, who attended, that there was strong support for immediate independence on the basis of the present Constitution, and that this support was widespread throughout the country. It was on the basis of this encouragement that the Prime Minister left for his London talks.'[2]

At Domboshawa the chiefs gave their unanimous support for immediate independence on the 1961 Constitution. The first chief who spoke stated: 'We want to be given independence; we do not want to come back and have to discuss it any more. All of us chiefs and headmen in the room today are speaking with one voice.' Chief after chief, headman after headman, repeated the same theme. There were no dissenting voices. The chiefs who spoke were unanimously behind the Government, but the question remained: did the chiefs represent the majority views of Africans?

The Southern Rhodesian Government described the British refusal to recognize the *indaba* as a 'startling change of heart' and stated: 'It is a reasonable assumption that the Conservative British Government (to avoid embarrassment at the election) had no real intention of permitting a situation whereby the Rhodesia Government could produce evidence of abundant African support for its independence claim'; and the Labour Government had followed suit. 'From the Rhodesian point of view this was a dismal retreat by the British Government from a position where it would have had to examine and face up to one of the most complex add difficult problems in Africa—how to sound African opinion—back to the comfortable (for Britain) doctrinate assumption that the ballot-box

---

[1] *The Rhodesia Herald*, 24 October 1964.   [2] *The Domboshawa Indaba*, p. 4.

is the solution.'[1] A letter from Mr. Wilson to a Southern Rhodesian African which had been given wide publicity was quoted in which Mr. Wilson had said the Labour Party was totally opposed to granting independence while a white minority government was in power and that the party's aim was 'to achieve a peaceful transition to African majority rule'.

With the R.F. success at the by-elections, with the *indaba* triumph, with the dismissal of General Anderson, and with the coming voters' referendum which Mr. Smith knew he would win, events seemed to be moving inexorably to U.D.I., but then on 27 October a statement by Harold Wilson, the new British Prime Minister, was published. Mr. Wilson said:

A declaration of independence would be an open act of defiance and rebellion and it would be treasonable to take steps to give effect to it. . . . An illegal declaration of independence in Southern Rhodesia would bring to an end relationships between her and Britain; would cut her off from the rest of the Commonwealth, from most foreign Governments, and from international organizations; would inflict disastrous economic damage upon her; and would leave her isolated and virtually friendless in a largely hostile continent.[2]

This statement may have delayed U.D.I. by a year.

On 5 November a referendum of voters was held at which they were asked: 'Do you want independence under the 1961 Constitution?' There was criticism of the referendum: criticism that no attempt was made to register additional voters, especially Africans who did not live in tribal areas (the Roll was closed as from 31 August); criticism that the 'A' and 'B' Rolls were voting together, so that there could be no separate indication of African opinion through the 'B' Roll; and criticism by the R.P. that the question, to which voters had to give a clear 'Yes' or 'No', was far too vague. The R.P. wanted it made clear that a 'Yes' vote supported independence by negotiation and not by unilateral action, and the party wanted an assurance that the principles of an independence Constitution would be the same as those in the 1961 Constitution, including

---

[1] *The Domboshawa Indaba White Paper*, p. 12.
[2] The statement was originally contained in a letter Wilson-Smith, 24 October 1964 (Cmnd. 2807). It was published by Southern Rhodesian newspapers on 27 October 1964.

the enshrinement of the entrenched clauses. The opposition's doubts were based upon well-founded rumours that the Government was considering constitutional changes which would give chiefs direct representation in the legislature, and which would 'fade out' 'B' Roll seats. (The number of 'B' Roll seats was not entrenched in the Constitution. One government proposal was that as an African was returned to an 'A' Roll constituency, so a 'B' Roll district seat would be removed. Naturally this would considerably delay the time when Africans could be expected to form a majority of the legislature.)[1] As the Government refused to change the terms of the referendum, the R.P. refused to campaign for it. This offered a means of escape for a party which was deeply divided within itself over support for the Government at the referendum.

Despite the Macheke speech, and despite an admission in a television talk that the Government had been weighing the pros and cons of U.D.I. the Prime Minister said very clearly that a 'Yes' vote was not a mandate for U.D.I. One R.F. poster read: 'To vote "Yes" means unity—not U.D.I.', and another: 'Don't let yourself become confused by talk of unilateral independence. It has nothing whatever to do with this Independence Referendum.' In a letter to voters Mr. Smith stated the case for supporting the Government. He said that Southern Rhodesia was fighting 'a struggle in which our established standards of political, public, and private morality and integrity are pitted against expediency and selfishness'. He spoke of the danger of these standards being lost to black extremists, and said:

unless we Rhodesians can unite to sever the final strings which tie us to Britain and which render us a pawn at the disposal of the British Government, we have no hope of survival. We either go under or break away and survive . . . We really have no choice when we face realistically what we see in Africa to the north of us today and when we consider the shameless behaviour of the British Government towards us.[2]

The referendum re-emphasized the solidarity of European

---

[1] Suggestions had been made by Mr. Smith in the London September talks (see Cmnd. 2807). Mr. Smith said he would like to see half the 'B' Roll seats elected by Chiefs' Council and a 'fade-out' clause.

[2] *The Rhodesia Herald*, 3 November 1964.

support for the Government. In a 61·6 per cent vote, 58,091 voted 'Yes' and only 6,096 'No'. The R.F. Government was convinced that by the *indaba* and the referendum, the 'responsible' sections of Southern Rhodesian society had demonstrated their support for independence on the Government's terms.

Such were the contradictions of Southern Rhodesian politics that the two main interest groups—the chiefs and the R.F. Government—which had pledged their support for independence on the 1961 Constitution both disliked that Constitution and wanted to make substantial amendments to it. The R.F.'s misgivings were already well known, and shortly after the *indaba* the chiefs added their criticism. In December, members of the Council of Chiefs advocated a coalition government of Europeans and chiefs, but noted that the main obstacle to their ambition was the present Constitution, which they said should be changed.[1] The R.F. and the chiefs accepted the Constitution as a basis for independence, not because they approved of it, but because it was the furthest they were prepared to go in placating the British Government. Their main determination was to prevent any increase in the strength of African elected Members.

[1] *The Rhodesia Herald*, 19 December 1964.

CHAPTER XII

The 1965 Election and Extreme European Opinions

During 1965 there was a further disintegration of formal opposition to the R.F. The two possible sources of opposition were the R.P. and the nationalists, but in 1965 neither presented a real challenge to the Government.

In the case of the nationalists the Government continued to counter the movement by security legislation and police action. Whenever there were signs of a revival, the Government acted quickly and surely. Three organizations—the Zimbabwe African Congress of Unions, the Zimbabwe Church of Orphans, and the United National Independence Party—were banned, because the nationalists were thought to be using them as fronts. In areas where trouble arose or was anticipated, emergency powers were invoked. In the Salisbury African townships the emergency regulations were extended deep into 1965. In Harare the emergency regulations remained in force until 4 April, while in Highfields they were not withdrawn until 21 May. Emergencies were also declared in two of the restriction areas where nationalist leaders were held: Nuanetsi and Lupane. This gave the Government, if it so wished, powers to detain rather than restrict, and also meant that access to the leaders was controlled, for it was suspected that the leaders had been sending out instructions to their followers via visitors to the restriction areas.

Also in the campaign against the nationalists, the Government extended yet again its repressive legislation. An amendment was made to the Law and Order (Maintenance) Act by which the Government's powers of restriction without trial were increased from one year to five years. The Minister, Mr. Lardner-Burke, explained that each case would be treated on its merits but said that a person who was a source of danger to the country might by 'intimidating witnesses or other opera- tions [be] able to avoid conviction and can then only be re- stricted for twelve months'. He claimed that the prospect of five years' restriction would be a real deterrent, but that re- strictions for such 'short' periods as three to twelve months had been 'laughed at'. But even the five-year restriction period did not completely satisfy Mr. Lardner-Burke, for he admitted, 'I would love to have preventive detention.'[1] The Minister was also reported to have said: 'I can restrict [a person] for fifteen years . . . every time he comes out I can restrict him again for no reason whatsoever.'[2]

The by-election defeats of 1964 had signalled the possible disintegration of the official parliamentary opposition, the R.P. The party's chances of a revival grew even weaker as the out- standing figures of the past retired into political obscurity. In December 1964 Sir Roy Welensky resigned as leader because he considered that the party should be led from inside the Legislative Assembly. At a party convention on 11 February 1965, two candidates were put forward to succeed Sir Roy. They were Sir Edgar Whitehead and Mr. David Butler, who had gained fame as an Olympic yachtsman and from his appearance at the United Nations in 1962. The party chose Mr. Butler and thereby virtually brought to an end Sir Edgar's political career, a career in which he had attempted to unite and reconcile the ambitions and aspirations of Africans and Europeans. Sir Edgar announced that he would continue to serve the party under the new leader but would not contest another election.

The new leader, Mr. Butler, announced that he would sup- port the existing Constitution and franchise, that he opposed U.D.I., but that he did not favour calling a new constitutional conference. He also hinted at a further moderation of Sir Edgar's 1962 policy, for while Mr. Butler thought that repeal of the Land Apportionment Act was the 'correct long-term basis' for Southern Rhodesia, he thought that it should not be repealed in residential areas until existing fears were dispelled.

[1] S.R.L.A. Hansard, 16 March 1965. (cols. 808–9, 810, and 1021).
[2] *The Examiner*, April 1965.

Mr. Butler did not have long to wait to test his skill as a leader and to test the strength of his party. At the end of March the Prime Minister announced that there would be an election on 7 May. Mr. Smith, who announced the election following a party caucus meeting, denied that the decision had been influenced by the state of the independence negotiations with the British Government, but there must be a strong suspicion that the negotiations did influence the decision. The election was announced almost immediately after receipt of a letter from Mr. Wilson in which the British Prime Minister referred to suggestions Mr. Smith had made to Mr. Bottomley and Lord Gardiner in private conversations on 3 March. Mr. Wilson commented: 'I believe that the suggestions which you made privately offer the germ of an idea but we should of course have to carry our Cabinets and Parliaments with us on any solution which might eventually emerge.'[1] Mr. Wilson suggested possible ways of pursuing the ideas without attracting too much publicity. What Mr. Smith's suggestions were, or whether they had become known to R.F. leaders, is unknown and they may have been unconnected with the calling of the election, but the coincidence of events suggests otherwise.

Mr. Smith said publicly that his aim in the election was to achieve a two-thirds majority in the Legislative Assembly so that his hand would be strengthened in negotiations with Britain and so that amendments could be made in the Constitution. After explaining that the Government had fulfilled its pledge to work within the existing Constitution, he said: 'It is obvious, however, that in some respects changes are essential. I give you an example: the cross-voting on the 'A' and 'B' Rolls.'[2]

The opposition R.P. said that the election was being fought on two basic issues: the threat of U.D.I. and the danger, with or without U.D.I., of Southern Rhodesia becoming a one-party state. Mr. Butler, after accusing the Government of following a policy which was leading inevitably to a U.D.I., announced that the R.P. offered 'the Third Choice'. This choice avoided the extremes of a U.D.I., or a quick hand-over to African nationalists. R.P. posters proclaimed 'Independence

---

[1] Cmnd. 2807, Wilson-Smith, 29 March 1965.
[2] *The Rhodesia Herald*, 1 April 1965.

by negotiation—maintenance of standards and responsible government—economic prosperity—racial harmony'. When these generalities were translated into a specific policy statement, the R.P.'s continued attempts to mollify European misgivings were apparent. Mr. Butler's pusillanimous attitude to the Land Apportionment Act was reiterated. It was stated that the Act should be retained 'in the residential areas until the public is satisfied that fears of its removal are groundless. Adequate safeguards for the maintenance of proper standards will be implemented'. The R.P. also advocated that education should remain segregated; that racial discrimination should be prohibited in public places, but that there would be freedom of association in private gatherings and clubs; that law and order must be maintained; and that the power and prestige of the chiefs should be enhanced.

As the campaign developed, the R.P. attack on the Government became centred on three main issues. First there was the continued opposition to U.D.I. Stemming directly from this was the second issue; that a U.D.I. would lead to economic disaster. The R.P. demanded that the Government should publish reports which had been made at the Government's request by agricultural, industrial, and commercial groups. Their publication, it was argued, was the only fair way of giving the public an accurate estimate of the economic consequences of a U.D.I. but also the publication could be of great service to the R.P., for it was widely rumoured that the reports were deeply pessimistic. One of the reports, that of the Rhodesia Tobacco Association, had been published by the Association before the election campaign started. This report estimated that, if unilateral action were taken, only half the tobacco crop would be sold and what was sold would only fetch a low price. Lord Graham, the Minister of Agriculture, attacked the report as an attempt 'to raise bogymen', and said its publication had been a disservice to the country. The Government countered the rumours of other gloomy reports by saying that those who now foretold economic disaster were the same people who had forecast similar disaster at the break-up of the Federation and at the R.F. election victory. Their present assessment was likely to prove as inaccurate as the previous ones.

However, the R.P. pressure decided the Government to

publish a White Paper containing its own assessment on the economic aspects of U.D.I. It was a brief, generalized report which was not really an assessment of economic consequences, but an assessment of whether the British threats of imposing economic sanctions were serious or practical. The White Paper said that the reports the Government had received had assumed that the threats would be carried out but 'if these proposals were not implemented then of course these reports would be of little relevance'. Reasons were then given why the threats would not be carried out: because Southern Rhodesia's northern neighbours would be hurt; because 'there is no sentiment attached to money' and therefore 'countries will continue to trade'; because the African states to the north were going under Communist influence and 'it is quite incredible, therefore, that Britain would attempt the destruction of the Rhodesian economy and the consequent overthrow of stable government. Other Western countries would not support Britain because of the threat.' If Britain did take action, the White Paper said that the Southern Rhodesian Government would take counter-measures, which might include the repatriation of non-indigenous labour (no details were given of how this enormous task of moving 300,000 men could be organized or what its consequences would be).[1] The White Paper had few merits as a strictly economic appraisal, but it helped to reassure the faithful, and it did emphasize the complex political and national interests which would be involved in imposing economic sanctions against Southern Rhodesia.

After the publication of the White Paper some of the industrial and business groups decided to publish their own findings. Among these, the Institute of Directors stated that the price of U.D.I. might be prohibitive, and that if Britain did no more than stop capital contributions and withdraw Commonwealth preferences the effects would be serious enough. Of the 294 members of the Institute only nineteen reported favourably on a U.D.I.[2] The Association of Rhodesian Industries (A.R.N.I.) reported that Mr. Wilson's threats must be taken seriously and there was no evidence to suggest that Southern Rhodesia could

---

[1] *The Economic Aspects of a Declaration of Independence* (Salisbury Government Printer C.S.R. 15, 1965).
[2] *The Rhodesia Herald*, 28 April 1965.

avoid a trade embargo by her northern neighbours or find alternative outlets in other countries. The report concluded: 'A.R.N.I. is convinced that the risks inherent in steps which would automatically lead to the loss of current trading opportunities cannot, on the known facts, be in the best interests of the people as a whole.'[1] The same tone of pessimism pervaded all the published reports.

In revealing the economic dangers of a U.D.I., the R.P. had gained a clear point, but it was uncertain whether the electorate would heed these gloomy prophecies or the insistent voice of the Government that independence was essential whatever its price.

The R.P.'s third line of attack was the accusation that the Government had no intention of abiding by the 1961 Constitution, that it was intended to change the whole constitutional balance. When Mr. Smith in his election announcement had suggested that constitutional amendments were necessary he was expressing the frustration of a government and party which had felt cabined and confined by the over-liberal Constitution. There was ample evidence of the frustration. In February Mr. Gaunt, the Minister of Local Government, had said:

The Constitution, which is our authority and which we have to carry out to the best of our ability so long as it remains a Constitution, is in certain respects completely and utterly unrealistic. It must have been drawn up by people who have either been so removed from the realities of life in a country like this where we have different communities who on the whole have reached different standards in life or it is made because it was never intended to last. It was intended as a stop-gap to the complete hand-over to African nationalist government.[2]

During the election campaign greater detail of the government constitutional plans was revealed. These plans all pointed in one direction—a slowing-down of the pace of advancement to African majority rule. At a private meeting between government leaders and R.P. leaders, it was reported that the Prime Minister had suggested some specific amendments. These were reported to be:

[1] *The Sunday Mail*, 2 May 1965.
[2] S.R.L.A. Hansard, 18 February 1965, col. 1711.

(1) the elimination of cross-voting between the rolls;
(2) an extension of the 'B' Roll franchise to embrace all tax-paying Africans;
(3) the provision of ten extra 'A' Roll and three 'B' Roll seats, but the three new 'B' Roll seats plus one of the existing 'B' Roll seats were to be filled by chiefs nominated by the Council of Chiefs;
(4) the removal of the restriction of the number of Cabinet ministers;
(5) a 'fade-out' clause for 'B' Roll seats;
(6) an amendment to the Declaration of Rights to permit preventive detention;
(7) the amendment of entrenched clauses by a two-thirds or three-quarters majority of the Legislative Assembly.[1]

When, during the campaign, the Government formally announced its proposals for constitutional changes, they were not as extensive as those discussed with the R.P. leaders. The most important of the proposals announced by Mr. Lardner-Burke were that chiefs should be permitted to sit in the Legislative Assembly; that the size of the Assembly should be increased, although the change in numbers or in balance between 'A' and 'B' Roll seats was unspecified; and that cross-voting should be abolished.[2] Whatever uncertainty there might be about the precise proposals the whole train of government thinking was that Africans' influence through directly elected members of the Legislative Assembly must be curtailed. This was, of course, the perfectly logical outcome of the success of the European (R.F.) party. To preserve European control for an indefinite period, constitutional changes were essential.

Although the R.P. pursued their campaign vigorously, it was clear that they had no chance of overthrowing the R.F. Government. Butler admitted that there was 'no ready belief in the country that it would be likely for us to form a government'. The party's chief aim was to prevent the R.F. gaining a two-thirds' majority. In the 'A' Roll constituencies the R.P. only fought twenty-five of the fifty seats. Of the sitting R.P. Members, only five sought re-election. The party's main hope was to win most of the 'B' Roll district seats, and add to these a handful of 'A' Roll constituencies.

The R.P. fought all the district seats, where only 'independents' opposed them. Unlike 1962, there were no R.F.

---

[1] *The Rhodesia Herald*, 26 April 1965.   [2] Op. cit., 24 April 1965

candidates nominated for the districts. There were two public reasons given for this. William Harper told an election meeting that the party was not nominating district candidates because the Government recognized the chiefs as the leaders of the African people.[1] The Prime Minister gave a different reason. He said that the 'B' Roll was designed for Africans to represent African interests. 'Therefore it is not the intention of the Rhodesia Front to submit any party candidates for the electoral districts. I believe that these members should be independent and free from any party ties to express the wishes of their constituents.'[2] The more probable explanation for the failure of the R.F. to nominate district candidates was that the Government did not want the odium of failure if the African vote went against them, as it had in 1962, and also they did not wish to recognize an electoral system which they disliked and hoped to change. In fact the R.F. gave covert support to some 'independents' who stood for district seats. A memorandum was circulated advising party members which of the district candidates should be supported by use of the cross-vote. This was probably an attempt to gain some African sympathizers in the Assembly, who would be useful in supporting constitutional changes and helping the party's 'image' abroad.[3]

The R.F. election campaign was directed to counter the opposition's attacks and to re-emphasize the party's well-established aims. An R.F. poster stated that 'the third choice' meant 'appeasement' and 'a black future for all'. The Prime Minister declared that R.P. policy was wishful thinking and an attempt to sit on the fence. He thought that Southern Rhodesians had two choices—a quick hand-over to 'one man, one vote', or the path the R.F. offered of independence at the earliest possible moment under a 'responsible' government. He asked: 'Does anybody really think that the extreme racialists are going to shelve their request for an immediate hand-over?'[4] In reply to the criticism that Southern Rhodesia was becoming a one-party state, Mr. Smith said: 'The true position is that in a one-party

[1] Public meeting at Allan Wilson School, reported by *The Rhodesia Herald*, 23 April 1965.
[2] *The Rhodesia Herald*, 1 April 1965.
[3] I am indebted to my colleague, Mr. L. W. Bowman, for these ideas on the 'B' Roll seats.
[4] *The Rhodesia Herald*, 2 April 1965 (speech at Umtali).

state no one is allowed to provide opposition. In Rhodesia today the Opposition, through their policy of vacillation and appeasement, is so bankrupt that they are incapable of providing opposition.'[1]

The R.F.'s direct appeal to the electorate made mention of the Government's successful economic record, but it was emphasized that the main issue of the election was independence. In a speech at Fort Victoria the Prime Minister said he hoped that it could be achieved by negotiation but 'in the circumstances we find ourselves the only practical appeal I can make is for an overall mandate to govern and act in what we consider to be the best interests of Rhodesia.' He saw the election as another phase in the battle for independence. 'Without independence', he continued, 'we cannot achieve the economic expansion or political stability which is so essential for the survival of civilized government in this country.' Negotiations would be tried but 'if in the end, we find we can make no progress and the negotiations end in deadlock then we must face up to the question of assuming our independence'.[2] Mr. Smith reiterated the same point on several occasions. He made clear that, while the election was not directly about a U.D.I., it was about independence and that unilateral action might be the only way to achieve this. In a broadcast on 4 May he said:

If we find we cannot get any further with negotiations and the time comes when the standards of civilization and the way of life we have built up are in jeopardy—the only thing we can see ahead of Rhodesia is to be handed over to extreme nationalists—then we will not, as the last government did, say we must plan a phased hand-over. No, we will then advise you differently and say we believe if it is going to be worth remaining in this country we have got to take matters into our own hands and that the answer is not to sit down in a slit trench and wave a white flag. The time may come when we will be forced to that decision—but it is not now. This election has nothing to do with a unilateral declaration of independence.[3]

The 1965 election was another major triumph for the R.F. If any doubts about the strength of European support for the

[1] Op. cit., 15 April 1965 (speech at Fort Victoria).
[2] Op. cit., 15 April 1965 (speech at Fort Victoria).
[3] Op. cit., 5 May 1965.

Government remained, they were dispelled at the election. The R.F. won all fifty 'A' Roll constituency seats, of which twenty-two were uncontested.[1] In the twenty-eight seats it contested, the R.F. drew 79·2 per cent of the 'A' Roll vote, against 21 per cent which the R.P. drew in the twenty-five seats it contested (three Independents stood against R.F. candidates); but again the minute size of the electorate is striking. In winning twenty-eight seats, the R.F. drew only 28,165 against the R.P.'s 6,377. The eclipse of the R.P. was even greater than the overall voting figures indicate, for the R.P. had only chosen to fight in the most favourable constituencies. In no single constituency did the R.P. come near to winning a seat. The closest contest was in Willowvale, which had a substantial Asian and Coloured vote, but even there B. Ponter, the R.F. candidate, had a majority of 318, obtaining 733 votes against G. J. Raftopoulos's 415 (R.P.) votes. In Bulawayo East, a traditional 'Establishment' stronghold, J. H. Allen (R.P.) could raise only 493 votes and lost by 367 votes. The R.P. leader, David Butler, lost in Highlands North by 545 votes.

In the 'B' Roll district seats the R.P. was much more successful, winning ten of the fifteen seats, the other five going to independents, two of whom were said to have received covert R.F. backing. But the paucity of voters in the districts was even more striking than in the constituencies. Only 14·4 per cent of the 'B' Roll electorate voted in the contested districts. In contesting fifteen seats, the R.P. obtained only 754 'B' Roll votes, yet won ten seats. The highest single number of votes received by an individual candidate was 129 ('B' Roll plus 'A' Roll devalued) for J. M. Gondo (R.P.) in Ndanga. The lowest poll was in Belingwe where the result was:

TABLE VI

BELINGWE DISTRICT—ELECTION RESULT 1965

Candidate	'B' Roll	'A' Roll	'A' Roll devalued	Total
J. S. Hove (R.P.)	37	353	7	44
S. Mazibisa (Ind.)	4	112	2	6
			Majority 28	

[1] For an analysis of the election results, see Appendix II.

19

In some districts the concentration of cross-voting by 'A' Roll voters for individual candidates was striking, and can be explained by the voters following R.F. advice, but the number of 'B' votes cast was so small that the 'A' votes were devalued to tiny proportions. In no district did the 'A' Roll cross-vote succeed in tipping the balance against 'B' Roll votes. Gokwe district provides one example, among others, of the ludicrous voting figures and devaluation of 'A' Roll votes, which resulted from the failure of the 'B' Roll electorate to register or vote. There the result was:

TABLE VII

GOKWE DISTRICT—ELECTION RESULT 1965

Candidate		'B' Roll	'A' Roll	'A' Roll devalued	Total
P.E. Chigogo	(Ind.)	74	122	1	75
D.S. Nkiwande	(Ind.)	34	3,085	29	63
L.L. Ndimande	(RP)	28	356	3	31

Mr. Chigogo's majority—12

With justification it could be argued that the district Members of Parliament virtually represented nobody. They were the residue of a constitutional failure.

The political trends of the 1960s—the European swing to the right, the predominance of 'the European party' in the Legislative Assembly, the African rejection of the constitutional arrangements, the disintegration of the multiracial party—culminated in the 1965 election. The African nationalist refusal to participate within the constitutional framework had left the parliamentary struggle open to 'the European party' and 'the multiracial party'. It was clear from the 1964 by-election results that 'the multiracial party' was collapsing as a political force, but the completeness of the collapse was not finally confirmed until the 1965 election. The election in fact signalled the failure of the 1961 Constitution, the Constitution of 'partnership', with its attempt to share power between the races. Perhaps it was a pious, unrealistic hope from the beginning, but the failure cannot be attributed simply to a mechanical failure of constitutional engineering. The real failure was the breakdown in support for 'the multiracial' party which per-mitted the R.F., the 'European party', to gain a tight grip on the Government.

After the election it was decided that the R.P. would be dis-solved and replaced by an all-African opposition party, the United People's Party (U.P.P.) led by J. M. Gondo, and a 'non-political pressure group', the Rhodesian Constitutional Association (R.C.A.). The R.C.A. represented the remnants of 'the Establishment' which within two and a half years had been transformed from the accepted ruling party to a small pressure group. The R.C.A. was 'to keep alive the principle of racial co-operation as the only long-term solution to Rhodesia's prob-lems'. The R.C.A. and the U.P.P. were associated by cross-membership; for example, Mr. Gondo sat on the steering com-mittee of the R.C.A. Speaking for the U.P.P. Mr. Gondo said that the new party would follow multiracial policies similar to those of the dissolved R.P., and added that 'we want to show that we are responsible parliamentarians who are capable of advancing the Constitution'.[1]

Because of the weakness of the opposition party, its division into the U.P.P. and the R.C.A. made little practical difference, but it was another sign of the failure of the two races to co-operate at a political level. Some African Members of Parlia-ment were incensed at the refusal of Europeans who had failed to gain parliamentary seats to remain within a party with an African leader and an all-African representation in the Legis-lative Assembly.

The election strengthened the Government's position in every way. Externally the Government felt stronger than ever in its negotiations with Britain; internally the parliamentary oppo-sition was very weak indeed. In the new Legislative Assembly some of the district Members who formed the opposition had experience of politics; men like Mr. Gondo and Mr. Chad Chipunza, ex-party whip of the U.F.P. in the Federal Assembly; and there was still Dr. Ahrn Palley, who had given a remark-able demonstration of political survival when he was returned as the Independent Member for Highfields district. But most

[1] *The Rhodesia Herald*, 1 June 1965.

of the opposition Members could offer only enthusiasm and goodwill, which could not compensate for their very limited experience and ability and even more for their lack of popular support.

The existence of the 'B' Roll African M.P.s had some direct advantages for the R.F. Government, for they could proclaim abroad that Africans sat in the Legislative Assembly. An air-mail letter printed after U.D.I. which Europeans were asked to post to friends overseas, said that charges of Southern Rhodesia being a police state were obviously untrue. 'Take a look at our Parliamentary system', the letter said, 'and you will see that it is blatantly untrue. For our Government is some-times accused of being intolerant of African opposition and surely, therefore, if this was a police state such opposition would be prevented? But it is not. Our Parliament already seats thirteen African Members of Parliament, and will un-doubtedly hold more in the course of time. As a parliamentary opposition, these M.P.s frequently oppose the Government both inside and outside the House and they remain free to do so.' This was the international image, but inside the country it was clear that the opposition of the African Members of Parliament could be indulged because it offered no real threat to the Government.

In the Legislative Assembly the old subjects and content of debates came up again and again. For example, on a motion seeking the repeal of the Land Apportionment Act, Mr. Chipunza said that the Act 'is bitterly resented by the entire African people because it has made them strangers in the land of their birth'. He said that 'both socially and economically . . . the African has suffered because of the implementation of this iniquitous piece of legislation'.[1] The evergreen Mr. Cary (R.F.) replied that the Act 'must be retained for generations, at any rate until such time as the Africans [were] able to look after their affairs better'. He challenged the opposition to sup-port throwing open the Tribal Trust Lands at the same time as repealing the Land Apportionment Act.[2] The debate could have been taken almost directly from the old U.F.P./D.P. days, but there was the vital difference that 'the European party' was

[1] S.R.L.A. Hansard, 11 August 1965, col. 97.
[2] Op. cit., 11 August 1965, col. 111.

now supreme, challenged only by a few independents and by 'an African party' which even its firmest supporters could never envisage as an alternate government. The very weakness of the parliamentary opposition has been seen by some R.F. members as justification for their claim that Africans are better represented by the chiefs than by parliamentarians.

In defending their position the African Members of Parliament have claimed that despite their minimal support they do provide a voice of African opinion in an otherwise white-dominated state, and they have claimed that they could form part of the foundation on which a reconciliation between the races could be built. So far there is little evidence to justify confidence in these views. The African Members have attracted little or no additional support during their period in Parliament; within Parliament they have revealed only limited skill in their hesitant, uncertain opposition to the R.F., and within their own ranks they have suffered from persistent faction and personality problems. They remain a collection of individuals inclined to conservatism and standing outside the mainstream of events.

The election victory gave Mr. Smith the opportunity to reshuffle his Cabinet. He dropped John Gaunt and Harry Reedman, neither of whom had distinguished themselves as Ministers. The deposed Ministers, both of whom were later given diplomatic posts, were replaced by John Howman, who had resigned with Winston Field, and Bernard Mussett.[1]

The election further emphasized a growing trend within the governing party. This was that with the R.F.'s commanding hold in the Legislative Assembly, the chief threats to, and the chief pressures on, the R.F. leaders came from within the ranks of their own party. Pressure from the party congress, the caucus meeting, and the branch offices carried much greater weight than that from the parliamentary opposition. These internal

---

[1] The full new Cabinet, in addition to Mr. Smith, was: Dupont (External Affairs and Defence: Deputy Prime Minister), Wrathall (Finance and Posts), Lardner-Burke (Justice, Law and Order), Mussett (Local Government and Housing), Lord Graham (Agriculture), Harper (Internal Affairs and Public Service), Van Heerden (Mines and Lands, Water Development), Rudland (Trade and Industry), McLean (Labour, Social Welfare and Health), Howman (Immigration, Tourism and Information), A. P. Smith (Education). See Appendix II.

pressures deterred the Government from any moderation of its policies.

The extent and nature of the pressure was clearly revealed at the party congress of August 1965. Before this congress, which was the first since 1963, there were rumours that the Government was to be challenged for compromising its position on the independence issue. There were even rumours that an attempt might be made to oust Mr. Smith and to replace him by a more reactionary leader. Mr. Smith, according to some of the party's right-wingers, had 'grown soft'. Two weeks before the congress met, there was a clear example of the R.F.'s insistence that Mr. Smith must place at least as much store on being the party leader as on being Prime Minister. Colonel M. Knox, the Party Chairman, issued a statement in which he said:

It may be of interest to know that, in view of certain articles which have appeared in the Press recently I called on the Prime Minister this morning and received his personal assurance first that the Government was not contemplating any action which could be construed as contravening the principles and policies of the R.F., and secondly that independence, whether it was through negotiation or not, would be—to use a colloquial expression—without strings.[1]

But rumour of right-wing pressure on the Government continued. A few days before the congress, *The Sunday Mail* reported an R.F. Member as saying that Mr. Dupont would have to be displaced because he was a moderating influence on the Prime Minister. 'Members', said the report, 'are growing suspicious of Mr. Dupont. In particular they are worried about his meeting Dr. Banda and his recent disclosure about overtures to President Kaunda.'[2]

The congress was a personal triumph for Mr. Smith. There was no overt attempt to challenge his authority. This may partially be explained by a closing of the ranks after the adverse publicity, but more important was Mr. Smith's increasing strength as a leader. He achieved this from a combination of personal popularity and an ability to reflect the predominant mood of the party, to identify himself with party aspirations.

[1] *The Sunday Mail*, 25 July 1965.   [2] Op. cit., 1 August 1965.

The Prime Minister received unanimous support, but he received the support because he made it clear that there would be no diversion from the party's aims. Personally he could not afford to tarnish his image as 'the tough man', the only Southern Rhodesian politician who had stood up to the British, and so he achieved his personal triumph by absorbing right-wing pressures. For the future this left him with little flexibility in his negotiations with the British Government. At the congress, the Prime Minister said that he would not be tied to a specific date but promised decisive action on independence. He said that, if unilateral action became necessary, the Southern Rhodesian Government would choose its own time. He admitted that to have seized independence in 1964 would have been disastrous. Then Mr. Smith moved on from independence to attack 'the enemies of the Government', who had been trying to undermine R.F. solidarity. He confirmed that the Cabinet was united behind him, with all the Ministers determined to fulfil the party's policies.

The strength of right-wing pressure on internal affairs was apparent in the congress debates on the Press and the new teaching hospital for the University College. An attack on the Press was an in-built characteristic of R.F. congresses. At this one K. B. Clarke from Hatfield declared that the men in senior positions in the Rhodesian Printing and Publishing Company 'have twisted minds . . . If they continue to work against the policy of the country we should automatically close them down, take over the Press and make it state-controlled'. The Parliamentary Secretary for Information, Mr. van der Byl, was sympathetic when it was suggested that all political articles should be signed by the authors.

When the plans for the new multiracial teaching hospital were debated, the congress abandoned itself to racial emotionalism and bad temper. The Minister of Health, Mr. McLean, was heckled when he said that a committee was investigating problems associated with the hospital. Mr. L. Dominion of the party executive was loudly cheered when he proposed that all building work on the hospital should stop. Mr. Dominion said that to establish a multiracial hospital was contrary to the R.F.'s principles and cause. He feared that all the best doctors would transfer to the new hospital and leave

Salisbury Central (European) Hospital without staff. 'We will', he was reported to have said, 'end up being presented with the alternative of going to a multiracial hospital or dying.' It was not reported whether Mr. Dominion indicated which of these terrifying alternatives he would choose in a crisis. Mr. Smith intervened to bring some sanity back to the debate. He told the congress that decisions should not be taken in an emotional atmosphere, that a full investigation should be made and only then could the future of the hospital be decided. After the Prime Minister's interjection, Mr. Dominion withdrew his resolution, but the congress adopted another which deplored the Government's failure to set aside funds in the current estimates for a new European hospital in Salisbury.[1]

The insistent voice of the far right wing was not confined to the R.F. congress. In Rhodesia, as moderate opinion has been silenced or has abandoned the contest, right-wing theorists have occupied the field. Those who hold these views cannot be dismissed as a lunatic fringe, for they are led by men holding important positions, such as Van der Byl, the Deputy Minister of Information, J. A. Newington, a Member of Parliament, Harvey Ward, the Director of News Broadcasts on the Rhodesian radio, and Ivor Benson, who has been employed as an Information Officer and was for a short time the Chief Government Censor after U.D.I. It would be wrong to imply that all Rhodesian Europeans or even all R.F. supporters accept every pronouncement by the high priests of the right, but it would be equally wrong to ignore the increasing acceptance of their ideas and the way in which aspects of their thinking can be detected with growing frequency in ministerial and government statements. The attraction of this thinking is that it rationalizes the existing social order, and lays a foundation of dogma for the myths upon which white domination is built. It defends and explains the increasing isolation of the Europeans of Southern Africa, and Southern Rhodesia in particular, and exonerates them from blame for the country's problems. The blame is laid squarely on evil outside influences and organizations.

[1] Accounts of the congress are contained in *The Sunday Mail*, 8 August 1965, and *The Rhodesia Herald* of 7 and 9 August 1965.

The basis of these extreme ideas is that Rhodesia is in the forefront of a battle, a battle to preserve Western civilization, Christian standards, justice, order, and truth. The battle is against 'forces of evil' which are threatening to eradicate Western civilization. As previously noted, Mr. Dupont expressed these fears when he introduced increased security legislation in 1963 and 1964.[1] Similar fears have been reiterated many times since. For example, the editorial of *Newsfront* for 4 October 1964 stated that: 'The arena is the world. The contest is white civilization versus barbarism . . . Today Southern Rhodesia, almost the last stronghold of this principle, finds herself cast to lead the counter-attack.'

In the battle Communism is the chief but not the only enemy. No clear or specific definition of Communism is given. Certainly its use is not confined to those who accept the theories of Marx, Engels, and Lenin. It is not unusual to hear a Southern Rhodesian say: 'All the black African states to the north are Communist.' The main use of 'Communist' appears to be as a smear, in the MacCarthy sense, for those who hold radically different views from predominant European thinking. The Communists are accused of using other men and institutions to achieve their ends but, while this is a generally accepted accusation in other Western societies, the right-wing theorists of Southern Rhodesia are quite exceptional in their claims of the extent of Communist infiltration and the individuals and organizations corrupted by it. It is essential, according to Mr. Benson, to 'know your enemy', and in Mr. Benson's view there are many, many enemies to know. They include, for example, 'liberals', who are either unwitting allies of the Communists or even Communists in disguise. Again, there is no clear definition of 'liberal', but it is usually applied to people, other than those identified as outright Communists, who believe that Africans should have more political, social, and economic rights than they enjoy in Southern Rhodesia at present. A. E. Stirton wrote:

As false prophets of new political and social theories, the liberals are dupes of sinister Masters, who, bent on world conquest have infected the universal body politic with a malignant view and in the

[1] See above, Chapter IX, p. 205.

battle for the mind of men . . . these obedient leftist professors, lecturers, teachers, journalists, authors, artists, lawyers, clergymen, etc. [barter] their service without scruple to the highest bidder in the slave market of the principal contenders in what is euphemistically termed the 'East-West Cold War'.

Mr. Stirton thought it was a sham fight, for the forces of evil were directed from both New York and Moscow.[1]

In unexplained ways such unlikely people and organizations as international financiers, the World Council of Churches, and the American Peace Corps have apparently formed alliances with the Communists. An example of the way in which diverse bodies and organizations are identified was given in an article in *The Citizen*, written after U.D.I. by Eric D. Butler. Mr. Butler said:

One of the first results of the Rhodesian stand has been to demonstrate the unholy alliance between international power groups which the average person does not realize have any connection. Just as the Goldwater challenge against the 'soft' attitude on international Communism resulted in powerful international financial organizations lining up with Communists and others against Goldwater, so the Rhodesia challenge has produced a unity of the same groups . . . The international financial groups have shown a persistent interest in the 'independence' campaign in Africa. The World Bank's activities have in some cases been openly subversive.'

Mr. Butler noted that the new Reserve Bank of Rhodesia set up by the British Government included 'Sir Sydney Caine, Director of the London School of Economics, the brain centre of political internationalism', but Mr. Butler saw profit for Southern Rhodesia in the campaign which had been mounted against her for it made her less dependent on international finance and 'free from the subversive influences of U.N.E.S.C.O. teachers and other officials of the U.N. Organization.'[2] Lieutenant-Colonel Macleod, the R.F. Member of Parliament for Eastern, made similar allegations about the connection between Communism and international finance. After stating that all revolutions since the time of Oliver Cromwell had been inspired by international financiers he said:

[1] *The Citizen*, 4 March 1966.   [2] Op. cit., 4 March 1966.

Finally we come to the greatest revolution of all, the Bolshevik Revolution of 1917. This revolution was financed and supported by international financiers in New York . . . these revolutions which have always been organized and carried out by the Communists always ended up with the international financiers in control. Russia is the international financiers' paradise.[1]

The ubiquitous forces of evil have penetrated, to a greater or lesser degree, the United Nations, the Commonwealth, the Organization of African Unity. Thus Rhodesia, except for her allies South Africa and Portugal, finds herself an isolated bastion of sanity and righteousness in an otherwise hostile world. Each week on the radio Harvey Ward warns of the evils which threaten Rhodesia and tells of the corruption and injustice in other countries and in international organizations. Within this picture the Commonwealth is seen as a combination of corrupt, Communist-dominated, new 'coloured' states, and weak, ineffectual, older 'white' states, which are prepared to appease the new states at almost any price.

The United Nations is no better. The world body was described by Fawcett Phillips, the M.P. for Hillside, as 'this forum of Communism, because it is nothing else . . . dominated, if I may say so, by thirty-three irresponsible African states.'[2] Speaking of the dangers of U.N.E.S.C.O. influence, Mr. J. R. Ryan, the R.F. Member for Salisbury Central, said: 'We have various institutions of the devil, as I call them, weaving their way into our society. It will be a sorry day if we are ever directly implicated in financing them and I wonder if this increase of the grant to the University in any way helps these institutions, these offshoots of the greatest communistic and devilish institution in the world known as the United Nations.'[3] The World Council of Churches has been described as 'an organization with a revolutionary political programme which it seeks to carry out in the name of Christianity', and which is under the control of 'those with leftish, liberal and Communist connections'.[4]

According to the right-wing theorists, one of the chief

[1] S.R.L.A. Hansard, 5 July 1966, col. 520.
[2] S.R.L.A. Hansard, 1 July 1966, col. 390.
[3] S.R.L.A. Hansard, 8 July 1965, col. 1088.
[4] 'Viewpoint', *Newsfront*, 1 and 15 May 1964.

weapons used by the Communists and their allies is insidious propaganda, which has already corrupted most nations and is now, 'in the fight for men's minds', being directed against Rhodesia. The Minister of Law and Order, Mr. Lardner-Burke, said:

This country is fighting a war on two fronts. One of these fronts is represented by the pressure and psychological warfare from abroad and the other is the internal campaign of subversion, destruction and sabotage much of it also inspired and directed from beyond our borders. We are determined to win this undeclared war, no matter what opposition we may encounter from the communist bloc and their fellow travellers both inside and outside our country.[1]

In March 1966 Mr. Howman, the Minister of Information, told a Rotary Club luncheon that, after the fall of the Nazis, Western nations had mistakenly 'dropped their guard', as they assumed the days of thought manipulation and brain-washing were over but, in fact, 'forces inherently every bit as evil as those we had vanquished—forces with a far greater potential for evil—embarked on a propaganda offensive which made the Nazi Propaganda war effort look like the work of bumbling amateurs. It took the form of a world-wide conspiracy.' At first there was an infiltration stage during which the institutions of capitalist society were corrupted, because it was realized that open Communist activity had limited value. 'I believe', he said, 'that immediately after the last war they [the forces of the Left] laid siege—quietly and without anybody ever realizing what was happening—to such institutions as broadcasting corporations, influential newspapers, seats of learning . . . even (and I say this with all deference and respect to the Churches) to world Christianity.' According to Mr. Howman, the Communist long-term plan is now bearing fruit, for 'the cub reporter of twenty years ago may well be the editor or the assistant editor of today'.

He said that it had not been a tight conspiracy in which every move had been controlled by Moscow, but 'a movement involving a loose alliance of all the elements of the Left, was under way, and thereafter carried itself and created its own momentum. I don't suppose many of the elements involved

[1] S.R.L.A. Hansard, 26 August 1964, col. 1278.

even realized themselves that they were part of such a movement, although undoubtedly there were the "faceless ones"
who knew all along the strategy which had been set afoot and
who applied such guidance and stimulation wherever and
whenever they could. Among these, for example, I would include the Fabians', and among the Fabians Mr. Howman
numbered the British Prime Minister, Mr. Harold Wilson.[1]

The threat of insidious propaganda has been a favourite subject of Mr. Newington. He told the Legislative Assembly that:

these hidden groups, hidden individuals, so often find their way to
radio news media and are never discovered and never known, and
it is never realized exactly what an insidious campaign they are
carrying on against the country that befriends them. We have not
realized that liberalism is now a cover name for Communism. We
have not realized that from positions of power and influence hidden
Communism is using education, the Church, radio, television, to
destroy us from within and all the woolly-minded idealists, all those
living in the twilight land of unreality, completely disregard this and
say it is not happening.

Mr. Newington concluded that 'it is absolutely essential that
Government has some means of protection'.[2] Mr. Ivor Benson
also thought that restriction must be placed on news media.
He asked: 'Can it [the Press] be left to do as it pleases, as in the
past?' He agreed that criticism could be a good thing but 'the
word criticism must be defined. It must be sound criticism.
That means that it must be criticism that springs from a set of
values and motives which belong to our society. Otherwise,
how can criticism further our own values and our interests?'[3]
For a period after U.D.I. Mr. Benson had the opportunity to
further 'our own values and our interests' when he became the
Government's Chief Censor.

The European extremists believe that within the country
itself the forces of evil may gain such a hold that even the parliamentary opposition may be used by them. Mr. Smith
warned of this danger in a speech which has already been
quoted.[4] Mr. Newington also had something to say about the
parliamentary opposition. He said: 'It is appalling to me that

---

[1] Rhodesian Government Press Release, 25 March 1966.
[2] S.R.L.A. Hansard, 12 August 1964, cols. 660–3.
[3] *Newsfront*, 15 May 1964.
[4] Chapter XI, pp. 255–6.

at a time when ruthless and unscrupulous propaganda outside our borders is attempting to undermine our unity, when subversive elements within and without willingly do the enemy's work, when Communism is mounting in Africa; I find it appalling that we have to spend our time in debates that only bring about disunity.'[1] The implication could be that all opposition is a form of subversion.

It is contended that Rhodesia, aided by her allies South Africa and Portugal, is fighting not only for herself but for all Western society. In this there is a message of hope, for it is said that in time the people of the Western countries will understand and applaud the Rhodesians for their courageous stand in upholding the virtues which have temporarily been lost to the Western world. Mr. Smith declared that if Sir Winston Churchill were alive today he would probably emigrate to Rhodesia, because all the qualities for which Churchill stood, 'all these admirable qualities and characteristics of the British that we believed in, loved, and preached to our children no longer exist in Britain', but they can still be found in Rhodesia 'to a greater degree than they ever existed before in the mother country'.[2] The light still burns in Southern Africa and will in time illuminate the world. In his independence speech Mr. Smith said:

I believe that we are a courageous people and history has cast us in a heroic role. To us has been given the privilege of being the first Western nation in the last two decades to have the determination and fortitude to say 'so far and no further'. We may be a small country, but we are a determined people who have been called upon to play a role of world-wide significance . . . We have struck a blow for the preservation of justice, civilization, and Christianity, and in the spirit of this belief we have this day assumed our sovereign independence.

Already, it is said, there are some signs of hope and frequently a distinction has been drawn between 'the people' of such countries as America and Britain, and their Governments. Increasingly it has been contended that 'the people' are seeing the folly of their Governments' hostility to the Europeans of Southern Africa and understanding that Rhodesia's

[1] S.R.L.A. Hansard, September 1964.
[2] *The Rhodesia Herald*, 29 October 1966.

battle is also their battle. According to Mr. Howman 'the truth'—and it is 'the truth' for which Rhodesia stands—'can be something of a shock treatment. Get one piece of incontrovertible truth through to a brain-washed zombie, and you may well suddenly turn him back to an angry human being—angry at the way he knows he has been fooled'.

But meanwhile these Western countries have themselves become riddled with the 'forces of evil'. This is most obvious in their Governments. Mr. Fawcett Phillips declared: 'The State Department like the British Government—when I say the State Department I mean, of course, the United States of America—are riddled, they are rotten with Communism. It is a question of infiltration into government utilizing the guise of democracy to achieve that purpose.'[1] But the infiltration has spread wider than the Governments; it has moved into the Churches, education, art, literature, music, radio, and television. In America these evil forces have been associated with the corrupting influence of big-business and financial interests; in Britain with the growth of the Welfare State, the influence of television, and the spread of socialism. Speaking of the B.B.C.'s independence and freedom from government restrictions, Mr. van der Byl said:

To suggest that the B.B.C., forming opinion in the minds of the people of England, has been an influence for good in any way, when you consider the criminality of large areas of London; when you consider the Mods and Rockers, and all those other things; when you consider the total moral underminings which have been taking place in England, much to all our distress, in the last fifteen to twenty years, the Hon. Member can hardly bring that up as an argument in favour of the freedom of broadcasting.[2]

Also in the Legislative Assembly, Lieutenant-Colonel Macleod said that Mr. Macmillan's phrase, 'You have never had it so good', '. . . is a perfect picture of the Welfare State and that, I submit, is the root cause of all the moral degeneracy

[1] S.R.L.A. Hansard, 1 July 1966, col. 390. Commenting on Mr. Fawcett Phillips' remarks, Mr. Lardner-Burke (Minister of Justice, Law and Order) said: 'What the Hon. Member said I would commend not only to Hon. Members of the house, but to all people in Rhodesia to read to ascertain exactly the manner in which this scourge, as it were, works and how it is being spread.' (Hansard, 6 July 1966, col. 576).
[2] S.R.L.A. Hansard, 12 August 1964, col. 694.

in the world today.'[1] On another occasion he said that because of the Welfare State, 'the national character suffers and finally with the introduction of pornographic literature and demoralizing drugs the stage is set for complete demoralization. With regard to the drugs perhaps all Hon. Members are not aware that one of Red China's main exports is these demoralizing drugs.'[2] Brigadier Dunlop said that: 'Spoonfeeding has been the beginning of the ruination of the greatest race that ever existed, the British race. Through the Welfare State they have degenerated fast and furiously.'[3] Harvey Ward, on the Rhodesian radio, suggested that, because Mr. Harold Wilson had visited Moscow so often, he must have Communist sympathies. R. R. Ellis wrote to *The Rhodesia Herald* to say that:

Few people seem to realize the effect on the British people of the Education Act of 1944. The personnel of the teaching profession in the U.K. from top to bottom are predominantly left-wing. In their ranks are many professed Communists, but a greater menace are the 'fellow-travellers' who have Communist ideas but lack the guts to declare them. After twenty years of state education almost all of the teachers have lived and been trained in a left-wing environment where all the old values which made Britain great are held up to ridicule or looked upon as something for which to apologize. Make no mistake about it, anyone in the United Kingdom below the age of thirty-five has been well steeped in the idealistic, optimistic, and above all fantastic doctrine of socialism.[4]

In the fight against Communism and its allies it is accepted that the Europeans of Southern Africa are gravely outnumbered, but this does not mean inevitable defeat. Will and determination can compensate for lack of numbers; will and determination not only to uphold 'civilized, responsible, Christian standards', but also to fight for them with all means available. Not all Southern Rhodesian Europeans would share Mr. R. Lawson's ambition to see 'the last Communist strangled with the guts of the last liberal',[5] but, at least in words, there has grown up a militant, aggressive attitude. Colonel Macleod told the Legislative Assembly: 'As Rhodesians we are ready to take up the challenge and prove to the world that we have the faith, the courage and the will to go forward against undoubted

---

[1] Op. cit., 17 March 1964, col. 875.   [4] *The Rhodesia Herald*, 25 March 1966.
[2] Op. cit., 3 September 1965, col. 1135. [5] *Newsfront*, 15 May 1964.
[3] Op. cit., 19 March 1964, col. 1100.

opposition and create here the real bastion for Christian civilization in Southern Africa.'[1] In a radio discussion programme Mr. Newington attacked America for sending grain to Russia at a time of famine because it was helping the Communists. Mr. van der Byl declared that:

The task of the Information Department is not merely to disseminate information from an interesting point of view but to play its part in fighting the propaganda battle on behalf of the country. 'Propaganda' is by no means the dirty word it is made out to be, but is in fact simply the propagation of the faith and the belief in any particular ideology or thing and that if the Information Department was to improve and strengthen the national ideology then indeed it was doing a worthwhile task.'

He gave another of the Department's tasks as 'the resuscitation of the determination of the European to survive and fight for his rights, the unification of the Europeans in this enterprise has been in a large degree successfully achieved.'[2]

Implicit in this right-wing thinking is the acceptance that, at least for the foreseeable future, Europeans as a race have abilities and values superior to Africans. This thinking appears from time to time in the correspondence columns of the newspapers. There have been letters trying to prove that Jesus was a white. There have been others rejecting the claim that Africans designed and erected the great buildings which now stand in ruins at Zimbabwe. Some Europeans just cannot accept that the race which they know today as servants, servants who forget to fill the salt-cellar or water the flowers, could have built such fine structures. They contend that a superior race must have directed the operations.

I had personal experience of this. While visiting the ruins a friendly but unknown European called to me: 'The niggers never built this, you know. They were used as slave labour by a superior race, the Phoenicians or somebody like that.' He must have detected hesitation in my eyes for, when I failed to reply, he said: 'Oh, I know you call the niggers "Africans" now, but the Africans never built these.' Similar doubts about Africans' abilities were expressed by 'Housewife' in the correspondence columns of *The Rhodesia Herald*. She wrote: 'I have contributed

[1] S.R.L.A. Hansard, 25 February 1964.
[2] Op. cit., 27 July 1965, col. 1418.

not inconsiderably towards "African advancement" at the expense of my pocket, my health, and my patience. Not only have I housed, fed, and clothed my servants, paying them the wages they asked but have taught them the rudiments of hygiene, cooking, and housework', and yet, she complained, 'they have no sense of responsibility or respect'.[1]

When the Bishop of Mashonaland suggested that in future a white skin could not be regarded as an automatic badge of authority, Lieutenant-Colonel Ichabod Alden wrote: 'If the European is ousted from his pride of place, it could only be done by an intelligent race—a requirement that precludes the African.' He thought that if Europeans withdrew from Africa then Asians would take over.[2] George Pile, a columnist in *Newsfront*, wrote of 'a triumvirate of black supremists', consisting of liberal Christians, big-businessmen, and democratic politicians, which had caused all the troubles among Africans, while 'every Christian who uses his eyes and brains knows without having to be told that Christianity itself could not survive without white supremacy.'[3]

It has been suggested that the right-wing theorists have created a new Dark Ages' philosophy, a philosophy in which there are devils lurking behind every tree, every bush, every building, and certainly behind every international organization. These evil ones are trying to lure men away from the paths of righteousness and using every conceivable means to do so. Not for a moment can a man drop his guard, because the evil comes in the most convincing and cunning guises. Most of mankind is smeared by the evil, but there are a few, the chosen, who will triumph in upholding the cause of good. There is hope for the future for, provided the righteous are brave and determined, provided they have the will to win, provided they understand the cause for which they fight and can identify the evil ones, provided they heed the correct doctrine and accept that the priests control what they hear and read—provided all these things are done, then the righteous, if not the meek, shall inherit the earth.[4]

---

[1] *The Rhodesia Herald*, 13 January 1960.
[2] *The Sunday Mail*, 19 August 1962.
[3] *Newsfront*, 3 April 1964.
[4] I am indebted to my colleague, Mr. P. Nursey-Bray, for this interpretation.

CHAPTER XIII

The End of the Road

The search for independence dominated 1965. The Government's determination to achieve it had been reinforced by the results of the chiefs' *indaba*, the referendum, and the election, but the chances of negotiating independence seemed remote and the external danger, the threat of hostile British and international reaction to a unilateral act, remained. This danger forced the R.F. Government to tread warily and apprehensively, to continue to pursue negotiations even when they realized that the prospects of gaining an agreement on their terms were almost hopeless. At times it seemed that the Government's talk of U.D.I. was a bluff, that they never would take the risk but would continue to use the threat as a source of pressure on Britain. There would be brave words but no action. But on other occasions the Government's resentment and frustration spilled out in such martial blasts and aggressive poses that a U.D.I. seemed imminent. According to mood or conviction, the pre-U.D.I. events were translated in either way. Was Mr. Reedman's posting to Lisbon as Southern Rhodesia's representative, in the teeth of strong British opposition, part of the brinkmanship game, or was it a clear indication that Southern Rhodesia intended to act independently?

The events of October 1964, with the British rejection of the chiefs' *indaba* and Mr. Wilson's warning of the consequences of a U.D.I., led to a further deterioration in the relations between the two Governments. Bitter recriminations and accusations dominated the official correspondence. In December Mr. Smith told Mr. Wilson that:

It is with regret that I have to record that during the short term of office of your Government in Britain there has been a drastic deterioration in relations between our two governments . . . Moreover the attempt on the part of your Government to intimidate us through the medium of economic blackmail and with threats to place us virtually in the category of an enemy state is something which has caused deep resentment in the minds of Rhodesians.[1]

Mr. Wilson replied: 'There was no threat to place Rhodesia "in the category of an enemy state": there was only a clear warning, which I am bound to repeat, of the consequences which would follow if Rhodesia should attempt, by unconstitutional actions, to place herself in the position of a territory in rebellion.'[2] Mr. Smith countered by saying: 'Your Government, under pressure, will accept nothing less than a hand-over of the reins of government to a small section of the community, openly advocating intimidation and violence.'[3]

And so it went on, with increasing acrimony but no progress. The only positive point to emerge from this early Smith-Wilson correspondence was a clarification by Mr. Wilson of his Government's policy. In one letter he wrote: 'We look forward to a peaceful transition to majority rule in Southern Rhodesia, but we do not seek ourselves to stipulate how this might be achieved or when that stage should be reached. I assure you that we have no preconceived plan that we wish to impose on your country.'[4] In another he wrote: 'We have an open mind on the timing of independence in relation to progress towards majority rule, to which, as I have said, we wish to see a peaceful transition, but the granting of independence must be on a basis acceptable to the people of the country as a whole.'[5] There was in fact little, if any, change from the previous Conservative Government's policy.

In the last months of 1964 Mr. Smith refused repeated offers to visit London and he refused to receive an all-party mission of senior Members of the British Parliament. The impasse was broken when Mr. Smith visited London to attend Sir Winston Churchill's funeral in January 1965. The visit gave the two their first opportunity to meet as Prime Ministers and surprisingly the meeting was a relative success. At this meeting Mr. Wilson suggested that Mr. Bottomley, the Commonwealth

---

[1] Cmnd. 2807, Smith-Wilson, 15 December 1964.
[2] Op. cit., Wilson-Smith, 21 December 1964.
[3] Op. cit., Smith-Wilson, 12 January 1965.
[4] Op. cit., Wilson-Smith, 17 November 1964.
[5] Op. cit., Wilson-Smith, 27 November 1964.

Secretary, and Lord Gardiner, the Lord Chancellor, should visit Southern Rhodesia. On his return Mr. Smith, after conferring with his Cabinet, confirmed that 'we are prepared to fall in with such an arrangement'.

The two British Ministers made their visit in late February and early March 'to obtain', in Mr. Bottomley's words, 'a balanced view of the state of opinion in Rhodesia and try to find a way forward in the discussions over the constitutional future of Rhodesia'.[1] During the visit the British Ministers met leaders from all sections of Southern Rhodesian society and heard their diverse opinions. Among Europeans they met the Government Ministers, the leaders of the opposition R.P., members of the farming community, and representatives of business and commercial interests. Among Africans they met the restricted nationalist leaders, and for five hours listened to chiefs at a specially summoned *indaba*, as they reaffirmed their support for independence on Mr. Smith's terms. Both the nationalist leaders and the chiefs claimed that they had support from the large majority of Africans.

The British Ministers' relations with the chiefs were particularly unfriendly. The chiefs had been offended by the British refusal to send observers to the October *indaba*, and by the British doubts about the chiefs' claims to represent majority African opinion. When members of the Chiefs' Council met the British Ministers some days after the *indaba* (i.e. the special *indaba* arranged for Mr. Bottomley and Lord Gardiner) it was reported that one chief, after explaining that Mr. Bottomley would not accept anything they said, had declared: 'If I had my way we would walk out of this meeting and leave Mr. Bottomley here alone.' When Mr. Bottomley had asked how the chiefs could demonstrate that they had majority African support, the chiefs had evaded the question by saying: 'It is not our custom to use a ballot or a piece of paper. It is a foreign custom.' When Mr. Bottomley had asked whether the chiefs wanted to be represented in Parliament and, if so, on what terms, a chief had said: 'I am not prepared to answer that question. It is something which is entirely our affair in this country and we feel it is not the concern of the British Government.'[2]

---

[1] *The Rhodesia Herald*, 11 February 1965.   [2] Op. cit., 3 March 1965.

The British Ministers left Southern Rhodesia wiser and no doubt sadder men. Almost everywhere they had met intransigence and fixed attitudes. In his final statement before leaving, Mr. Bottomley reaffirmed that British policy was not to impose immediate majority rule nor to break the constitutional convention by taking unilateral action. Britain, he said, was seeking a 'peaceful transition to majority rule', but did not stipulate how or when this would be achieved. He reaffirmed Britain's opposition to unlawful and unconstitutional acts whether they came from nationalists or adherents of U.D.I. He admitted that he had found a 'hardening of attitudes', but whatever the difficulties 'the search for a constitutional solution must continue'.[1]

The visit of the British Ministers failed to resolve the deadlock between the two Governments. After their return to Britain, correspondence between the Governments continued and, although the tone was now much more polite, and although at one point there appeared to be hope of progress on private suggestions made by Mr. Smith,[2] no real progress to a solution was made. In June the British Government was under renewed pressure at the Commonwealth Prime Ministers' Conference where, according to Mr. Wilson, there was 'solid unanimity of feeling on the need for a speedy democratic settlement', but the British Prime Minister wrote to assure Mr. Smith: 'We have maintained our ground on the British Government's sole responsibility in the matter of Rhodesia's independence and the Prime Ministers have reaffirmed this. We have made clear our own approach to the problem and refused to be deflected from negotiations between the two Governments as the next step.'[3] Mr. Smith replied: 'I am pleased to see that you have been successful in keeping the way open for negotiations in spite of pressure to undertake various commitments.'[4]

The next step in the negotiations was a visit in July by Mr. Cledwyn Hughes, the British Minister of State for Commonwealth Relations. The 'hard-core' R.F. attitude to negotiations

---

[1] *The Rhodesia Herald*, 4 March 1965.
[2] See Chapter XII, p. 270.
[3] Cmnd. 2807, Wilson-Smith, 25 June 1965.
[4] Op. cit., Smith-Wilson, 28 June 1965.

at the time of Mr. Hughes's visit was expressed by Mr. Newington, who said :

I think it is most essential that we reiterate that this party was put in power on clearly defined principles and policies and there will be no retreat therefrom. I think again we should make it clear that we are completely and entirely willing and have always shown ourselves willing to negotiate but not with the object of watering down those principles and those policies on which we were returned to this House . . . From this there can be and will be no retreat.[1]

Mr. Newington's blinkered approach to negotiations was shared by many R.F. members, including some Ministers. Negotiations were seen as a means of persuading the British Government to accept R.F. terms, not as a means of reconciling differences by compromise or by new approaches.

No way was found during Mr. Hughes's visit to bridge the gap between British and Southern Rhodesian attitudes. Mr. Hughes was left with no delusions about the size of the gap when he was seriously asked in a television interview whether General de Gaulle was a Communist sympathizer.

As the abortive negotiations dragged on, the obsession with independence grew. Independence became a be-all and an end-all; all the country's ills, all tensions and worries, would be over if only it could be achieved or seized. In people's minds the act became isolated and divorced from other problems. Yet, even excluding the international reactions, independence by itself could not solve Southern Rhodesia's main problems of establishing satisfactory relations between the two main races and re-forming the society to accept the changing social and economic circumstances. It could perhaps set these problems in a new framework, although there must be some hesitation even about this, for they were principally internal problems, which had emerged while Southern Rhodesia was internally self-governing. Certainly, with a U.D.I., the very act, with its implication that Europeans had seized power to impose their own settlement, could only deepen the division between the races and convince both sides that the future held little more than a direct racial clash for power. However, hiding behind the shield of 'independence means all', the delusion grew that somehow

[1] S.R.L.A. Hansard, 21 July 1965, col. 1284.

problems would be solved, or be changed, or mysteriously disappear. Most Europeans were caught in a wave of self-deception, a wave which R.F. Ministers had helped to create and had then become caught in themselves.

The Government's excessive concentration on independence left it vulnerable to friend and foe alike. The supporters wanted action and evidence of progress; the opponents to jeer at the Government's failure. It was probably the increasing pressure from all sides and the increasing frustration within the Government itself which decided Mr. Smith to bring matters to a head by visiting London in October 1965. He went saying that, 'sweet or bitter', these London talks must be the end of the independence negotiations. Once Mr. Smith took this decision the train of events was rapid and dramatic. The London negotiations ended in deadlock. Mr. Smith returned once again frustrated and disillusioned, but this time probably determined to seize independence. He was quickly followed to Southern Rhodesia by Mr. Wilson, who said he was going 'to do a job of work', to break the independence deadlock. Mr. Wilson spent the last week of October in Salisbury in concentrated talks and negotiations. He encountered the old intransigence and extremism but, when the British Prime Minister returned to London, he hoped that a U.D.I. had been averted. In general terms it had been agreed that a Royal Commission would be set up, but the detailed terms of reference for the Commission had not been finalized. Misunderstanding and disagreement arose about how broad the Commission's investigations should be and the method of reporting to the Governments. There must, however, be a strong suspicion that by that time the Southern Rhodesian Government had decided to seize independence come what might, for the disagreement about the Commission did not appear irreconcilable. After a dramatic but futile last-minute telephone call from Mr. Wilson, Mr. Smith, in a lunch-time broadcast on 11 November, declared that by a unilateral act Southern Rhodesia had declared herself an independent state.

The October negotiations in London and Salisbury were intricate and detailed. They centred around five main principles laid down by the British Government, which were:

(1) The principle and intention of unimpeded progress to majority rule, already explained in the 1961 Constitution, would have to be maintained and guaranteed.

(2) There would also have to be guarantees against retrogressive amendments of the Constitution.

(3) There would have to be immediate improvement in the political status of the African population.

(4) There would have to be progress towards ending racial discrimination.

(5) The British Government would need to be satisfied that any basis proposed for independence was acceptable to the people of Rhodesia as a whole.[1]

Around these points there were frank and forceful discussions. There could be no complaints that there was vagueness or uncertainty on either side. At that time both Prime Ministers, although recognizing their inability to agree, also publicly stated their mutual admiration for the way in which the negotiations had been conducted. The actual negotiations were so detailed and complicated that they warrant a study in themselves, but some general issues emerged, issues which made it clear that the failure to agree was based not upon any mechanical defects in the method of negotiation but upon differences of aims and principles.

Although the personalities of the two Prime Ministers added flavour to the already tense and dramatic negotiations, there was no major clash of personalities. Both Mr. Smith and Mr. Wilson had considerable political experience and neither was reluctant to seize opportunities to further their personal political ends, but in these negotiations they were not just playing for personal ends. They each sincerely believed that their particular policy was the right one to ensure successful and peaceful development in Southern Rhodesia. They believed that to abandon their principles would be disastrous for all Southern Africa.

The greatest difference was over African political rights. On this question the two Governments had widely different objectives. The British had set no time-limit for achieving majority rule but insisted that the pace of African political development must be speeded up. Therefore the British, as well as proposing

[1] Cmnd. 2807, Bottomley-Smith, 21 September 1965.

constitutional changes, made other proposals which would speed up African participation in government. They suggested that Africans should be given experience in top administrative posts, and offered substantial financial aid for African education whereby greater numbers of Africans would soon achieve the franchise qualifications. The Southern Rhodesian Government was unsympathetic to these British aims. It continued to lay emphasis on slow, unforced evolution, upon retaining control in responsible hands. Its emphasis implied a slowing-down in the pace of African political advancement. Thus in the negotiations Mr. Smith repeated his Government's hopes to abolish cross-voting and to 'fade out' 'B' Roll seats as Africans were returned to 'A' Roll seats.

The constitutional discussions were centred on the 1961 Constitution. Inevitably the two Governments viewed this Constitution from conflicting angles. At the London talks Mr. Smith said that he '. . . must make it clear that the Government Party in Rhodesia did not believe in majority rule. They accepted that the 1961 Constitution would eventually bring it about, but they would not take any action to hasten the process. The criterion of fitness for majority rule must be a criterion of merit, i.e. a criterion in terms of those standards of civilized behaviour which other independent African countries were not succeeding in observing.'[1] Mr. Smith frequently mentioned that Africans had denied themselves the opportunity to participate in politics and government by boycotting the 1961 arrangements. It would be ludicrous, he said, to grant further concessions after this stubbornness and extremist attitude.

In contrast Mr. Wilson said: 'I cannot accept that the grant of independence simply on the basis of the 1961 Constitution would satisfy the five principles you and I have accepted.' 'Further', he continued, 'both we and our predecessors have made it clear to you that progress under the 1961 Constitution has not yet resulted in sufficiently representative institutions to satisfy the British Parliament that the grant of independence would be justified.' He accepted that it was regrettable that Africans had refused to participate under the Constitution, but contended that 'it is no reason for depriving them of all voice

---

[1] Cmnd. 2807, London talks, 7 October 1965, pp. 72–3.

in the future of their country'.[1] To the Southern Rhodesian Government the 1961 Constitution represented a dangerous and over-liberal concession to African extremists' claims. To the British Government it represented the first but not the last step to increased African participation in government.

Because the two policies were based on conflicting principles, opinions about the reasonableness of each case and the degree of compromise each government was prepared to make depended upon which set of principles an individual accepted. Thus the Southern Rhodesian Government's proposal that there should be an all-African senate of twelve chiefs which could sit with the fifteen 'B' Roll members to form a 'blocking third' on constitutional changes, and the proposal that all adult taxpayers could vote for 'B' Roll seats, could be seen as major concessions or, alternatively, it could be argued that these proposals represented no change of substance for direct African representation was not increased and there was still no guarantee that the number of 'B' Roll seats would not be reduced. Thus the British acceptance that Southern Rhodesia could have independence before majority rule was achieved, provided it was clear that the country was moving steadily towards it, could be interpreted either as a major concession or as no real concession because there was still the insistence upon a guaranteed increased pace in African political advancement.

The conflict over principles reinforced the continued distrust between the two Governments. Mr. Smith, who could see no compromise between rule by the R.F. and rule by the black nationalists, believed that the British Government planned a quick hand-over to African extremist rule, while the British suspected that the R.F. Government's aim was to perpetuate indefinitely white domination.

Another of the underlying causes of dispute was the different context in which the two Governments continued to see the dispute. For Mr. Smith and his Ministers, backed by a right-wing party, the problem was a very personal one, related to the society they wished to preserve. Speaking for his fellows Mr. Smith said:

Their country and their lives are at stake. If Britain had considered all that might have happened to her in 1939, she might not

[1] Cmnd. 2807, Wilson-Smith, 21 October 1965.

have gone to war. Rhodesia might be relatively insignificant, but
the issues were just as important for her people. If they did not
obtain independence, they would have to leave Rhodesia. They
would rather fight it out than go voluntarily.[1]

Mr. Wilson saw the problem in the context of international
problems. He foresaw the danger of an international crisis
which might lead to war: 'It was a dangerous illusion', he said:

. . . to think that the situation could be contained within the
borders of Rhodesia . . . Mr. Smith had perhaps been right in
saying that the United Kingdom Government were remote from
realities of the position in Rhodesia; but perhaps the Rhodesian
Government themselves were not as closely in touch with international opinion as the United Kingdom. They did not seem to
realize the irresistible passions which might be aroused . . . had
they considered the more indefinable consequences if wide areas of
Africa were opened up to conflict?'

He warned of the dangers of Russia and China seizing the
opportunity to intervene. 'Here lay a great danger—almost,
perhaps, a probability. He feared a terrible conflict and bloodshed.'[2]

During his exhaustive discussions in Salisbury the British
Prime Minister saw at first hand that political attitudes in
Southern Rhodesia were firmly polarized. There were, at least
for the present, only two political powers: the very real and
obvious power of the R.F. Government, and the suppressed but
potentially enormous power of the African nationalists. Neither
was prepared to compromise and, despite all his attempts at
persuasion and pressure, Mr. Wilson achieved no substantial
shift of attitude by either group. This left the British isolated for,
while British policy was directed towards achieving majority
rule, it hoped to move towards this by a middle course, by a
sharing of power between the races. However, there was no
bridge, no multiracial party, no party of compromise on which
the British could build their solution. In 1965 Mr. Smith's
assessment of the immediate choice was an accurate one. In-
stinctively Mr. Wilson fought for time, in the hope that with
patience the hardened attitude would become more flexible.

[1] Cmnd. 2807, London talks, 8 October 1965, p. 84.
[2] Op. cit., London talks, 8 October 1965, p. 83.

He was not given the time and so his attempt to avert a U.D.I. failed.

The Unilateral Declaration of Independence was in character with the pattern of politics which Southern Rhodesians, both African and European, had created for themselves in the 1960s. It was part of the 'all or nothing at all' spirit, the politics of desperation. It stemmed from fear and mistrust and suspicion. In hard reality, neither race had been prepared to trust the other, and so eventually a white government risked isolation, international alienation, economic sanctions, and perhaps armed conflict, rather than risk offering equal economic, social, and political rights to their fellow, black Rhodesians. Mr. Wilson may not have succeeded in preventing a U.D.I., but he did succeed in capturing the mood and the spirit of this desperation. In his Press conference at the end of his Salisbury talks he said:

There can be no doubt, I am afraid, that the situation is hypercharged with emotion; and this is not conducive to getting the right answer for, among those emotions, predominant is the emotion of fear, with the attendant emotions of distrust and suspicion and of unfounded rumour. And fear is a bad counsellor, when the primary need is for wise advice and cool and rational and statesman-like judgment.

He rightly advised: 'The first freedom that Rhodesia needs to achieve, the foundation of all the others, is freedom from fear; and from that will develop the freedom that has flowered in the twentieth century, freedom from contempt based on the dignity of man.'[1]

---

[1] *East Africa and Rhodesia*, 4 November 1965.

Appendix I

Southern Rhodesia Cabinets 1960-65

The U.F.P. Cabinet, 1960–62

The Cabinet, from the beginning of 1960 to September 1962, was:

Prime Minister	Sir Edgar Whitehead, K.C.M.G., O.B.E.
Minister of Labour, Social Welfare, and Housing	Abraham Eliezer Abrahamson
Minister of Local Government and Native Education	Ralph Milton Cleveland, O.B.E.
Minister of the Treasury and Mines	Cyril James Hatty
Minister of Justice and Internal Affairs	Reginald Knight, Q.C.
Minister of Roads, Irrigation, and Lands	Albert Rubidge Washington Stumbles
Minister of Native Affairs	Herbert Jack Quinton

There was a Cabinet re-shuffle in September 1962. The new Cabinet retained office until the U.F.P. election defeat in December of the same year. In the re-shuffle Sir Edgar Whitehead and Mr. Abrahamson retained the same portfolios. Messrs. Knight and Cleveland left the Cabinet, while Messrs. Ellman Brown and Ewing came in. The changes gazetted on 28 September 1962 (Gazette Notice No. 1072 of 1962) were:

Minister of Mines and Industrial Development, and of African Education and the Public Service	Cyril James Hatty
Minister of Justice and Internal Affairs, and Roads	Albert Rubidge Washington Stumbles
Minister of Agriculture, Lands, and Natural Resources	Herbert Jack Quinton
Minister of the Treasury and Irrigation	Geoffrey Ellman-Brown, C.M.G., O.B.E.

Minister of Native Affairs,   Blair Ewing
   District Administration, and
   Local Government

The R.F. Cabinet, 1962–65

The first Cabinet formed after the election victory of December
1962 was:

Prime Minister and Minister   Winston Joseph Field, C.M.G.,
   of the Public Service   M.B.E.
Minister of the Treasury   Ian Douglas Smith
Minister of Justice, Law,   Clifford Walter Dupont
   and Order
Minister of Mines and   John Gaunt
   Industrial Development
Minister of Agriculture, Lands,   James Angus Graham (7th Duke
   and Natural Resources   of Montrose)
Minister of Irrigation, Roads,   William John Harper
   and Road Traffic
Minister of Internal Affairs,   John Hartley Howman
   Local Government, and
   African Education
Minister of Labour and Social   Ian Finlay McLean
   Welfare

The following additions were made later to Mr. Field's Cabinet:

Minister of Trade, Industry,   George Wilburn Rudland
   and Development   (Appointed 2 August 1963, Gazette
                          Notice No. 783 of 1963)
   (On Mr. Rudland's appointment Mr. Gaunt lost the portfolio
   of Industrial Development but remained Minister of Mines)

Minister of African Education,   John James Wrathall (First
   Education, and Health   appointed as Minister of African
                          Education 11 October 1963,
                          Gazette Notice No. 1075 of 1963)

In April 1964 Mr. Smith replaced Mr. Field as Prime Minister.
He formed the following Cabinet:

Prime Minister and Minister   Ian Douglas Smith
   of Defence
Deputy Prime Minister and   Clifford Walter Dupont
   Minister of External Affairs

Minister of Local Government and Housing	John Gaunt
Minister of Agriculture	Lord Graham
Minister of Internal Affairs and the Public Service	William John Harper
Minister of Justice, and Law and Order	Desmond William Lardner-Burke
Minister of Health, and Labour and Social Welfare	Ian Finlay McLean
Minister of Roads, Immigration, and Tourism	Harry Reedman
Minister of Trade, Industry and Development, and Transport and Power	George Wilburn Rudland
Minister of Education	Arthur Philip Smith
Minister of Mines and Lands, and Water Development	Philip van Heerden
Minister of Finance and Posts	John James Wrathall

After the R.F. election victory of May 1965, Mr. Smith made Cabinet changes which were gazetted on 4 June 1965 (Gazette Notice No. 811 of 1965). Mr. Gaunt and Mr. Reedman left the Cabinet and two new Ministers were appointed. Mr. Dupont, who remained Deputy Prime Minister, also received the portfolio of Defence from Mr. Smith, as well as retaining External Affairs. The new Ministers were:

Minister of Immigration and Tourism and Information	John Hartley Howman
Minister of Local Government and Housing	Bernard Horace Mussett

Appendix II

Election Results

1962 ELECTION

(1) *The State of the Parties*   (Number of candidates in parentheses)

	Constituencies	Electoral Districts	Total Seats
Rhodesian Front (R.F.)	35 (50)	— (15)	35
United Federal Party (U.F.P.)	15 (49)	14 (15)	29
Independents (Ind.)	— (6)	1 (1)	1
Central Africa Party (C.A.P.)	— (1)	— (13)	—

(2) *Votes Cast in Constituencies*   (First Preference)[1]

	'A' Roll Votes	'A' Roll Percentage	'B' Roll Votes	'B' Roll Percentage
R.F.	37,920	56·36	362	15·11
U.F.P.	28,517	42·38	1,946	81·22
C.A.P.	75	0·11	29	1·21
Ind.	776	1·15	59	2·46
Total	67,288		2,396	

(3) *Votes Cast in Districts*   (First Preference)
(Before devaluation of 'A' Roll votes)

	'A' Roll Votes	'A' Roll Percentage	'B' Roll Votes	'B' Roll Percentage
R.F.	35,070	54·03	306	11·87
U.F.P.	28,055	43·23	1,870	72·57
C.A.P.	1,764	2·72	359	13·93
Ind.	15	0·02	42	1·63
Total	64,904		2,577	

[1] Preferential, transferable voting was permitted but, as it made no difference to any results, only the first preference votes are recorded.

(4) *Percentage Poll*

	Constituencies 'A' Roll	'B' Roll
Total Electorate	90,785	10,632
Votes cast	67,288	2,396
Percentage Poll	74·12	22·54

	Districts 'A' Roll	'B' Roll
Total Electorate	90,785	10,632
Votes cast	64,904	2,577
Percentage poll	71·49	24·24

1965 ELECTION

(1) *State of the Parties*

	Constituencies	Districts	Total Seats
R.F.	50 (50)	—	50
Rhodesia Party (R.P.)	— (25)	10 (15)	10
Ind.	— (3)	5[1]	5

(2) *Votes cast in Contested Constituencies* (The number of constituencies which the parties fought in parenthesis)

	'A' Roll Votes	Percentage	'B' Roll Votes	Percentage
R.F. (28)	28,165	79·2	206	28·6
R.P. (25)	6,377	20·9	509	70·8
Ind. (3)	964	20·7	4	0·6

(3) *Votes cast for R.P. in Thirteen Contested Districts*

	'A' Roll Votes	Percentage	'B' Roll Votes	Percentage
R.P.	12,886	41·5	754	52·2

Votes for R.F. or Independents in the districts are not given, since some Independents, while not official party candidates, were given R.F. support.

---

[1] Two of the Independents who won district seats were said to have received R.F. backing.

(4) *Percentage Poll*

	Constituencies *'A' Roll*	*'B' Roll*
Total electorate in 28 contested seats	55,025	5,656
Total effective vote	35,506	719
Percentage Poll	64·5	12·7

	Districts *'A' Roll*	*'B' Roll*
Total electorate in 13 contested constituencies	75,255	10,032
Votes cast	31,036	1,443
Percentage vote	41·2	14·4

Appendix III

Southern Rhodesia Legislative Assembly Composition and Franchise

1957–61

Until the introduction of the 1961 Constitution, the Assembly had a Speaker and thirty members. Under the Electoral Act of 1957 the franchise was:

Ordinary qualifications	Special qualifications
(a) £720 p.a. income salary or wages or ownership of property valued at £1,500 *or*	(a) £240 p.a. income, etc. *or*
(b) £480 p.a. income, etc. or ownership of property valued at £1,000 *and* completed Primary education *or*	(b) £120 p.a. income, etc. *and* two years' completed Secondary education. (N.B. This category to fall away when numbers of voters with special qualifications equalled 20 per cent of those with ordinary qualifications. No further registrations were then to be permitted.)
(c) £300 p.a. income, etc. *or* ownership of property valued at £500 *and* four years completed Secondary education.	

1961 onwards

With the introduction of the new Constitution (the first election under the new Constitution was fought in December 1962) the Assembly contained a Speaker and sixty-five members (fifty from constituencies and fifteen from districts). The new electoral system was based upon two voters' rolls—an 'A' Roll and a 'B' Roll. *Each* voter had the right to cast a vote in a constituency and in a district, but the influence of votes could be restricted. In district seats the 'A' Roll votes could not exceed 20 per cent of the total votes cast—they were devalued if they did exceed 20 per cent—and conversely 'B' Roll votes in constituencies could not exceed 20 per cent of the votes.

The franchise introduced by the 1961 Constitution was:

Qualifications common to both Rolls

(1) Citizenship of Rhodesia and Nyasaland;
(2) Twenty-one years of age or over;
(3) Two years' continuous residence in the Federation and three months' residence in the constituency and electoral district concerned immediately preceding application for enrolment;
(4) Adequate knowledge of the English language and ability to complete and sign the registration form except in the case of duly appointed chiefs and headmen;
(5) The following additional qualifications are required:

'A' Roll

(a) Income of not less than £792 during each of two years preceding date of claim for enrolment or ownership of immovable property of value not less than £1,650; *or*

(b) (i) Income of not less than £528 during each of two years preceding date of claim for enrolment or ownership of immovable property of value not less than £1,100;
and
(ii) completion of a course of Primary education of prescribed standard; *or*

(c) (i) Income of not less than £330 during each of the two years preceding date of claim for enrolment, or ownership of immovable property of value not less than £550;

'B'

(a) Income at the rate of not less than £264 per annum during the six months preceding date of claim for enrolment or ownership of immovable property of value not less than £495; *or*

(b) (i) Income at the rate of not less than £132 p.a. during the six months preceding date of claim for enrolment, or ownership of immovable property of value not less than £275;
and
(ii) two years' Secondary education of prescribed standard; *or*

(c) Persons of over thirty years of age with:
(i) Income at the rate of not less than £132 p.a. during the six months preceding the date of claim for enrolment, or ownership of immovable property of value not less than £275;

and

(ii) four years' Secondary education of prescribed standard; *or*

(*d*) Appointment to the office of Chief or Headman.

and

(ii) completion of a course of Primary education of a prescribed standard;
or

(*d*) Persons over 30 years of age with income at the rate of not less than £198 p.a. during the six months preceding the date of claim for enrolment, or ownership of immovable property of value not less than £385; *or*

(*e*) All kraal heads with a following of twenty or more heads of families; *or*

(*f*) Ordained ministers of religion with university degree or five years of full-time training or two years' training and three years' service.

Notes:

(1) In terms of Section 13 of the Electoral Act (which provision was permitted by Section 9 (3) of the Constitution) the Governor has prescribed that the means qualification as enacted in the Act and the Second Schedule to the Constitution should be increased by 10 per cent. See Governor's Proclamation No. 32 of 31 August 1964 in Southern Rhodesian Government Notice 658/64. The Electoral Act does not therefore reflect the present franchise qualifications.

(2) Note that 'owner', for purposes of the 'B' Roll only, includes a hire-purchaser if such person has been in continuous occupation for three years, is not in arrears, and has paid not less than 10 per cent of the purchase price of such property (Section 11).

(3) The value of board and lodging may be included in computing salary (Section 12).

(4) Except in the case of wives of Chiefs and Headmen, a married woman is deemed to have the same means qualifications as her husband. However, only the first wife under a system permitting of polygamy is deemed to have such qualifications (Section 14).

Appendix IV

Registered Voters in Southern Rhodesia, May 1961–January 1965

		31 May 1961	*31 August 1962*	*31 May 1964*	*31 January 1965*
Europeans:	'A' Roll	77,717	86,720	89,278	92,405
	'B' Roll	429	614	608	587
Asians:	'A' Roll	972	1,151	1,231	1,242
	'B' Roll	55	147	114	120
Coloureds:	'A' Roll	999	1,281	1,308	1,307
	'B' Roll	63	151	176	181
Africans:	'A' Roll	1,397	1,920	2,263	2,330
	'B' Roll	3,231	9,585	10,466	10,689
	Total	84,863	101,569	105,444	108,861

(Extract from Palley *op. cit.*, p. 421.)

Bibliography

Among books, publications, and reports consulted are the following:

(1) NEWSPAPERS AND PERIODICALS

> *The Rhodesia Herald*
> *The Times* (London)
> *The Central African Examiner*
> *East Africa and Rhodesia*
> *Newsfront*
> *The Citizen*
> *The Daily News*
> *Ukuru*
> *Democratic Voice*
> *The Sunday Mail* (Rhodesia)

(2) SOUTHERN RHODESIA AND CENTRAL AFRICAN FEDERATION
GOVERNMENT AND PARLIAMENTARY PUBLICATIONS

> *The Rhodesian Legislative Assembly Hansard*
> *The Central African Federation Hansard*

Annual Reports of Chief Native Commissioner, 1950–62
Annual Reports of Secretary for Internal Affairs, 1963 and 1964
Annual Reports, Secretary for Law and Order, 1963 and 1964
Annual Reports, Secretary for Local Government, 1960–4
Annual Reports, Secretary for African Education, 1960–4
Annual Reports, Director of African Administration, Salisbury, 1960–4

> *Annual Reports*, Director of Housing and Amenities, Bulawayo, 1960–5
> *Parliamentary Select Committee on Political Boycott* (L.A.S.C. 8–65)
> *Report of Commission of Inquiry into the Organization and Development of the Southern Rhodesian Public Service* (Paterson Commission), C.S.R., 35, 1962
> *African Local Government in British East and Central Africa* (Howman Report), December 1951
> *Report of Mangwende Reserve Commission of Inquiry, and Minority Report*, 1961

Local Government and Community Development: The Roll of Ministers and Co-ordination, C.S.R. 44–65

The Domboshawa 'Indaba', Government Printer, 1965

The Rhodesian Community Development Review, Vol. 1, No. 1, March 1966

Second Report of the Select Committee on the Resettlement of Natives, L.A.S.C. 3, 1960

Phillips' Report on Economic Development, L.A.S.C. 15, 1962

African Census, 1962 (published June 1964)

Non-African Census, 1961, Government Printer (n.d.)

Monthly Digest of Statistics, 1961–1965, Central Statistical Office

Economic Aspects of Declaration of Independence, C.S.R. 15, 1965

(Pamphlets and news sheets issued by the Southern Rhodesian Information Department have also been consulted)

(3) BRITISH GOVERNMENT AND PARLIAMENTARY PUBLICATIONS

House of Commons Hansard

The Monckton Commission (Cmnd. 1148, 1960) and *Record of Evidence* (Cmnd. 1149–1152)

Correspondence between the Southern Rhodesian and British Governments (Cmnd. 2073 and Cmd. 2807)

Report on Central Africa Conference (Cmnd. 2093)

(4) PUBLISHED WORKS

(i) *History*

GANN, L. H., *A History of Southern Rhodesia Early Days to 1934,* London, Chatto and Windus, 1965.

GRAY, R., *Two Nations,* London, Oxford University Press, 1960

HOLE, H. M., *The Making of Rhodesia,* London, Macmillan, 1926

HOLE, H. M., *Old Rhodesian Days,* London, Macmillan, 1928

MASON, P., *The Birth of a Dilemma,* London, Oxford University Press, 1958

PALLEY, C., *The Constitutional History and Law of Southern Rhodesia 1888–1965,* London, Oxford University Press, 1966

THOMSON, H. C., *Rhodesia and its Government,* Smith, Elder & Co, 1898

(ii) *Autobiographies, Biographies and Memoirs*

ALPORT, Lord C., *Sudden Assignment,* London, Hodder and Stoughton, 1965

GANN, L. H., *and* GELFAND, M., *Huggins of Rhodesia*, London, Allen and Unwin, 1964

LOCKHART, J. G., *and* WOODHOUSE, C. M., *Rhodes*, London, Hodder & Stoughton, 1963

MILLIN, S. G., *Rhodes*, London, Chatto and Windus, 1952

WELENSKY, Sir R., *4,000 Days*, London, Collins, 1964

(iii) *Politics and writing on recent and contemporary events in Central Africa*

BRELSFORD, W. V. (*Ed.*), *A Handbook of the Federation of Rhodesia and Nyasaland*, London, Cassell, 1960

CLEGG, E. M., *Race and Politics. Partnership in the Federation of Rhodesia and Nyasaland*, London, Oxford University Press, 1960

KEATLEY, P., *The Politics of Partnership*, London, Penguin Books, 1963

LEYS, C., *European Politics in Southern Rhodesia*, London, Oxford University Press, 1959

MASON, P. *Year of Decision: Rhodesia and Nyasaland in 1960*, London, Oxford University Press, 1960

PECK, A. J., *Rhodesia Accuses*, Salisbury, The Three Sisters, 1966

RANGER, T., *Crisis in Southern Rhodesia*, London, Fabian Commonwealth Research Bureau, No. 217, 1960

REA, F. (*Ed.*), *Southern Rhodesia: The Price of Freedom*, Bulawayo, Manning, 1964

SHAMUYAYIRA, N., *Crisis in Rhodesia*, London, Deutsch, 1965

SITHOLE, N., *African Nationalism*, London, Oxford University Press, 1954

SOREF, H. *and* GREIG, I. *The Puppeteers*, London, Tandem, 1965

SYMONDS, A., *Southern Rhodesia: Background to Crisis*, London, Oxford University Press for R.I.I.A. 1965

WILLSON, F. M. G. (*Ed.*) *and* PASSMORE, G. C. *and* MITCHELL, M. T., *Source Book of Parliamentary Elections in Southern Rhodesia 1898–1962*, Salisbury, U.C.R.N., 1963

(5) UNPUBLISHED MATERIAL

ARRIGHI, A., 'The Political Economy of Rhodesia'.

BOWMAN, L., 'Trends in Rhodesian Politics, with Special Reference to African Advancement and the Independence Question'.

GARBETT, G. K., 'The Chief's Dilemma: Government Officer or Tribal Leader?' (Now published in *Race*, Vol. VIII, No. 2,

October 1966, as 'The Rhodesian Chief's Dilemma: Government Officer or Tribal Leader'.)

GARBETT, G. K., 'Religious Aspects of Political Succession among the Valley Korekore (N. Shona)'.

——, 'Spirit Mediums as Mediators in Valley Korekore Society'. (Now published in Stokes, E. *and* Brown, R., *The Zambesian Past*, Manchester University Press for University of Zambia, Institute for Social Research, 1966.)

Index

DATE DUE

9-3			
DEC 8: 1972			
MAR 1 4 1980			
GAYLORD			PRINTED IN U.S.A.